Models & Methods for Youth & Young Adult Ministry

"A deeply irenic and practical book grounded in theology and best practices for ministry. This is a great survey of the major models and methods that will continue to shape work with adolescents and young adults. Those that hear, heed and integrate these models will find a deep reservoir to draw pastoral care and pedagogical insights for transformative work with young people."

—MIKE SEVERE, Associate Professor, Taylor University

"This book is a thoughtfully constructed offering to all of us who are invested in seeing adolescents well formed as followers of Jesus Christ. It's a fresh resource that will enhance my own efforts to develop the leadership potential in others. With exemplary humility and zeal for Christian unity, Art Canales led me to enrich my perspective about youth ministry practice by exploring four different models."

—DAVE RAHN, Senior Ministry Advisor, Youth for Christ

"I wholeheartedly endorse the book Models and Methods for Youth and Young Adult Ministry for several reasons. As a youth pastor for over 20 years, I have seen paradigm shifts occurring in the field of youth and young adult ministry and had been looking for a resource that articulated what was happening . . . This book is a must have youth ministers in the field, educators in youth ministry and any pastoral agent in churches that is trying to incorporate a Twenty-First-Century model into their current programs."

—RICARDO GONZALEZ, Youth Minister, St. Edward Catholic Church

"Arthur Canales has a deep passion for re-visioning the way we value and minister to young people in our world. His book carefully examines the current major modes of youth and young adult ministry and offers theologically grounded insights for shepherding and equipping Christian youth workers."

—BRENDA SNAILUM, President of the Association of Youth Ministry Educators

"This book will provide today's youth and young adult ministers with the high challenge of thinking through, not only their methodologies, but the theological thinking underlying their ministry. Any eager reader will profit from this book, but it will prove even more valuable when discussed in group or class situations."

—DEAN BORGMAN, Professor, Gordon-Conwell Theological Seminary

"In an era that situates youth and adolescents as a side act in many regards—worth only the branding and marketing value they present—Art Canales calls those of us who work with this population to better understand and act on the theoretical frameworks, models, and theologies that drive youth ministry. Canales has given us a great volume in order to better serve the Church and young people within this post-civil rights era."

—DANIEL WHITE HODGE, Associate Professor, North Park University of Chicago

"Canales' book is exquisite for many reasons, but especially because of the writer's open ecumenical attitude and understanding of the different orientations inside the field of Christian youth work. Thus, this book is useful for people from every Christian denomination, and even for people from other world religious traditions or non-religious, if they are interested in learning to understand the positive possibilities, which lie in work with adolescents."

—Jouko Porkka, Lecturer and Researcher, Diaconia University

Models & Methods for Youth & Young Adult Ministry

Ecumenical Examples and Pastoral Approaches for the Christian Church

ARTHUR DAVID CANALES

CASCADE *Books* • Eugene, Oregon

MODELS & METHODS FOR YOUTH & YOUNG ADULT MINISTRY
Ecumenical Examples and Pastoral Approaches for the Christian Church

Copyright © 2018 Arthur David Canales. All rights reserved. Except for brief quotations in critical publications or reviews, no part of this book may be reproduced in any manner without prior written permission from the publisher. Write: Permissions, Wipf and Stock Publishers, 199 W. 8th Ave., Suite 3, Eugene, OR 97401.

Cascade Books
An Imprint of Wipf and Stock Publishers
199 W. 8th Ave., Suite 3
Eugene, OR 97401

www.wipfandstock.com

PAPERBACK ISBN: 978-1-5326-3019-4
HARDCOVER ISBN: 978-1-5326-3021-7
EBOOK ISBN: 978-1-5326-3020-0

Cataloguing-in-Publication data:

Names: Canales, Arthur David

Title: Models and methods for youth and young adult ministry : ecumenical examples and pastoral approaches for the Christian church / by Arthur David Canales.

Description: Eugene, OR: Cascade Books, 2018 | Includes bibliographical references and index.

Identifiers: ISBN 978-1-5326-3019-4 (paperback) | ISBN 978-1-5326-3021-7 (hardcover) | ISBN 978-1-5326-3020-0 (ebook)

Subjects: LCSH: Church work with youth. | Church work with young adults. | Youth—Religious life. | Young adults—Religious life.

Classification: BV4447 C15 2018 (print) | BV4447 (ebook)

Manufactured in the U.S.A.   MAY 21, 2018

To my hero—my dad—Alex Canales (1929–2011)

and

To my two sons, Alex & Albert

Contents

List of Figures and Tables xi

Acknowledgments xiii

Introduction:
Situating Youth and Young Adult Ministry 1

Chapter 1:
Theological Models and Methods 15

Chapter 2:
The Biblical-Hermeneutic Model 32

Chapter 3:
The Servant-Leadership Model 60

Chapter 4:
The Liberation Model 88

Chapter 5:
The Christian Discipleship Model 120

Conclusion:
The Journey of Youth and Young Adult Ministry 155

Bibliography 163

Epilogue 171

About the Author 173

Index 175

Figures and Tables

Figures

Figure 1: Ministry Methodology 24

Figure 2: The Hermeneutical Process for Interpreting Scripture 34

Figure 3: The Biblical Interpretation Process 38

Figure 4: Servant-Leadership Circle 84

Figure 5: Liberation Framework and Youth and Young Adult Ministry 95

Figure 6: The Movement of Christian Discipleship 139

Tables

Table 1: Models for Youth and Young Adult Ministry 29

Table 2: Ten-Week Biblical Cinema Series 50

Table 3: Ten Theological Characteristics of Servant-Leadership 69

Acknowledgments

Models and Methods for Youth and Young Adult Ministry: Ecumenical Examples and Pastoral Approaches for the Christian Church has been in the back of mind for over a decade now and has become a tedious labor of love. This book has taken over ten years to write, research, and finalize for various reasons, both personal and professional. Personally, my father, a brilliant scientist and virologist, had a seven-year bout with dementia and Alzheimer's disease, which was painful for my family to endure. Second, I moved eight times in eight years, went through an awful divorce and a bitter custody dispute, and had to overcome a battle with prostate cancer; in all of those skirmishes I came out on top. Professionally, I had to take two jobs that removed me from academia and I had to endure a lay-off from one position in 2010, which kept me out of full-time work for almost two years. Despite all the personal and professional setbacks, the book is now complete—thank God!

Other acknowledgments that I need to make are for the four chapters dealing with models. Originally, these chapters were written for academic journals, but have been redacted, rewritten, and lengthened for this book. Therefore, I owe these journals and their editors a salute for first publishing the work and allowing for reworking and reprinting in this book. Chapter 2 was originally published in *The Bible Today*. Chapter 3 was originally published in *Journal of Youth & Theology*. Chapter 5 was originally published in *Journal of Religious Education*. I am grateful to the following editors: Donald Senior, CP, Nicholas Shepherd, A. (Jos) de Kock, and Peta Goldburg.

This is not my first book and conventional wisdom dictates that no book writes itself. There are always numerous people who deserve much gratitude and credit for their suggestions and assistance along the way. First, I am tremendously blessed by the Triune God: God the Father/Mother who created and loves me; God the Son, Jesus the Christ, my Lord and Savior who redeems me (daily sometimes); and God the Holy Spirit who sustains and guides me (when I decide to listen), and who has granted me with the powerful gifts of perseverance and tenacity!

Second, I have an awesome family, both immediate and extended. However, a special debt of gratitude and gratefulness must go to my beautiful bride Tanya, who always supports me and loves me beyond words, and for her encouragement, which has not wavered over the years, or on this project.

Third, much indebtedness is owed to my present employer, Marian University in Indianapolis, for granting me the opportunity to teach, the office space to research and write, and most poignantly, the faculty within the university's Department of Theology and Philosophy where this book was written, researched, redacted, and completed. Most importantly, though, were the various theological and pastoral conversations regarding certain ideas, strategies, and chapters of this book, particularly professors Mark Reasoner, Donna Proctor, and Andrew Hohman.

Fourth, the faculty within the Department of Theology and Philosophy at Silver Lake College of the Holy Family, Manitowoc, Wisconsin (where I taught from 2000 to 2006), merits much gratitude for their encouragement and support where this book originated through various articles, lectures, and catechetical essays. I am especially grateful to Francettee Riebe, OSF, Kay Elmer, OSF, Rev. Dr. Jeremiah J. Cullinane, and Dr. Robert Berchmans.

Fifth, the library staffs at both institutions, Marian University and Silver Lake College, deserve special thanks, particularly for helping me gather information and material in the stacks and numerous sources through interlibrary loan.

Sixth, a measure of appreciation must go out to my initial proofreader Mr. Don Manly from Jacobs Writing Consultants. Also, of course, to my editor and publicist Dr. D. Christopher Spinks of Cascade Books, whose ideas and insights regarding this book have been most valuable.

Seventh, warm and sincere appreciation goes to the countless individuals: students (present and past), colleagues in theology and ministry, Christian youth and young adult ministers, and adolescent ministry scholars, who have all offered insights, suggestions, and constructive criticisms alone the way.

Last, but certainly not least, many thanks to my old and good friend, Mr. Joseph F. Barrero, CEO of Cornerstone Financial Education of Austin, Texas, for a small grant and financial contribution to make this book a reality. His incredible generosity has helped me to work on and complete this book over the past summer.

Introduction:
Situating Youth and Young Adult Ministry

> *The Church's mission is threefold: (1) to proclaim the good news of salvation; (2) to offer itself as a group of people transformed by the Spirit into a community of faith, hope, and love; and (3) to bring God's justice and love to others through service in its individual, social, and political dimensions.*[1]
>
> Department of [Catholic] Education
> *A Vision of Youth Ministry*, 1976

Preliminary Remarks

Hopefully, *Models and Methods for Youth and Young Adult Ministry: Ecumenical Examples and Pastoral Approaches for the Christian Church* will help to fulfill the church's mission quoted above. Youth and young adult ministry has always been a passion of mine because as a young man I began my ministry career in the church working as a youth minister. While in graduate school in my early twenties, I attended and received my spiritual edification and catechesis in a parish young adult ministry in Miami, Florida. While in my twenties, I served as an adolescent catechist for two years in one parish and then became a full-time youth minister for a neighboring parish for three years before continuing my graduate education in theology and ministry at the Catholic University of America in Washington, DC.

---

1. Department of [Catholic] Education, *Vision of Youth Ministry*, 3. This document will be referred to henceforth as *Vision*.

While working on advanced degrees in my late twenties and early thirties, I also served as a youth minister for another six years at two different churches, providing me with valuable learning experiences. All in all, I worked in youth and young adult ministry for nearly sixteen years and most of those ministries started from "scratch," that is, as an inaugural youth ministry new to that particular church. Each of them was a very different ministry based in three different areas of the country (Miami, Florida, Washington, DC, and Beltsville, Maryland). Each of the ministry settings was different and diverse. One was in a suburban setting, one was in an urban setting, and one was in a rural setting, and they all provided me with opportunities for growth and all had their set of challenges.

I have also served as a campus minister and as a young adult minister in Miami, Florida, and as a diocesan director of youth and young adult ministry in Austin, Texas. Both positions had their own set of unique and challenging issues. Since my full-time days in youth and young adult ministry, I have continued to predominately research, write, and lecture on various themes within the field of youth and young adult ministry because I believe they are the *most* important ministries in the Christian Church.

I consider myself a pastoral and liberation theologian who specializes in adolescent ministry; hence, I am an adolescent ministry scholar. My sincere hope is that this book is a helpful theological and pastoral tool in advancing the study and field of Christian youth and young adult ministry in *all* denominations: Orthodox, Catholic, Protestant, and Evangelical.

I believe this book is insightful and useful to all mainline Christian youth and young adult ministers. However, it may also be applicable and appropriate to other world religious traditions. Consequently, though I am a Roman Catholic, this book has a largely Catholic orientation to it, both in its theological scope and in theological references. This, of course, does *not* mean that I do not use Protestant and other Christian theologians and sources, because I do. Nor does it mean that I am not open to ecumenical dialogue, issues, and concerns, because I am. It simply means that I am proud to be a Roman Catholic Christian and that I strongly believe that Catholic insights on youth ministry and young adult ministry have much to offer the worldwide Christian community. In fact, it is my ecumenical desire that all Christian youth and young adult ministers from every Christian denomination read, enjoy, and integrate the models and methodologies into their ministries.

Introduction: Situating Youth and Young Adult Ministry

The aim of this book is not to be merely a theological, cerebral, academic exercise. It is meant to be both an academic book, and a pastoral and practical book, as well, that is undergirded by sound theology and solid pedagogical insights and pastoral strategies. In addition, I do *not* want this book to be solely a book with "good ideas" that encourages youth and young adult ministers to think "outside the box." I also hope to inspire congregational youth and young adult ministers and diocesan directors of youth and young adult ministry to move into *action* and begin to integrate the models and implement the methodologies the book proposes.

Moreover, this book is not only a book filled with solid pedagogical and theological methods about youth and young adult ministry; it is a book that deserves to be read by every so-called Christian youth and young adult minister, discussed in small gatherings of youth and young adult ministers, and passed down to catechists and volunteers to solidify its importance within a parish community.

Furthermore, this book is meant to create more effective youth and young adult ministers. Youth and young adult ministers who are in these fields, which, in my mind, are most valuable to the Body of Christ.

Finally, this book will attempt to chart a new course that gently nudges forward the possible within Christian youth and young adult ministry because this ministry *cannot* exist by doing things the same way, year-after-year, with the sad mantra: *we have always done it this way*. There is an absolute need and a strong desire to rekindle the spirit of young people in the Church and the world today. The conditions are ripe to challenge the *status quo* within Christian youth and young adult ministry.

Since adolescence represents a transition from childhood to emerging adulthood and from emerging and young adulthood to adulthood, the transition for many young people is not an easy time. Youth and young adult ministry can provide a safe and stabilizing influence for today's teenagers, emerging adults, and young adults. Christian youth and young adult ministry *always* strives to reach out to embrace all young people: those in the congregation and those beyond the congregation. The parish youth and young adult ministry must *not* be a social club or an elitist group, but one that nurtures, empowers, and challenges adolescents and young adults to become more productive Christians in the church and citizens in the world. Therefore, it is critical that youth and young adult ministers be properly and theologically educated and spiritually formed to do the important pastoral work of serving, guiding, and ministering to and with young people.

Defining Some Terms

This book is about young people between the ages of fifteen and thirty-five years, and that is a tremendous age gap! There are entire volumes of books and countless academic journals and popular magazines dedicated to the various developmental stages of that age grouping. Therefore, this book will not try to reconstruct those findings. Instead, it maintains a stylistic conformity that addresses the overall "big picture" of youth and young adult ministry without doing disservice to either ministry or developmental periods. I have tried to use models and methods that will undergird adolescent, emerging adult, and young adult ministry. The fact of the matter is that there are a lot of people wearing two ministry hats at their church anyway: a youth minister's hat on one night and wearing a young adult minister's hat on another night. In other words, lots of ministers in Christian congregations are working in two similar, but unique, ministries: youth and young adult.

Young People

Throughout the book the term young people will be employed to refer to three populations: (1) adolescents, ages 15–18; (2) emerging adults, ages 19–25; and (3) young adults, traditionally ages 26–35. I recognize that is a large span of time of human growth and development. Although I use the term *young people* as a shorthand, the intent here is not to "shortchange" any of these three young populations of people. The unique distinctions of each group can be further nuanced by the psychologists and sociologists who are experts in these various classifications of human development and culture.

Youth and Young Adult Minister

Other important terms used throughout the book are the terms youth minister or youth pastor, and young adult minister. I employ the terms *youth pastor* and *youth minister* as synonymous and equivalent terms. Although the term *youth minister* is commonplace in the Catholic Church and in the majority of Protestant churches, ecumenically, I recognize that there are distinctions in some denominations. Some Protestant and Evangelical churches distinguish between *youth minister* and *youth pastor* by either advanced pastoral degrees (Masters of Divinity or Masters in Pastoral Studies) and/or by ordination within their respective communities. Therefore, in some Protestant and Evangelical churches, the *youth pastor* is an ordained minister serving as a pastor to young people of that particular congregation, but doing much of the same work as a non-ordained youth minister in another Christian community. Nevertheless, I will use this term interchangeably, mainly as an ecumenical equalizer. There is no disrespect intended in anyway whatsoever on my part.

The phrase youth and young adult minister will be used for the person or persons who do either in part or in whole, the work of ministering to and with any of the three populations of people listed above: (1) adolescents, (2) emerging adults, and (3) young adults. In this book, the terms ministry and minister, for the most part, are restricted to those adults who are charged with and carry forward the mission of the Christian churches and the ministry of Jesus the Christ to young people. Therefore, *youth and young adult ministry* falls under the umbrella of Christian ministry, and has its own special and genuine style, context, and qualities that make it applicable and appealing to young people.

Finally, throughout this book the terms *youth*, *adolescents*, and/or *teenagers* are used interchangeably and as synonymous terms. These terms are used to designate middle adolescence, ages 15–18, or the typical high school years in the United States. The use of these words is intended to be used as all-encompassing, gender-neutral, and inclusive, reflecting a certain age category within the infrastructure of Christian youth ministry. Consequently, then, this book does not consider younger teenagers or early adolescents, 11–14 years of age.

Parish/Congregation/Community

Other terms that are utilized in this book are *parish/parishes*, *community/communities*, and *congregation/congregations*. All three terms are used as interchangeable and intermeshing terms, and are not meant to confuse the audience or readership of this book. The terms are used as identical ecclesiological realities even though some Christian denominations may use one term more than another.

Describing Young People Today

It is difficult, if not pompous, to try and pinpoint the exact climate and culture of young people today. Nevertheless, I will try to give some brief insight to these different periods of human growth and development.

Adolescence

The question, "What is adolescence?" also seems to merit brief attention. Within the Western world adolescence or the "teenage years" is a stage of life that fits into the larger matrix of human development. A widely held position among adolescence scholars is that "adolescence is the period of transition between childhood that involves biological, cognitive and socio-emotional changes."[2] Certainly, the period of adolescence can be further divided as well: early adolescence, ages 11–14 (the middle school years); middle adolescence, ages 15–18 (the high school years); and late adolescence, ages 19–25 (often called "emerging adults" today).[3]

Over the decades, adolescence has become a homogenized and domesticated institution. Besides family guidance and school influences there are a myriad of outside stimuli that help to shape teenage values: music, advertising, social media, peer groups, globalization, and postmodernism.[4] Along with changing influences and outside stimuli come new trends: sex with no rules, materialism, consumerism, the prevalence of substance abuse, increased risk-taking behavior, the rise in teenage violence and destructive behavior, the epidemic of adolescent depression and suicide, and smorgasbord spirituality.[5] Without being jettison, it is worth noting that *not* all North American adolescents bend toward materialism and consumerism. *Not* all cultures and classes of youth are captured by consumption-ism and dependent upon the media or social-media for attention.

For the most part, common, secular, youth culture today is free of biblical and Christian underpinnings. Youth today have life spaces and social choices that constitute their own culture, including personal styles, choice of clothes, music, television, bedroom decorations, dance, rituals

---

2. Santrock, *Adolescence*, 17.
3. Canales, *Noble Quest*, 30–34.
4. Mueller, *Youth Culture 101*, 48–51.
5. Ibid., 53–58.

for romance, and subculture styles.⁶ Youth culture today is recognized as being present in some form or fashion in every corner of the globe.⁷ This book hopes to help youth ministry move youth culture "from a culture of entertainment and pleasure" to a culture of grace and mercy.⁸ Therefore, youth culture is part of the institution of adolescence. Understanding youth culture can empower a youth minister about the period of adolescence, which can enhance Christian youth ministry.

Emerging Adults and Young Adults

Today emerging adults are seen as ages 19 to 25, the typical college-age person. The term was coined in 2004 by Jeffrey J. Arnett and his book *Emerging Adulthood*. Arnett maintains emerging adulthood and young adulthood are quite different from adolescence. There are five key features that distinguish emerging adults and young adults from adolescence: (1) identity exploration, (2) instability, (3) self-focused, (4) feeling in-between, and (5) thoughts of possibilities, hopes, and unparalleled opportunity.⁹

In their document, *Young People, the Faith, and Vocational Discernment*, the Catholic Bishops state that emerging adults today live in a "hyper-connected generation" that offers great opportunities, but also great risks.¹⁰ Emerging adults are bombarded with an array of choices everyday though social media and regular routine relationships. Matters of faith and discerning life's vocation should seem important, but they are a group, for the most part, that are concerned with choosing this or that today, and worrying about the consequence tomorrow.¹¹

American Protestant adolescent ministry scholar Thomas E. Bergler wisely notes that American congregations—Protestant or Catholic, African-American or Caucasian—have *not* done an adequate job of helping emerging adults reach spiritual maturity. The reason is partly because "churches, seminaries, and theologians are just beginning to grapple with

---

6. Jacober, *Adolescent Journey*, 82.
7. Ibid.
8. Crosby, "Reformed View of Youth Ministry," 46.
9. Arnett, *Emerging Adulthood*, 8.
10. Synod of Catholic Bishops, *Young People*, 13. Hereafter *Young People*.
11. Ibid., 14–15.

the realities [and complexities] of the new emerging adulthood."[12] Emerging adults is a relatively new phenomenon.

When it comes to matters of faith, emerging adults like to keep their options open and see religion and church attendance as many choices and options within their lives. Sociologist Christian Smith maintains that faith and spirituality of emerging adults can be sorted into six religious types:

1. Committed Traditionalist (15 percent)
2. Selective Adherents (30 percent)
3. Spiritually Open (15 percent)
4. Religiously Indifferent (25 percent)
5. Religiously Disconnected (5 percent)
6. Irreligious (10 percent)[13]

These groupings of emerging adults may help to shed light on the way emerging adults think and understand religion. The second group of emerging adults—Selective Adherents—is the largest grouping and usually comes from reasonably strong religious upbringings. Emerging adults are now in the process of picking and choosing the things in life they want to keep and discarding the parts of life they do not want in terms of faith and spirituality.

Bergler uses the terms *missional typology* to describe the different "tribes" that emerging adults correspond with because in his mind these "new types reflect a more careful distinction between those with more and less positive affective connections to their faith."[14] Bergler, unlike Christian Smith, is more concerned with emerging adults and their emotional connection with God. Bergler calls his emerging adult tribes: (1) transitioning believers, (2) wavering believers, (3) seekers, (4) the unreached, (5) the indifferent, and (6) the alienated.[15] Bergler maintains that emerging adults can move around between tribes over time.

Emerging adulthood is *not* a universal period for all cultures; in most countries adulthood begins with marriage.[16] Emerging adulthood has been

---

12. Bergler, *From Here to Maturity*, 102, 113.
13. Smith, *Souls in Transition*, 166–68.
14. Bergler, "Mapping the Missional Landscape," 87.
15. Ibid., 88–91.
16. Arnett, *Emerging Adulthood*, 24.

regarded as a "new period" in human development, individual exploration, and personal exploration. This new phase of life is typically brought about by social, cultural, and economic changes that have affected young adults around the world.[17] Emerging adults seem to be faced with two undergirding themes (1) instability and (2) value shifts.[18] The markers for emerging adult instability are: career instability, relationship instability, financial instability, and physical instability.[19] The markers for emerging adult value shifting are uncertainty of truth, easy access to information, global awareness, and an embrace of diversity, provisional connections, and personalized spirituality.[20]

What does all this mean? It means that emerging adults are still growing cognitively and are still trying to find their place in the world. Emerging adults are moving toward greater maturity, and will embark upon full young adulthood and adulthood by experiencing life and by making the right choices in life.

Young adulthood is typically seen as ages 26–35, which seems old enough to be considered an adult, rather than a *young* adult. However, since the period of adolescence is extending, it only makes sense that young adulthood is also extended. Chronology of age does not usually serve as a consistent factor when determining young adulthood or adulthood.

With young adulthood comes the capacity to make meaning of one's life. It is a more stable period than the emerging adulthood typical of one's college years. Young adult ministry scholar Sharon Daloz-Parks states that there are three modes of awareness that comes with young adulthood: "(1) becoming critically aware of one's own composing of reality, (2) self-consciously participating in an ongoing dialogue toward truth, and (3) cultivating a capacity to respond—to act—in ways that are satisfying and just."[21] For most young adults, they are distinguished from emerging adults in terms of their seriousness about life and their level of commitment to work, relationships, and education.

The US Catholic Bishops highlight four key developing areas that help shape young adults from their late twenties to their mid-thirties. The four areas are developing personal identity, developing relationships, developing

---

17. Dunn and Sundene, *Shaping the Journey*, 24.
18. Ibid., 31.
19. Ibid., 31–33.
20. Ibid., 34–36.
21. Daloz-Parks, *Big Questions, Worthy Dreams*, 6.

a meaning of work, and developing a spiritual life.[22] Typically, young adults experience self-sufficiency and discover new roles in society, work, family, and the church. Young adulthood moves from dependency to independency and young adults become comfortable making their own life choices.[23]

Hopefully, the defining and describing of these various terms helps the reader to understand my rationale, as well as to situate youth and young adult ministry properly within the framework of this book. Finally, before getting into the heart of the book, it might be wise to briefly address the role and purpose of youth and young adult ministry.

Youth and Young Adult Ministry

I want to distinguish between youth and young adult *ministry* and the youth and young adult *minister*. The former caters to a specific population of people and works to benefit young people for the betterment of the Kinship of God. The latter is about the function of the person doing ministry in the Christian Church as a vocation and life-calling.

The Ministry of Youth and Young Adults

A reasonable question is what is youth and young adult ministry? Youth and young adult ministry, as I like to tell my students, is not rocket science. If it was, I would not be doing it or enjoy it so much.

First and foremost, youth and young adult ministries flow directly from God and God's grace of God's favor. Second and simultaneously, youth and young adult ministries are ministries of the Christian Church and move from the mission of the Christian Church, which is to usher in the Kinship of God. Third, youth and young adult ministries are, as the esteemed Dean Borgman (sometimes referred to by his colleagues as the "grandfather of youth ministry") points out, are "remedial functions of the Christian Church. If all other systems—families, communities, schools, and churches—were functioning holistically, youth [and young adult] ministry as a profession and academic discipline would not be needed."[24]

---

22. USCCB, *Sons and Daughters*, 8–16. This document will be referred to henceforth as *Sons and Daughters*.

23. Ibid., 7–8.

24. Borgman, *Foundations for Youth Ministry*, 8.

Introduction: Situating Youth and Young Adult Ministry

Fourth, since families, communities, schools, and churches are highly dysfunctional and will remain this way for the foreseeable future, youth and young adult ministry will continue to play an active role in guiding young people on their faith and life journey. Fifth, youth and young adult ministry can take place anywhere and at any time. Youth and young adult ministry can take place in an urban, rural, or suburban setting. Youth and young adult ministry can happen with a large gathering on the church grounds, with a few people at a coffee shop, or a restaurant in a train station.

Sixth, quality youth and young adult ministry are comprehensive and systematic in scope. Areas and components of importance and competence include: advocacy, catechesis (biblical, liturgical, moral, sexual, and theological), community life, evangelization (mission in the Protestant churches), justice and service, leadership development, pastoral care, prayer and worship, spiritual development, and stewardship.[25] Seventh, worthwhile youth and young adult ministries have various intersecting dimensions or themes that undergird its ministry. Significant areas of concentration and specialty include: family friendly, intergenerational, inculturation, multicultural, interreligious openness, collaboration with the larger societal community, provide Christian leadership, adaptable and flexible programming.[26]

Eighth, youth and young adult ministry would be wise to offer these quality avenues to increasing Christian identity, spirituality, and faith: mentoring, pastoral care and counseling, prayer experiences, retreats, days of reflection, service and social justice opportunities, spiritual activities (bible studies, prayer meetings, small faith sharing groups), and social activities.[27]

The Minister of Youth and Young Adults

It is equally important to discuss the youth and young adult minister as a minister of the Christian church. Such positions within Christian congregations are quintessential to the faith, moral, and spiritual development of a young person.

First, youth and young adult ministers are servants, that is, they serve the Christian Church and the church's mission. In its broadest sense, ministry is to be understood as service or *diakonia* (Greek) to the people of

25. USCCB, *Renewing the Vision*, 26–47. This document will be referred to henceforth as *Renewing the Vision* or *RTV*.
26. Ibid., 19–25.
27. Canales, *Noble Quest*, 81–99.

God.[28] The understanding that ministers are servants of the church is an ecclesiology that is firmly rooted in the reality that youth and young adult ministers are called to serve, guide, and lead young people (disciples) to encounter God's goodness (mercy), to experience God's favor (grace), and to engage in God's being (ontology).[29]

Second, youth and young adult ministers have a genuine vocation (life's calling) to ministry. The desire to help young people on their spiritual and faith journey is a vocation. The vocation of youth and young adult minister is "to help young people choose life (Deut 30:19) by equipping them with the faith, hope, and love needed to recognize God's forgiveness and embrace the life God intends for them."[30] There are seven primary functions that youth and young adult ministers do for young people: (a) they lead young disciples toward Jesus the Christ; (b) they enact and embody certain ministerial practices—teaching, preaching, worship, pastoral care, social concerns, and administration; (c) they live in relationship with God's mission; (d) they act as discernible public figures in word, deed, and symbol; (e) they work and are servant-leaders on behalf of a particular Christian community; (f) they are publicly recognized and acknowledged by a particular Christian community; and (g) they practice their vocation in a diverse array of ecclesial settings, contexts, and relationships.[31]

Third, youth and young adult ministers must possess the following intentional virtues: (a) character, (b) charity, (c) justice, (d) fidelity, (e) self-esteem, (f) prudence, (g) gratitude, (h) generosity, (i) compassion, (j) humility, (k) holiness, and (l) courage.[32] These virtues help to intentionality shape and solidify the integrity of youth and young adult ministers as professionals serving, guiding, and leading young people toward Jesus the Christ in their Christian communities.

Fourth, there are certain things that youth and young adult ministers will find useful, especially during their first two years of ministry. Veteran youth and young adult ministry expert Doug Fields shares a worthwhile list of commitments that youth and young adult ministers would do well to recognize, remember, and recite to themselves:

---

28. Unites States Conference of Catholic Bishops, *Co-Workers in the Vineyard*, 20.
29. Root, "Regulating the Empirical in Practical Theology," 59.
30. Root and Creasy Dean, *Theological Turn in Youth Ministry*, 14.
31. Cahalan, *Introducing the Practice of Ministry*, 57–67.
32. Gula, *Just Ministry*, 48, 83–115.

Introduction: Situating Youth and Young Adult Ministry

a. I will move slowly and cautiously (Prov 14:15–16).
b. I will regularly check motives and evaluate my heart (Prov 20:8–12).
c. I will steer clear of the number's game (Matt 18:12).
d. I will not criticize the past or my predecessor (Phil 3:13).
e. I will avoid the comparison trap with another person or ministry (Gal 6:4).
f. I will focus on priorities (Matt 22:36–40).
g. I will pace myself as to not burn-out (Heb 10:36).
h. I will serve and be a servant-leader (Matt 20:26–28).
i. I will be a good learner and be coachable (Prov 4:5; 13:20).
j. I will pursue contentment and joy (Phil 4:11).[33]

The fruits these ten commitments will yield personal results and the ability for youth and young adult ministers to balance their lives within and outside the ministry, and the capability to form the foundation of a thriving and lasting ministry.

Fifth, healthy youth and young adult ministers must take care of themselves before giving to others. This means doing things like: reading for pleasure, having fun, spending time with family and friends, praying often, seeking regular pastoral supervision (for several years) with an older and wiser person in ministry, continuing education and study, making personal retreats, seeking out pastoral counseling or spiritual direction, and taking time for self-reflection and introspection.

This section is by no means exhaustive in scope and practice. I have tried to highlight some of the distinctions between the *ministry* and the *minister*. I like to tell my students that God cares more about the minister than the ministry. We are created in the *imago Dei* (the image and likeness of God)! Therefore, God wants to see God's children healthy and thriving, not necessarily succeeding in an individual ministry. Please, do not get me wrong; good ministry is also extremely important, but just like any good parent, God cares more about the person and not the person's achievements.

---

33. Fields, *Your First Two Years in Youth Ministry*, 37.

CHAPTER 1

Theological Models and Methods

> *[A] model for ministry involves three sources of religiously relevant information: (1) Christian tradition, (2) the experience of the community of faith, and (3) the resources of the culture.... The model of theological reflection in ministry suggests resources that can help in ministry to respond faithfully and effectively to the concerns that challenge the community of faith.*[1]
>
> James D. Whitehead and Evelyn E. Whitehead
> *Method in Ministry*

Preliminary Remarks

This chapter maintains that theological models are fantastic to integrate and implement into youth and young adult ministry. Models and methods are fantastic because they offer students and scholars alike a way to comprehend information regarding a particular study of inquiry. Therefore, the field of youth and young adult ministry can benefit from various models and methods of theology. Hopefully, all Christian youth ministers, emerging adult ministers, and young adult ministers, can appreciate various models and methods for practicing and approaching ministry with young people.

This chapter presents the theological rationale for integrating models in the Christian church that will serve as an underpinning for youth and young adult ministry. Both the academic study and the pastoral framework

---

1. Whitehead and Whitehead, *Method in Ministry*, 13, 21.

for adolescent ministry and young adult ministry will be highlighted. Youth and young adult ministers must be willing to think differently about the manner in which youth and young adult ministry is being conducted across the United States in diverse and multicultural churches. Models that focus on practical ministry encourage independent thinking and the willingness to do Christian and ecumenical youth and young adult ministry with a renewed sensibility and with new felt awareness.

Models are more than mere ideas; models are grounded concepts that arise from theological constructs which help shape human understanding. In addition, models can serve as living images and reflections of a reality whose essence sometimes is not easily accessible to human perceptions. The scope of this book is to represent the best meaning of theological interpretation with the intention of making the message understandable and meaningful for all parties: the student, the practitioner of youth and young adult ministry, and the academic adolescent ministry scholar (I am thinking of the work done by my wonderful colleagues at the Association of Youth Ministry Educators and the International Association for the Study of Youth Ministry).

Understanding and Mastering Models

This section will briefly examine three theologians, Avery Dulles, S.J., John F. O'Grady, and Kevin W. Irwin, for their insights on theological models. This chapter will also highlight three others, Sallie McFague, Thorwald Lorenzen, and Stephen B. Bevans, whose theological works on various models have influenced the twentieth century theology, and continue to influence the twenty-first century Christian thought and ministry praxis. The rationale for reviewing these theologians is to: (1) glean insights for the importance of models in theological and pastoral discourse, and (2) provide parameters for utilizing models with ministry to adolescents and young adults, either in local congregations or perhaps high school and college campus ministries.

Models of the Church

Conceivably the real "master" of the modern day model is the late Jesuit systematic theologian Avery Dulles whose international best seller *Models of the Church* is truly ecumenical in scope and a landmark book for its

Theological Models and Methods

contribution to ecclesiology. Dulles offers five models of the church that find significant support in the documents of the Second Vatican Council (1962–65) or Vatican II.[2] Dulles's models of the church are: (1) institutional, (2) mystical communion, (3) sacrament, (4) herald, and (5) servant.

In his later edition, the 1987 text, Dulles adds an important sixth model, community of disciples, which is a foundation for all pastoral and ministry models. Like his other models it has its strengths and limitations.

In the interim, Dulles writes his *Models of Revelation*, which explores the theology of revelation and moves beyond pre-Vatican II understanding of revelation as predominately apologetic. Dulles's models of revelation are: (1) doctrine, (2) history, (3) inner experience, (4) dialectical presence, and (5) new awareness. Unfortunately for Dulles, *Models of Revelation* never reached the status of *Models of the Church*, nor was it widely acclaimed as he had hoped. Both of Dulles's books would be good for youth and young adult ministers to read to expand their ecclesiological horizons because these books are considered staples for ecumenical ecclesiology.

Both of Dulles's books are still incredibly insightful, and continue to be used, studied, and integrated into ecclesiology and theology classrooms at universities and seminaries across the United States. Dulles utilizes various models to view and interpret numerous theologies through different and alternative theological lenses, demonstrating his keen ability to master theological models. During the course of this book I will endeavor to communicate diverse "models" as a way to assist Christian youth and young adult ministers, and volunteer catechists in the important work of ministering with and to young people. As Dulles points out:

> The method of models is applicable to the whole of theology, and not simply to ecclesiology. . . . *The method or types, I believe, can have great value in helping people to get beyond the limitations of their own particular outlook,* and to enter into fruitful conversation with others having a fundamentally different mentality. Such

---

2. The Second Vatican Council also referred to as Vatican II (1962–65) was a watershed event for the Catholic Church in particular and perhaps in general to the rest of the Christian Church. Vatican II changed the face of the Catholic Church in the modern world; its main task was to recapture the biblical and liturgical roots of early Christianity and to help situate the medieval church into the twentieth century and beyond. The Second Vatican Council produced sixteen documents, which rank high in terms of "pecking order" for Catholics to adhere to as authoritative; first and foremost, in terms of authoritative texts, is of course the Bible.

conversation is obviously essential if ecumenism is to get beyond its present impasses. (emphasis added)³

Dulles's words are as true today as they were forty years ago.

Models are an approach for theology and the theological method, but also a way of approaching pastoral theology, practical theology, or ministry praxis. Dulles's works continue to be a fortification for Catholic and Protestant theologians and he is rightly considered an authority when it comes to theological models. Most books that utilize models in theological discourse owe a bit of gratitude to his insights.

Models of Jesus

Catholic Scripture scholar John F. O'Grady wrote a best-selling book on models revolving around Jesus: *Models of Jesus*. O'Grady's book insists that models are inclined to synthesize people's existing experiences or the faith experience that they have come to believe.⁴ He maintains that theological models will manufacture the "biblical experience as well as the experience of centuries of lived faith in the history of Christianity."⁵ O'Grady is concerned with adapting images for Jesus of Nazareth, which he successfully accomplishes in six models for Christology: (1) Jesus as the Incarnation of the Second Person of the Blessed Trinity; (2) the Mythological Christ; (3) Jesus the Liberator; (4) the [Person] for Others; (5) Jesus, Lord and Savior; and (6) the Human face of God.

O'Grady insists that the investigative use of models includes a specific theological task of "breaking new ground" and offering a means for the Christian Community to benefit from the new discoveries.⁶ Therefore, models must bring fresh insights to the academic discipline they represent, as well as the larger community which supports the field of inquiry. O'Grady's work is objective and balanced, and his insights offer much wisdom on the topic of Jesus. O'Grady's *Models of Jesus* continues to be a mainstay for those interested in Christology. This is a wonderful book for

---

3. Dulles, *Models of the Church*, 12. Dulles's monumental work, *Models of the Church*, was originally published in 1974.
4. O'Grady, *Models of Jesus*, 22. Originally published in 1980.
5. Ibid.
6. Ibid., 23.

youth and young adult ministers to read to enlarge their understanding of Christology.

Models of the Eucharist

Catholic liturgical and sacramental scholar Kevin W. Irwin published the book *Models of the Eucharist*, which is a theological, liturgical, and pastoral investigation of the celebration of Sunday Eucharist. For Irwin, Sunday worship is "the jewel in the crown of [Christianity]."[7] Irwin addresses ten models that are constitutive for the issues that surround and shape popular piety, religious education, and Eucharistic exacerbation in terms of lacking proper theological and liturgical understanding. Irwin's models of the Eucharist include: (1) Cosmic Mass, (2) the Church's Eucharist, (3) the Effective Word of God, (4) Memorial of the Paschal Mystery, (5) Covenant Renewal, (6) the Lord's Supper, (7) Food for the Journey, (8) Sacramental Sacrifice, (9) Active Presence, and (10) Work of the Holy Spirit. Irwin argues that these ten models are designed to help people view the way Christians pray at the Eucharist, and to understand the liturgy, its meaning, and its unique impact upon everyday spiritual life.[8] Irwin's book is too new to conceive its impact upon Christianity, but it is greatly respected by this author, and if it is an indication of his previous work, it will impact both liturgical academia and ecclesial ministry.

Other Theological Models

It is also worthwhile to mention three other theological works which investigate models: (1) Protestant and feminist theologian Sallie McFague's *Models of God: Theology for an Ecological, Nuclear Age*, which received the 1988 American Academy of Religion Award for Excellence; (2) Baptist Scripture scholar Thorwald Lorenzen's *Resurrection and Discipleship: Interpretive Models, Biblical, and Theological Consequences*; and (3) practical theologian Stephen B. Bevans's highly acclaimed book *Models of Contextual Theology: Faith and Cultures*.

McFague utilizes three models for God in her text: (1) God as Mother, (2) God as Lover, and (3) God as Friend, which have been seen as feminist

---

7. Irwin, *Models of the Eucharist*, xiii.
8. Ibid., 30.

models and interpretations of God, and highly valuable to feminist theology, practical theology, and ministry.

Lorenzen integrates four models for the Resurrection of Jesus: (1) the "Traditional" Model: Fact and Reason, (2) the "Liberal" Model: Word and Faith, (3) The "Evangelical" Model: Fact and Faith, and (4) the "Liberation" Model: Promise and Praxis. All of his models give biblical foundations to understanding and interpreting the Resurrection and Christian discipleship.

Bevans examines six models of contextual theology: (1) the Translation Model, (2) the Anthropological Model, (3) the Praxis Model, (4) the Synthetic Model, (5) the Transcendental Model, and (6) the Countercultural Model. His models are important because they help ministers to understand the richness of doing theology in context and help to situate contextual theologies today.

These three theologians cannot be studied in any depth here, but they help to illustrate the importance of theological models to theology and ministry and to every Christian denomination.

Conversely, my prevailing intent with using models in youth and young adult ministry is fourfold: (1) to be faithful to the Christian principles and components that help to shape and guide youth and young adult praxis in the United States, (2) to ensure that these models can be integrated as part of a systematic, intentional, and comprehensive youth and young adult ministry, (3) to provide solid theological and pastoral rationale for *doing* Christian youth and young adult ministry, and (4) to enrich the fields of practical theology and youth and young adult ministry studies, an emerging discipline that transcends denominational boundaries. The models that are presented in this text are integral not only to the field of youth and young adult ministries, but may also be integrated and utilized in both campus ministry and adult ministry, and perhaps may be developed for the larger umbrella of pastoral ministry.

Furthermore, there are criteria that have been used to study each of these models: (1) compatibility with Christian theology and the Bible; (2) ecumenically open-minded in theory, as well as being able to integrate into multiple church traditions with similar harmony, depending upon the model; (3) supportive of catechetical integration into Christian youth and young adult ministry, Christian high school campus ministry, and/or college campus ministry; and (4) correspondence to the religious faith experiences of adolescents and young adults as a fruitful implementation of the various pastoral strategies.

These criteria are not infallible by any means, nor are they exhaustive. However, they do give brief guidelines for each model, and either the pastor, youth minister, and/or young adult minister will have to decide which models are worthy of more attention, integration, and implementation on any given year.

The Importance of Models for Christian Youth and Young Adult Ministry

An important question for our discussion is: *why models for Christian youth and young adult ministry?* This is a fair question to ask. Models for pastoral and practical theology and ministry, at least in my mind, if not also for Dulles, McFague, and Bevans, are important and serve a real pastoral need. In the context of youth and young adult ministry, models serve to support and simplify the sometimes hectic and complex world of ministry while providing concrete theology in the process.

Franciscan and systematic theologian Ewert H. Cousins explains clearly the importance of models within the discipline of theology:

> Theology is concerned with the ultimate level of religious mystery which is even less accessible than the mystery of the physical universe. Hence our religious language and symbols should be looked upon as *models* because even more than the concepts of science, they only approximate the objects they are reflecting.[9]

Cousins is persuaded that models contribute positively to theology and its various branches of theology such as pastoral and practical theology, and therefore, ministry.

Protestant practical theologian Ray S. Anderson reminds us that "ministry always precedes and produces theology, not the reverse."[10] *Why is this true?* Because ministry and pastoral work are determined and put forward by God's initiative and God's personal ministry of revelation and reconciliation with the world, in and through Jesus the Christ and the Christian churches of God.[11] All Christian ministries are the work of God

---

9. Cousins, "Models and the Future of Ministry," 81.
10. Anderson, *Shape of Practical Theology*, 62.
11. Ibid.

and God's own ministry. Therefore, theological models used for ministry can help situate and better understand the practice of ministry. For our purposes, these models give youth and young adult ministers particular practical knowledge for pastoral care and ministry.

Catholic practical theologian Kathleen A. Cahalan writes that "the particular knowledge that is unique to ministry is called practical theological interpretation, and its task is to engage the context of ministry."[12] The four models within this book will support youth and young adult ministers in their important work with young people as they interpret various ministerial situations, contexts, and initiatives.

The four models that will be discussed within the context of this book fall under the context of Christian youth and young adult ministry. I offer four ecumenical ways of participating in comprehensive ministry with young people. The four models proposed in this body of work are indeed models, in the sense of being representative prototypes of Christian practical theology and pastoral ministry. In other words, the four models are types of pastoral approaches for adolescent and young adult ministry that include both a theoretical component (theology) and a practical component (ministry). The models are also appropriate for a ministerial framework for constructing youth and young adult ministry.

Borrowing from Avery Dulles:

> A distinction must be made between experimental models, which can actually be constructed and used in a laboratory, and the theoretical models, which are excogitated with the help of creative imagination, have a merely mental existence, and are used for the development of theories.[13]

According to Dulles's framework, the models in this text represent both experimental and theoretical models because they allow youth and young adult ministers the ability to integrate and implement a specific methodology for each model in the "field." Moreover, each model will give youth pastors and young adult ministers the theological background to support their ministerial practice and integration of a particular model.

Of course, models must be tested by the community at large to be proven reliable and worthy. If a model has been estimated to be a viable and reputable source of intellectual inquiry by members within the community, in this case the field of youth and young adult ministry, the hypothesis it

---

12. Cahalan, *Introducing the Practice of Ministry*, 122.
13. Dulles, *Models of the Church*, 31.

advocates may benefit from a certain conjecture in their favor, but any such hypothesis must then be appraised by the methods and criteria proper to the disciplines in question.[14] Again, in this case, the models presented in this book must be appropriate to those interested in the field of youth and young adult ministry: college students, catechists, pastors, congregational youth and young adult ministers, diocesan directors of youth and young adult ministry, practical theologians, and adolescent ministry scholars.

These models, then, are for those engaged in serious work with young people involved in youth and young adult ministry. Christian youth and young adult ministry models are designed to assist, in an analogous way, those engaged in ministering to adolescents, emerging adults, and young adults. Models of Christian youth and young adult ministry are typically built upon three independent components: (1) a traditional understanding of the sacred Scriptures and Christian orthodoxy; (2) the cognitive, moral, spiritual, and emotional development of young people; and (3) service, outreach, and social justice initiatives.[15]

Finally, models for youth and young adult ministry are valuable practical and pedagogical tools because they will give pertinent theological reflection and method to assist youth pastors and young adult ministers. However, the models addressed in this study will also allow youth pastors and young adult ministers the ability to employ different denominational contexts for their important ministerial work to be carried forth. Youth and young adult ministry is a rich pastoral field and deserves far more critical attention by the Christian community or *sensus fidelium* (sense of the faithful) than it receives. Hence, with the glimmer of light that this book provides, it hopes to further illuminate the discipline of youth and young adult ministry education.

The Methodology for Youth and Young Adult Ministry

The methodology that this book engages is one that seeks to improve the quality of ministry practice by utilizing three areas: (1) tradition and Scripture, (2) personal experience, and (3) cultural information and social sciences. The method has genuine concern for ministry and aiding in the practical approaches for ministry implementation. Figure 1 below illustrates the ministry methodology that helps to shape this book.

14. Ibid., 32.
15. Arzola, *Toward a Prophetic Youth Ministry*, 31–32.

FIGURE 1

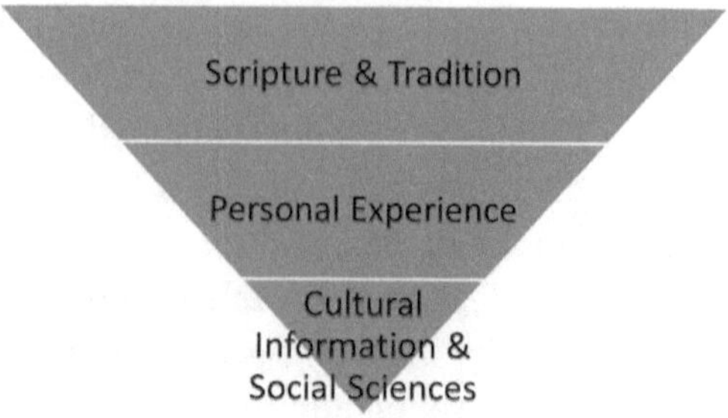

- Scripture & Tradition
- Personal Experience
- Cultural Information & Social Sciences

The result of these three areas is that pastoral care and ministerial concern for young people is the driving-force of this method. Scripture and tradition are integral components for Christianity as a whole to reflect upon and for understanding history and theology as deposits of faith.[16] It is difficult to speak of one without the other: Scripture and tradition are the bedrock of Christianity. Personal experience brings into play the skills of awareness, introspection, and listening, and these skills are a critical stage in the overall spiritual developmental component of self-actualization.[17] Personal experience of the young person as faith-seeker, and the larger youth and/or young adult community and the wider congregation of faith also bring a dynamic to the religious experience of a young person.

Cultural information and social sciences provide valuable data that help to shape ministry formation. Cultural information and social sciences offer a different lens for being able to understand other societies, religious traditions, and cultural ambiguities.[18]

The integration of each individual model, vis-à-vis pedagogical approaches or pastoral strategies, is the prescriptive section of this work or methodological component. The methods for this book come after the theological model has been discussed. According to the American practical theologian Andrew Root, "Method, by definition, seeks not reality, but rather takes reasoned steps to reduce reality, so that it might say something particular."[19] Or, in the case of this book, the methodology seeks to help the youth and young adult minister see something practical and pastoral and in ways which the method can be implemented and utilized. The imple-

---

16. Whitehead and Whitehead, *Method in Ministry*, 14–15.
17. Ibid., 18–19.
18. Ibid., 20–21.
19. Root, "Regulating the Empirical," 48.

mentation of a methodological approach for a particular model is up to the discretion of the youth and young adult minister who has a particular ministerial concern that must be met. To help situate an exact model within youth and young adult ministry, a brief example of a ministry vignette will be illustrated.

Ministry Vignette

Jackson Johnson is a thirty-three-year-old African-American youth minister working in a a medium-sized, racially and culturally diverse church on the east side of Indianapolis, Saint Phillip Methodist Church. Jackson works with about fifty high school students participating in various programs throughout the week. He is also blessed with five committed adult catechists (volunteers) to help him with various projects and activities. One of the areas that has concerned Jackson in his two years of working at Saint Phillip's is that there is not as much spiritual depth in the programs as he had hoped. Jackson would like to begin the following year with being more intentional and systematic about incorporating more of the Bible and biblical themes and activities throughout the year. Perhaps focusing a little less on fun activities and service projects (albeit important) and being more deliberate about weaving the Scriptures into the curriculum. From Jackson's perspective, he would be wise to examine and implement the biblical-hermeneutic model in this book. This laconic case study is merely a sample of the type of ministry scenario that will help contextualize the models and methodologies for youth and young adult ministers.

The Four Models for Christian Youth and Young Adult Ministry

This book proposes four models for Christian youth and young adult ministry. All the models that I introduce and examine are not exhaustive, but taken together they are a significant theological, pastoral, and spiritual tool for youth and young adult ministry.[20] The proposed models are *not* listed

20. For the purposes of this book, I am taking for granted that these four models will be integrated and implemented into comprehensive Christian youth and young adult ministries in the United States of America. In addition, each of these proposed models will not be the totality of a youth or young adult ministry gathering. I am presuming that a typical youth and young adult ministry evening/gathering would include most

or studied by order of importance or by particular merit. They are simply investigated as theological, catechetical, and pedagogical prototype in order to assist youth pastors and young adult ministers in their important pastoral work and care with young people.

It is my strong contention that no one model is superior to another; all four models have strong merits and solid ministerial attributes. All the models are compatible with the others and to say otherwise would be misguided and an inadequate assumption. Likewise, to choose exclusively one model over others or to blatantly reject other models appears to be arbitrary and not entirely comprehensive.

Therefore, no one model is better or worse than the other. It is solely up to the discretion of the congregational youth minister, campus minister, and/or young adult minister to adopt an appropriate model. The appropriation of each model depends on the adolescent and young adult population for a given community, and it is for the youth pastor and young adult minister to best determine which model to integrate and which strategies to implement.

My sincere hope is that youth and young adult ministers of every color and stripe—youth pastors, volunteer catechists, parish directors of Christian education, campus ministers, diocesan directors, and ordained ministers—will benefit from the models presented in this exposition. As previously alluded to, it is possible to expound upon all the plausible models in existence, but the goal of each model is to assist the youth pastors and young adult ministers with theology, methodology, and pedagogical strategies to empower young people to achieve moral and spiritual transformation.[21] Furthermore, ideally, these models with their own emphases and viewpoints may be interchangeable with any of the other models.

All four models are distinct yet complementary. Each model acts as a reference point or accountability factor for the manner in which a youth ministry operates. The four models for youth ministry and young adult

---

of the following: prayer, ice-breakers, games to play, skits, music, Scripture reflection, catechetical talk or presentation, faith-sharing small discussion groups, social time after the gathering, and the offering of food and refreshments. Furthermore, I am maintaining that a comprehensive youth and young adult ministry has two or three weekend retreats and days of reflection per year in order that a larger spectrum of adolescents and young adults many participate in spiritual encounters. Finally, I recognize these are large assumptions!

21. As noted, these models are not exhaustive; in fact, there are many possibilities. There are other models that could *possibly* be explored in a subsequent volume.

Theological Models and Methods

ministry are as follows: (1) biblical-hermeneutic model, (2) the servant-leadership model, (3) liberation model, and (4) the Christian discipleship model. Each of these models will correspond with a chapter in this book. Before examining each model in greater depth, each of these models will be considered individually and briefly.

1. The biblical-hermeneutic model: A method that investigates and interprets the sacred Scriptures so the holy texts have meaning and purpose for adolescent and young adult religious experience and expression. Biblical narratives are life stories, action stories, and universally relevant stories that impact contemporary worldviews. The Bible informs, forms, and transforms the human consciousness. Therefore, the principle of the biblical-hermeneutic model informs, forms, and transforms the reader by private interpretation that has been shaped by culture, community, and tradition. Youth ministers and young adult ministers will have to adopt reading methods and Bible study strategies that allow biblical narratives to address young people's issues and concerns, as well as develop biblical spirituality and biblical literacy.

2. The servant-leadership model: Probably the most difficult to realize because most of its fruits will not be seen until after students graduate from high school and college and move on from the youth and campus ministry setting. Servant-leadership can also be viewed as threatening because it implies that the one who serves the most is the leader. Leading by serving others is one of the main reasons Jesus of Nazareth threatened the religious establishment of his day. By its very nature servant-leadership puts the subordinate first, the followers first, the employees first, the students first, the children first, the poor first, the illiterate first, etc., and this can be a threatening proposition. The three backbones of servant-leadership are listening, acceptance, and empathy. A good leader listens well, but an exceptional leader listens well, with acceptance and empathy. The goal of servant-leadership is to encourage and empower adolescents and young adults to become servant-leaders within their home, school, community, neighborhood, and society, thus transforming their spheres of influence and the world.

3. The liberation model: Liberation is a theological concept that emphasizes human response to the invitation of salvation in Jesus the

Christ. Liberation theology calls the Christian Church to tolerance, compassion, justice, and peace. In the context of this book the themes of inculturation, multiculturalism, and interreligious openness will be stressed as liberation topics. Liberation motifs also imply the inquiry that takes as its primary concern the idea of emancipating oppressed peoples from unjust political, economic, racial, and/or social subjection. Liberation has its roots in the South American liberation theology of Gustavo Gutiérrez. Liberation is a bold theology of reflection and pastoral praxis that identifies with the gospel commitment of love, care, and action. Liberation is born of shared vision to abolish unjust situations, to build a better society and a more free and humane world.

4. The Christian discipleship model: Throughout the centuries, discipleship has been continuously affirmed and held in high esteem as being the predominant paradigm for devout and dedicated Christians. There are other Christian paradigms such as virginity, martyrdom, and monasticism, but discipleship appears to be the measuring stick for authentically committed Christians. Christian discipleship, which has many interpretations, comes from the word "disciple" meaning the "one who learns" or the "pupil who follows" the Master. Christian discipleship and all that it entails are at the very heart of the gospel: "Come, follow me" (Matt 4:19; Mark 1:17). All Christian discipleship has Jesus the Christ as its unifying center and creative power; that is, all Christian discipleship flows from Jesus Christ, the fountain and wellspring of life.

Each of these models will assist youth and young adult ministers in their noble work with young people. Below is a table that will help situate each of the four models. The chart helps to characterize and give meaning to a given model's specific nature and scope within the framework of youth and young adult ministry. The table is designed to be interpreted and classified by type, distinction, theological objective, and pastoral outcome, and it will guide readers through some of the foundational aspects offered in each model.

Theological Models and Methods

Table 1: Models for Youth and Young Adult Ministry
Specific Characteristics of Each of the Four Models

MODELS	DISTINCTIONS	THEOLOGICAL OBJECTIVES	PASTORAL OUTCOMES
1. Biblical-Hermeneutic	Interpreting the Bible for pastoral reflection and ministerial praxis.	1. Deepen the knowledge-base and appreciation of the Scriptures. 2. Empower the reading and studying of the word of God as a "living book." 3. Engage in the biblical-hermeneutic process.	1. Higher biblical literacy and Scripture comprehension within the youth ministry. 2. Become inspired to read, study, and lead Bible discussions as they feel comfortable. 3. Overcome biblical complacency and to experience power of the Scriptures.
2. Servant-Leadership	Learning the art of leadership through service and service-learning.	1. Raise the consciousness about the theory and practice of servant-leadership. 2. Teach the ten characteristics of a servant-leader. 3. Develop an ethic of caring for individuals and community.	1. Learn to choose service over self-interest and to lead through service. 2. Become empowered to become servant-leaders within the society. 3. Become agents of change through servant-leadership.
3. Liberation	Focusing on the poor, the marginalized, and the disenfranchised in society.	1. Encourage a theological praxis to take shape within the ministry. 2. Establish pedagogy from the three areas that help to contextualize liberation theology. 3. Teach inculturation, multiculturalism, and interreligious openness.	1. Become attuned to the process of inculturation in their lives and in the church. 2. Encourage to appreciate, value, and promote cultural diversity. 3. Learn to be open-minded toward people who believe in another religious tradition.
4. Christian Discipleship	Living as a Christian disciple within a community of faith.	1. Foster Christian adolescent conversion. 2. Teach about the eight areas of Christian discipleship. 3. Empower behavior on the vertical, horizontal, and internal levels for Christian growth.	1. Develop a conscience for Christian responsibility and living a life of faith in Christ. 2. Live as an authentic Christian disciple in the world, but not of the world. 3. Faithful to God's call in one's own life.

The model distinctions, theological objectives, and pastoral outcomes are *not* exhaustive by any means and there may be some overlap with some models, but overall the table does indicate the richness and diversity of each model. All four models are equally significant and contribute to youth and young adult ministry, even though they are not all on identical levels or "playing fields" theologically, spiritually, and pastorally. These models are a means to the ever-elusive aim of Christian ministry renewal, communal self-transcendence, and becoming witnesses to God's rule and reign in the world. Increasingly, of course, these models may be indirectly applicable to every ministry within the Christian Church.

The four models for youth and young adult ministry are *not* specifically designed to choose one over another as conceptually more appealing. Each simply indicates different ways of viewing the church and illuminating diverse aspects of ministry in its ecclesial relationship with community and young people.

The differing models reflect different theologies, ecclesiologies, and pastoral relationships between the youth ministry, collegiate campus ministry, or young adult ministry, and the particular Christian institution or community at the local level of the congregation. Therefore, different models elucidate different aspects of ecclesial ministry.

No model is complete in and of itself, theologically or theoretically. One model can, however, offer critical insights, assessments, and synthesis of those aspects of youth and young adult ministry not accounted for in another particular model. The construction of new models, as purposed in this book or the reconstruction of existing models, is for shaping youth and young adult ministry relationships in terms of equality and collegiality with other ministries within Christianity. The creation of new models is often accomplished with critical observation, dialogue, and discernment. Sometimes new models emerge from an already older conceptualization of an existing framework within the church.

Parting Remarks

As aforementioned, it is my hope that the academic community, that is, youth ministry educators and adolescent ministry scholars in particular, embrace this book for their own edification, research, and courses. However, even more so, that the pastoral community, that is, youth ministers, campus ministers, adult volunteer catechists, directors of Christian

Theological Models and Methods

education, young adult ministers, and pastors will benefit from these four pastoral and theological models. Ideally, these models have their own emphases and viewpoints, and stand independently apart from other models; however, they may be used interchangeably with any of the other models out of pastoral necessity. These four models provide valuable theological content and pastoral context that will provide Christian youth ministers and young adult ministers with resources that will empower them to faithfully and effectively minister to the needs and challenges that young people face today.

These four models characterize a theological system coupled with a systematic and pastoral integration schematic. In addition, they represent a relevant and sensible blueprint for youth pastors, campus ministers, and young adult ministers to build upon and to utilize as a practical guide. Moreover, the four models represented are merely *theological organizing frameworks* and *modes of action* that may become part of a minister's field of vision and sphere of influence to engage, enthuse, and empower young people to move beyond themselves. Finally, each model reflects certain aspects within culture, and of course, is conditioned as such. However, each model is timeless as each addresses the human consciousness and the great quest to become closer to God.

The subsequent chapters will offer a deeper investigation of each of these models, and will independently examine the theological relevance of each model and offer insights on various approaches for integrating each model into a pastoral framework. Furthermore, each model will offer four or six methodological approaches and pedagogical strategies for implementation, which youth and young adult ministers may find useful as ministerial devices in their imperative work of ministering to young people. Beyond studying the theology, integration principles, and pedagogical strategies, each of the four models will have a brief section explaining the strengths and limitations of the model under consideration. Finally, there will be fictitious youth or young adult ministry case studies based upon real scenarios, although the names, churches, and cities have been changed—presented at the end of each chapter to help the reader identify with various pastoral circumstances that exist within the life of Christian youth and young adult ministry. Ultimately, these four models will bring new insights and understandings into the meaning of faith for those who minister to adolescents, emerging adults, and young adults.

CHAPTER 2

The Biblical-Hermeneutic Model

> *Concern for young people calls for courage and clarity in the message we proclaim; we need to help young people to gain confidence and familiarity with sacred Scripture so it can become a compass pointing out the path to follow. Young people need witnesses and teachers who can walk with them, teaching them to love the Gospels and to share it, especially with their peers, and thus to become authentic and credible messengers.*[1]
>
> Pope Benedict XVI
Verbum Domini, n. 104

Preliminary Remarks

Before getting started there are a few preliminary remarks that need to be addressed. First, in this chapter, the terms "Bible" and "Scripture" are synonymous and are used as interchangeable words, as well as the derived adjectives "biblical" and "scriptural." The words "Bible" and "Scripture" will be capitalized to demonstrate respect for their place as a source of theology and as a mode of divine revelation; however, the terms "biblical" and "scriptural" will *not* be capitalized. Second, the terms "biblical" and "hermeneutic" need to be addressed before exploring further the nature and scope of this model. Third, the phrase "word of God" is meant to be tantamount to the two terms "Bible" and "Scripture." It is worth mentioning that mainline New Testament scholars, Protestant and Catholic, use the lowercase expression *word of God*, as I have done, to be interpreted as sacred Scripture or

---

1. Benedict XVI, *Verbum Domini*, n. 104.

The Biblical-Hermeneutic Model

the Bible, that is, the book itself, the actual text, and its private reading or public proclamation. The phrase *Word of God*, using capital letters (i.e., capital "W"), denotes the Second Person of the Holy Trinity, that is, Jesus the Person Incarnate and the mystery of the divine self-revelation and self-communication of God, whether in Scripture, "in Jesus" at prayer, or in some other consciousness.[2]

The term "biblical" refers to the body of literature commonly referred to as the holy "Bible" or a sacred "Scripture." In the Christian tradition, the Bible is the word of God, inspired by the divine and expounded upon through human authors, and it is an expression of God's holy revelation on the printed page, designed to bring people into a deeper and more meaningful life experience. As the fourth Gospel states, the word of God, like Jesus himself, "came so that [humanity] might have life and have it more abundantly" (John 10:10b). Therefore, the adjective "biblical" refers to the art of understanding, interpreting, and engaging in various topics, principles, and ideas that surround the sacred texts contained in the word of God.

The word "hermeneutic" is derived from the Greek word *Hermes*, "messenger of the gods." *Hermes* can also mean "to make something understandable," but it is loosely or colloquially translated as "interpretation."

In this chapter, hermeneutics is the theory and practice of understanding and interpreting the sacred texts, passages, and pericopes[3] within the Bible. Hermeneutics addresses the phenomenon or problem of biblical interpretation and offers systematic reflection upon the historical, theological, and spiritual meaning of the Scriptures. Primordially, hermeneutics is a process and Scripture scholars refer to this as the "hermeneutical circle," a process that begins with God and a particular event. After the particular event happens, for example, the liberation of oppressed people, people who witnessed the event and remember it, tell the story to preserve the narrative (oral tradition). Then, after some time (generations), the oral story is written down by human authors to help preserve the stories as sacred texts. Next, the process is handed down to the ecclesiastical community (Protestant or Catholic), which is the interpreter of the sacred texts. Finally, the process moves on to the rest of humanity (the People of God), to whom

---

2. Schneiders, *Revelatory Text*, 7.

3. The word *pericope* (pe·ric·o·pe / pə-'ri-kə-pē) is a French term and it actually means a "slice of literature" or "an extract from a text." In this case, we mean a "slice of biblical literature." Scripture scholars and biblical theologians have been using this word for decades now, and a pericope can mean a small verse within a chapter or it can mean an entire chapter contained in a book of the Bible.

the faith is proclaimed and lived out or fused with everyday life. Individuals and faith communities begin to understand and interpret the sacred texts and apply them to their lives. This appropriation of the sacred texts also allows for faith in God to grow and for God to reveal God's self to the people or interpreters of the texts, both as individual and as a community of believers.[4] Figure 2 below illustrates the hermeneutical process of interpreting sacred Scripture.

FIGURE 2

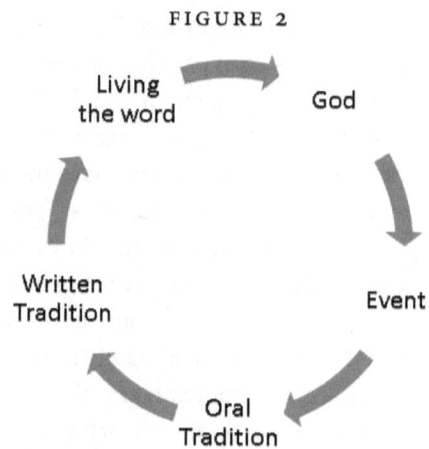

This hermeneutical process has been a model of interpreting Scripture for the Jewish community and has been transmitted and preserved as authoritative for the Christian tradition. Jesus himself acknowledged and emphasized this biblical-hermeneutical model and its normative nature (Matt 5:17–19; John 10:35)[5], and yet simultaneously Jesus claimed his own authority over this model (Matt 5:21–28). Jesus' message was to uncover anew the Scriptures' character and integrity as a central message of God's divine revelation (Matt 19:4–8; Matt 21:12–46).

The Bible is indispensable as a theological, spiritual, and catechetical tool for youth and young adult ministers. Youth and young adult ministers are in the privileged position to help young people live holier lives, and become spiritually empowered by witnessing and teaching the Bible's content and message to adolescents and adults alike. This chapter offers three ways

4. De La Torre, *Reading the Bible from the Margins*, 102–3.

5. All Scripture passages in this book are taken from *The Catholic Bible: Personal Study Edition*, New American Bible translation (New York: Oxford University Press, 1995).

The Biblical-Hermeneutic Model

for Christian youth and young adult ministers to implement the Bible into their respective ministries: (1) to use the Bible as object of study and as a lens through which to understand one's self and one's cultural context, (2) to use Christian precedents for appropriating Scripture in various ways in order to utilize the Bible effectively in the lives of young people, and (3) to empower youth and young adult ministers to help young people absorb the biblical message actively in their own lives.

The primary aim is to try to have youth and young adult ministers bolster the biblical imagination and spirituality of today's young people by providing a variety of pedagogically and methodologically appropriate strategies for integrating sacred Scripture into the lives of young people. This chapter examines only one model that can be effectively integrated into youth and young adult ministry on the prescriptive level through various pastoral and pedagogical strategies. Likewise, this chapter is meant to be ecumenical in nature as its aim is to promote a better understanding of the possible integration methods for the Bible into Christian youth and young adult ministries. Finally, it is worth noting that I write from a Catholic perspective, but the material and insights that are contained in this composition are applicable to all Christian youth and young adult ministries.

Not Merely Words on a Page

The biblical-hermeneutic model is a ministerial and methodological experience that investigates and interprets the Scriptures in order that they have meaning and purpose for adolescent, emerging adult, and young adult religious experience and expression. Biblical narratives are life stories, action stories, and universal relevant stories that impact contemporary worldviews. The Christian faith comes from God's revealing word as conveyed by the testimony of the church, albeit, among the readership of the Bible, there exist innumerable interpretations of individual pericopes of Scripture and these interpretations are often irreconcilable with one another. In youth and young adult ministry, any biblical passage needs fluid comprehension for its theological and pastoral content, but equally the passage needs to be applicable and relevant to adolescent culture and lifestyle.

A Catholic understanding of the Bible is that the Bible must be possible for all people, for all reading levels, and for all ages in every generation. If youth and young adults are going to understand and appreciate the Bible, especially if church leadership desires young people's lives to be transformed by its message, then the Bible and its message must be accessible and made relevant for the twenty-first century. Therefore, it is imperative that the Bible not be viewed as mere words on a page, but a living word that informs and inspires. An individual may read the biblical text primarily for information, that is, to be intellectually enlightened, or one can read the Scriptures for personal transformation with the aim being *metanoia* and conversion.[6] As the Vatican II Constitution *Dei Verbum* (1965) points out, "The sacred books of [God] who is in heaven comes lovingly to meet [God's] children, and talks with them."[7] Therefore, it is the proper task of youth and young adult ministers to challenge and engage adolescents with the word of God.

Because the ideological aim of the Bible is liberation, youth and young adult ministers may assist young people in rereading the Bible, which encourages them to "act locally and think globally" regarding certain issues. Moreover, the liberation nature of the Scriptures empowers young people to make-meaning out of the sacred texts that move them to action and commitment toward others in the community.

Youth and young adult ministers are expected to catechize young people that the Scriptures are both a sacred text as well as a literary classic. This makes the Bible a "living book," not merely words on a page, but the living, breathing word of God, albeit open to critical examination and investigation. I have heard it said, and have read it in print many times, that the Bible is the number one best-selling book, year-in and year-out, across the globe.

Essentials of the Biblical-Hermeneutic Model

Essentially, the biblical-hermeneutical model is a method for youth and young adult ministry that incorporates the Bible as its core curriculum.

---

6. For an excellent survey of *metanoia* and conversion see Canales, "Rebirth of Being 'Born-Again,'" 98–119. *Metanoia*, the Greek term for "change of mind," "repentance," and "conversion," but the term is far more encompassing. Canales states that the "classical definition of *metanoia* is a change of the mind, that is, 'change the way you think.' The Jewish understanding of *metanoia* is a change of heart, that is, 'change your attitude or feelings'" (102). The definition of *metanoia* that Canales uses is quite appropriate for the interior change that adolescents may experience through the biblical-hermeneutic model. For Canales *metanoia* is twofold: "(1) a radical change of mind and heart, and (2) a total turning away from sin and the world and embracing God. Ultimately, *metanoia* refers to the transformation of the total person: changing of the heart, renewing of the mind, and informing of the conscience through Jesus Christ" (102).

7. *Dei Verbum*, 762–63, no. 21.

The Biblical-Hermeneutic Model

This model asks youth and young adult ministers to infuse the word of God more purposefully into the activities and programs in the youth and young adult ministry. Theologically, the biblical-hermeneutic model offers adolescents a solid theological base that will incorporate the various narratives, parables, miracle-stories, and other inspirational and revelatory material contained within the word of God. Ecumenically, the biblical-hermeneutic model is extremely rich for teenagers because it is all-encompassing.

While Catholics and many Protestants today realize that everyone needs a tradition and lens to guide the reading of the Bible, it must also be personally appropriated. Therefore, the biblical-hermeneutic model fully accepts and appreciates the Bible's relevance for every Christian and its foundational nature for the life and faith of every Christian. Morally, this approach takes seriously the Bible and it is capable of providing a worldview for young people to appropriate into their lives. Young people can ask a very basic question: How should I live my life according to the Scriptures?

I am not tacitly implying that the Bible is a moral manual, but it can provide questions to ethical dilemmas. Pastorally, the biblical-hermeneutic model offers young people a solid grounding in sacred Scripture; although it is not an exhaustive academic study, but a personal appropriation of the Bible that will benefit a young person's faith life and journey with God. If adolescents or emerging adults are going to learn and grow into mature Christians, then it would be most prudent to afford them the opportunity to learn to live by the ethical and social justice standards that are embedded in the Scriptures.

Understanding the Biblical-Hermeneutical Circle

The integration of the Scriptures for adolescent and young adult ministry serves to deepen the faith-life of teenagers and adults. Predominately, the way that the biblical-hermeneutical model will be integrated into youth ministries is through weekly or semi-monthly Bible studies. The goals of Bible studies are twofold: "(1) to engage students in pragmatic biblical theology, and (2) to empower them for Christian discipleship."[8] The Bible study, although primarily a catechetical instrument, also rejuvenates adolescent and adult spirituality. Hence, youth and young adult ministers can "crack open" the Bible and study from it just about anywhere: at the beach, inside a ski lodge by a cozy fireplace, camping along a lakeside, in the school

---

8. Canales, "Spiritual Significance of the Nicodemus Narrative," 29.

cafeteria, or at the local coffee shop. There is no hard and fast rule that a Bible study, geared for youth or young adults, has to be done on church property; thus, the creativeness of the Bible study can also be the location.

Again, as previously mentioned, the hermeneutical circle is a process that begins with God and is then transmitted to the authors of the sacred texts. Next, the process is handed down to the ecclesiastical community (Catholic and Protestant), which acts as the interpreter of the sacred texts. Finally, the process moves on to the rest of the people of God (in this case existing within the Christian community) who believe and belong to the larger family of the Christian faith who practice their faith and live it daily through prayer, ritual, and worship. Figure 3 below illustrates the biblical interpretation process.

FIGURE 3

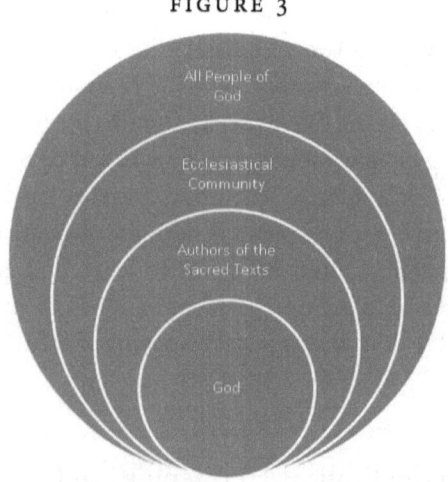

Understanding and interpreting the Bible is an excellent opportunity for young people to mature as Christians. Youth and young adults have the potential to experience meaningful and life-changing effects through small Bible study gatherings of twelve to fifteen peers. Moreover, there are two avenues that facilitate adolescents and young adults learning through the biblical-hermeneutic model: (1) Bible-centered, faith-sharing groups led by the youth or young adult minister (or an adult catechist), and (2) Bible-centered, faith-sharing groups led by peers (young people themselves).[9] Both approaches will empower young people to be committed to Christ, the church, and Christian discipleship. Youth and young adult ministers

9. Strommen and Hardel, *Passing on the Faith*, 200–202.

The Biblical-Hermeneutic Model

can profit greatly from the biblical-hermeneutic model because it helps young people develop strong Scripture-based knowledge as well as cultivating biblical spirituality.

The biblical-hermeneutical model is likened to Greg Stier's *Gospel Advancing View of Youth Ministry*. In Stier's scriptural system, if young people read and study the Bible: (1) it equips teenagers for relational evangelism; (2) it helps youth share stories; (3) it gives the gospel priority in youth gatherings; (4) it adheres to the 10 percent rule (which is essentially that with just 10 percent of a group's population holding an unshakable faith, this confidence will hopefully be adopted by the other 90 percent over time); (5) it tries to "Gospelize" everything; and (6) makes prayer a big deal.[10] These six points are part of a larger matrix of evangelization and catechesis which try to shape young people into Christian disciples.

The Bible can be used as great tool for instruction, catechesis, evangelization, and discipleship. So, what is the biblical-hermeneutical circle? The biblical-hermeneutical circle in youth and young adult ministry refers to the word of God being interpreted: (1) as universal truth, (2) by the culture, (3) is accessible to all Christian denominations, (4) an expression that helps discern the will of God, (5) that designates that which is necessary to believe (theology), and (6) establishes for its readers proper conduct for their lives (discipleship). Hispanic theologian Miguel A. De La Torre states, "Biblical interpretation is deductive; that is, the universal truth of the Bible or the teachings of the church is the starting point, a first step that leads to a second step, which is the application of biblical truth."[11] The Scriptures have much to teach us and there is much to learn from its pages, but in order to capture the essence of the Bible it needs to be read, comprehended, and utilized into action in daily life.

Many of my youth ministry students have told me that they were hesitant to conduct Bible studies with youth because they did not understand everything within the Bible. I usually responded back with something along these lines: "You cannot be an affective youth minister without knowledge of the Bible," or, "You have to know how to do a Bible a study if you want to be a youth minister," or, "Once you prepare your first Bible study, you will be on your way to becoming a good youth minister."

Comprehension of the Bible is absolutely necessary to becoming a quality, professional youth and young adult minister. Not being able to

---

10. Stier, "Gospel Advancing View of Youth Ministry," 9–12.
11. De La Torre, *Reading the Bible*, 102.

create ice-breakers or be able to play games with young people, those are secondary to a good, proper understanding of sacred Scripture.

The typical biblical-hermeneutical circle interprets from the center of society and *not* from the fringes of society, and the center or dominant is usually concerned with self-preservation, maintaining the *status quo*, and in gaining more possessions (for example white, suburban, middle-class to upper-class, educated, patriarchal, heterosexual, etc.). Interpreting the Bible from the margins reverses the dominant methodology of biblical interpretation and allows for authentic liberation to be experienced as action (pastoral practice) and contributes to the expansion of a theological perspective that underscores the sociorelational, socioreligious, socioeconomic, and sociopolitical context of those who are doing the biblical reading.

What does this have to do with youth and young adult ministry? Plenty! Everything! Youth and young adult ministry is at the service of adolescents and emerging adults; therefore, it must strive for quality catechetical programs such as Bible studies.

The typical youth and young adult ministry methodology for the biblical-hermeneutical circle, as mentioned, is Caucasian, male-prevailing, affluent, and in a suburban parish. To reinterpret the Scriptures from a non-dominant youth and young adult ministry perspective is to shift the reality of the reader or audience. In youth and young adult ministry, the reader and audience are young people who, for the most part, have not been consumed by life's hardships and struggles, but certainly can benefit from another worldview. Therefore, a new pedagogical method for youth and young adult ministry utilizing the biblical-hermeneutical circle incorporates the minority perspective: Hispanic/Asian/black, female-oriented, homosexual, low income, and in an urban parish. This different and new approach can be advantageous for youth and young adult ministry to glean a fresh perspective on life and to gain a positive outlook on the marginalized and ostracized.

The Integration of the Biblical-Hermeneutic into Ministry

It should come as no great surprise that the Bible deserves a high priority of integration into a comprehensive youth ministry. The first ecclesial document written about comprehensive Catholic youth ministry in the United States was *A Vision of Youth Ministry* (1976), which articulated seven components for *doing* youth ministry. The document is out of print and pretty

The Biblical-Hermeneutic Model

much out of use as well. The original *Vision* document maintained that the word of God is a major component for Catholic youth ministry, stating, "Although the ministry of the word of God in the Church touches more than youth ministry, it is a very important component of ministry with young people."[12] Therefore, the effective use of integrating the word of God within youth ministry is essential on many levels: sharing, proclaiming, listening, preaching, teaching, catechizing, and evangelizing. Remarking on the fruitfulness of the Bible, the document notes the following:

> The ministry of the word is the sharing with others of the Gospel message, the good news of God's love, [liberation], and salvation as shown to us in Jesus Christ. This sharing involves elements of what are commonly known as evangelization and catechesis.... In some cases, the ministry of the word involves the initial proclamation of the faith, preceded by "the first means of evangelization . . . the witness of an authentic Christian life," and followed by the communication of the gospel message.[13]

It is clear that *A Vision of Youth Ministry* upholds the importance of the word of God and its various applications within adolescent ministry. Integrating the sacred Scriptures into youth and young adult ministry can be accomplished on a variety of levels:

- Listening to the word being taught as catechetical instruction
- Thinking about the word during a rally or conference
- Praying the word on a weekend retreat
- Hearing the word proclaimed during a worship service
- Contemplating up the word *lectio divina*
- Studying the word in a large or small Bible study group
- Reflecting the word the Stations of the Cross during Lent

An updated version of the original *Vision* document—*Renewing the Vision: A Framework for Catholic Youth Ministry* (1997)—also emphasizes the importance of using the Bible with adolescents. *RTV* suggests that Scripture is best situated within revelation and tradition.[14] *RTV* supports adolescents having rudimentary knowledge of the Bible in these areas:

12. *Vision*, 13.
13. *Vision*, 13.
14. National Conference of Catholic Bishops, *Renewing the Vision*, 32.

- *Old Testament*—developing the knowledge and tools to read the Old Testament and to understand its meaning and challenge for us today.

- *The Gospels*—developing the knowledge and tools to read the gospels and understand their meaning and challenge for us today.

- *Paul and His Letters*—developing the knowledge and tools to read the letters and understand their meaning and challenge for us today.[15]

Thus, *RTV* calls for integration of the Bible into youth ministry, but it is limited.

A third youth ministry document, *The Challenge of Adolescent Catechesis: Maturing in Faith*, stresses that adolescent catechesis must focus on integrating Scriptures into youth ministry. "The catechesis for each faith theme is grounded in Scripture. This fosters in adolescents a deepening knowledge and appreciation of Scriptures in the Church's tradition and in their own lives."[16] The document clearly calls for the integration of Scripture into an adolescent curriculum.

Unfortunately, the U.S. Catholic Bishops' documents for emerging adults *Empowered by the Spirit: Empowering Campus Ministry*, and for young adults *Sons and Daughters of the Light: A Pastoral Plan for Ministry with Young Adults*, offer virtually nothing regarding scriptural formation and biblical catechesis. This is a major flaw in each of these documents and provides ammunition for the untrue adage that "Catholics don't understand the Bible."

It may be possible for youth and young adult ministers to purchase a Christian high school curriculum on the Bible from various publishers to help in developing and guiding young people in this biblical-hermeneutical model of ministry. Publishers typically use the language of *scope* and *sequence* to determine educational aims, goals, and outcomes. However, biblical knowledge and scriptural comprehension is measured in scriptural stories, doctrinal concepts, theological views, and religious introspection.[17] Nevertheless, a good biblical curriculum might be a worthwhile investment for a youth and young adult minister to have to help integrate the biblical-hermeneutical model more fruitfully.

---

15. Ibid., 33.

16. National Federation for Catholic Youth Ministry, *Challenge of Adolescent Catechesis*, n. 25.

17. Sedwick, "Teaching for Adoptive Ministry," 307.

The Biblical-Hermeneutic Model

Anglican practical theologian Dean Borgman often called the "grandfather of youth ministry" in this country, maintains that the Bible is one of the core youth ministry foundations. Borgman insists that youth and young adult ministers know the various ways to utilize the Bible and refers to this ability as "the practice of interpretation."[18] For youth and young adult ministers to be able to effectively and efficiently use the Bible with young people they would be wise know a few things:

1. Learn to exegete the biblical text; for example, what is the story about? What is the historical context of the story? What does the text mean today? How can I apply it to my life?

2. Learn the ways of biblical interpretation, not as a Scripture scholar, but in a rudimentary way, as a pastoral person working with young people.

3. Use the Scriptures to dissect pop-culture such as music, magazines, television, films, and social media.[19]

Borgman sees self-awareness of the minister as critical to understanding the Bible. Self-awareness is key to developing a deeper biblical-hermeutical mind-set. Young people deserve to have their youth and young adult ministers help them to integrate the Bible into their lives in meaningful and creative ways.

It seems sensible that a solid scriptural foundation is needed for young people to cultivate their spirituality. The biblical-hermeneutic model calls youth and young adult ministers to think innovatively and imaginatively, using the Bible as the predominant paradigm. Today's teenagers and emerging adults deserve pedagogical strategies for integrating the Bible. Failure to appropriate the word of God effectively into one's life may lead to a depleted biblical spirituality and nominal Christianity—a bitter foe of the church.

Cultivating Biblical Spirituality

Cultivating biblical spirituality is an aspect of the Christian life that merits attention. Biblical spirituality focuses primarily on the sacred Scriptures for personal nourishment and sustenance. It is the daily reading and meditation upon a particular Bible pericope—verse or passage. One method of

---

18. Borgman, *Foundations for Youth Ministry*, 24.
19. Ibid., 25–38.

reading the Scriptures that I encourage young people to integrate into their lives is the daily reading and meditating of certain books of the Bible.

For example, over the years I have encouraged my students (former and present) to read one psalm daily and since there are 150 psalms, a person could finish the entire Psalter in six months. I also encourage young people to read from the book of Proverbs daily, and since there are thirty-one proverbs, a person could repeat the book every month for a year. I also like to encourage youth and young adults to read and reflect upon a chapter from a particular Gospel or the writings of the Apostle Paul; for instance, to annually read the Gospel of John during the liturgical season of Lent, or perhaps to read the Gospel of Matthew during the season of Advent. There are abundant ways to enhance young people's biblical spirituality.

In addition, some Christians might want to participate in church-based or home-based Bible studies to help "dig" deeper into the Scriptures. Some young adults might want take a college course on a particular book of the Bible or on various books to further increase their awareness of the Prophets, Synoptic Gospels, Pauline literature, apocalyptic literature, etc. The beauty of cultivating one's biblical spirituality is that it can be easily accomplished if truly desired. It is my sincere hope that youth and young adult ministers will encourage their young people to take advantage of Bible courses and Scripture studies as they are offered. Another great asset of cultivating biblical spirituality in young people is that it is always constant and dynamic; biblical spirituality grows and flows as a person gleans knowledge from the Scriptures and develops in holiness.

Pedagogical and Pastoral Methodologies for Implementation

The method used in this section is prescriptive because it provides tangible examples to be implemented. The biblical-hermeneutic model is most effectively utilized when Scripture is creatively woven through the youth and young adult ministry as a source of proclamation, as a reference for catechetical presentations, as narrative to be shared, and as a tool of personal growth such as a Bible study.

Before delineating pastoral strategies for this model, it may be useful for youth and young adult ministers to adopt a few pragmatic suggestions regarding the Bible. First, youth and young adult ministers should have a good comprehension of the Scriptures, that is, more than a cursory familiarity with the Bible. Second, it may be advantageous for the youth or young adult minister to enroll in a university Scripture course in order to become more proficient in biblical studies. Third, youth and young adult ministers might want to invite local theologians to come and speak to the catechists and core youth leaders in the youth ministry about biblical themes and concepts. Fourth, it may be edifying if the youth and young adult ministers were involved in a peer Bible study with other ministers in the area—Protestant and Catholic—to share insights and ideas, to understand different theologies, and to gain a network of colleagues.

The word of God is extremely important to Christian faith and identity. Christians are a people who believe the sacred Scriptures are the inspired word of God and the Bible is the book of the church.

The Five Strategies

Before addressing these five implementation strategies for youth and young adult ministries it is important to keep in mind this famous Scripture pericope: "All Scripture is inspired by God and is useful for teaching, for refutation, for correction, and for training in righteousness, so that one who belongs to God may be competent, equipped for every good work" (2 Tim 3:16–17). Therefore, whatever strategy works best for individual ministers and for a particular ministry is good. No one strategy is better than the other; using the sacred texts is the truly important factor of the biblical-hermeneutical model for youth and young adult ministry. For example, a young adult minister in Minneapolis, Minnesota, may want to implement Strategy 5 relatively soon based on her/his ministry needs, while a youth minister in Mobile, Alabama, may want to begin to use Strategy 3 right away based on her/his youth's needs.

Strategy 1

One pedagogical method for implementation is to offer a monthly Bible study which consists of a four-week series on various biblical themes. The month of September could focus its discussion on God's Creation:

- Week 1: the first creation story (Gen 1:1—2:4)
- Week 2: the second creation story (Gen 2:5—3:24)
- Week 3: developing creation spirituality (Ezek 47:1–12; Rev 21:1—22:6)
- Week 4: understanding ecology-spirituality (Rom 8:18–30)

The month of October could concentrate its discussion on God's liberation and the giving of the Decalogue, which will help reinforce in adolescents their Judeo-Christian heritage.

- Week 1: the call of Moses (Exod 3:4–22)
- Week 2: the plagues of Egypt (Exod 7:1—11:9)
- Week 3: the Exodus event (Exod 12:37—14:31)
- Week 4: the covenant at Mount Sinai (Exod 19:1—20:26)

Each month the biblical theme and studies rotate with different emphases, all focusing on the needs of the adolescent population. The most important aspects of the biblical-hermeneutic approach involves four steps: (1) understanding the text, (2) making meaning out of the text's interpretation, (3) validating the correct interpretation for its fruitfulness, and (4) appropriating the text for transformative understanding.[20] These four steps will need to be part of the youth and young adult minister's scheme for developing biblical methodology as well as creating a meaningful biblical curriculum for young people.

Strategy 2

A second pastoral procedure is to fully focus on one or two larger biblical themes for the entire academic year. This methodology will focus *all* youth and young adult ministry endeavors—retreats, Bible studies, social activities, days of reflection, lock-ins, service and outreach, and social justice initiatives—toward that particular effort.

A good example might be that the second half of the year (mid-January through mid-June) could consist of interpreting and living out Jesus' Sermon on the Mount or Beatitudes (Matt 5:1–12). Some weeks, the youth or young adult minister might have teenagers acting out one of the Beatitudes or have a skit that concentrates on a particular Beatitude. Implementing the Beatitudes in youth and young adult ministry programs will require dedication and it is quite an undertaking, one that will occupy approximately twenty weeks. The suggestion below is for the primary catechetical youth ministry gathering. For this strategy Michael Crosby's book *Spirituality of the Beatitudes: Matthew's Challenge for First World Christians* is a great ministerial tool.

---

20. Schneiders, *Revelatory Text*, 157–72.

The Biblical-Hermeneutic Model

- Month one: The relevance of the Gospel of Matthew and the reign of God
  » Week 1: The context of Matthew's Gospel
  » Week 2: The problems facing the Matthean community
  » Week 3: Addressing the Reign of God
  » Week 4: Entering the Reign of God today
- Month two: Blessed are the poor in spirit and blessed are those who mourn
  » Week 1: Poverty in Spirit, the *anawim*, and the abandoned
  » Week 2: Analyzing social sin, structures, and cultural addictions
  » Week 3: Mourning and comfort in our individual lives
  » Week 4: Mourning and comfort in our relationships
- Month three: Blessed are the meek; they shall inherit the land and those who hunger and thirst for justice, they shall be satisfied
  » Week 1: Biblical spirituality: integrating the word and the world and prayer and ministry
  » Week 2: Meekness and violence: two ways of living in the land
  » Week 3: The constitutive and normative dimensions of justice
  » Week 4: Not being satisfied until justice is fulfilled
- Month four: Blessed are those who show mercy; they shall receive mercy, and blessed are the pure of heart; they shall see God
  » Week 1: Mercy: the sign of God's perfection and compassion
  » Week 2: Mercy: the foundation for Word and worship
  » Week 3: Achieving purity of heart
  » Week 4: The blessedness of seeing God
- Month five: Blessed are the peace-makers; they shall be called God's children, and blessed are those who are persecuted for justice's sake; the reign of God is theirs
  » Week 1: Jesus: sign of God's favor and messianic peace
  » Week 2: Making peace in a war-driven world
  » Week 3: Persecution from the world and prophetic witness
  » Week 4: Prophetic spirituality and living as a Christian disciple

Part of this strategy would be to incorporate some pastoral activities on the non-catechetical nights, which could be an evening that includes spending the night at a homeless shelter or interacting with residents of a poverty-stricken area of the city. Although interacting with "undesirables" might seem a bit too risky for some ministries to attempt, it is a rewarding experience nonetheless. Another possibility is to involve the young people in the spiritual practice of Almsgiving during the liturgical seasons of Advent and Lent. This ministerial tactic is a powerful pedagogical tool for youth and young adult ministers, but requires faithfulness to the Beatitude principle, one of incorporating biblical spirituality and personal experience. Such an experience of youth and young adult ministry would help solidify a young person's understanding of the Gospel of Matthew and social justice.

Strategy 3

A third pragmatic proposition is to offer a weekend retreat that centers on the Scriptures. Retreats are an excellent spiritual and pastoral tool for teenagers. "Retreats increase discipleship, particularly areas of faith and spirituality, and have the ability to captivate, inspire, and motivate adolescents into a more meaningful relationship with God."[21]

The retreat theme could be the "Word of God" retreat or the "*Sacra Pagina*" (sacred page) retreat. The retreat could offer a variety of presentations on various topics of Scripture such as "How to Read and the Bible?" or "Understanding the Prophets" or "What is Wisdom Literature?" The list of retreat topics and themes is endless and the retreat could be as broad or narrow as the youth minister discerns.

The retreat may also facilitate a fifty-minute Bible study on a topic that mirrors a regular weekday study to showcase the practice's importance for young people. Again, the topics are limitless, but could include discussions focusing on "the parables of Jesus" or "the miracles of Jesus."

Furthermore, the retreat may provide a spiritual communal mediation centered on the Bible such as *lectio divina* (divine reading). *Lectio divina* can be a powerful spiritual tool for youth and young adult ministers to utilize with their young people because "*lectio divina* is a crucial means of perpetual and vigilant receptivity to and engagement with the word of God, which has a formative effect on the mind and heart."[22] Those who had utilized *lectio divina* recognize its transformative power and although the process is methodical and time consuming for most young people, it does yield benefits.

Finally, the retreat might also pray the Rosary, highlighting certain Scripture as an accompaniment. Although the Rosary is more particular to Catholics than Protestants, it still offers great scriptural benefits. Again,

---

21. Canales, "Christian Discipleship: The Primordial Model," 42.
22. Angel, "Vineyards and Landscapes," 19.

The Biblical-Hermeneutic Model

though, praying the Rosary can be a bit tedious and time consuming for youth and young adults.

Retreats are great avenues to bolster biblical spirituality in young people. Since retreats take place during a weekend format, they have greater potential to transform teenagers and call them more deeply into a relationship with God through the sacred Scriptures.[23]

Strategy 4

A fourth practical approach is to have a film series on biblically based themes or persons. The movie would be set within the parameters of a ministry gathering; therefore, a two-hour film is recommended for this methodology. Unfortunately, that leaves out classics like *The Ten Commandments* (1956), *Jesus of Nazareth* (1976), *Peter & Paul* (1981), and the *Left Behind Trilogy* (2004). The cinema series could be titled "Discovering the Bible through Film," and each week the young people are introduced to a different Bible character and/or biblical theme. The following is a suggestion for a ten-week biblical cinema series.

---

23. Canales, "Noble Quest," 72.

Table 2: Ten-Week Biblical Cinema Series

Weeks	Movie Titles	Discussion Theme
Week 1	Esther (1999)	Ahasuerus (Xerxes I), King of the Persians, whose empire now extends from India to Egypt after the defeat of the Babylonians, is holding a celebratory banquet for his people in the citadel of Susa to display his wealth and splendor. When he summons his attractive wife Vashti, to show off her beauty to the guests, the proud queen refuses to come. The king promptly bans her from ever entering his presence again and gives orders for the most beautiful young virgins in the land to be brought to him. The young Jewess Esther, adopted daughter of her uncle Mordecai, is among the girls selected; they are told to beautify themselves in the royal harem and prepare to spend the night with the king. Esther succeeds in enchanting the king with her extraordinary beauty and charm, and he makes her his queen.
Week 2	Samson and Delilah (1949)	When strongman Samson rejects the love of the beautiful Philistine woman Delilah, she seeks vengeance that brings horrible consequences they both regret.
Week 3	Ben Hur (1959)	When a Jewish prince is betrayed and sent into slavery by a Roman friend, he regains his freedom and comes back for revenge.
Week 4	King David (1985)	This is a movie about the life and times of Israel's great king—David.
Week 5	Joseph in Egypt (1995)	The biblical story of Joseph, who was sold to slavery by his brothers who were jealous of his prophetic abilities to analyze dreams and of his being their father's favorite.
Week 6	The Greatest Story Ever Told (1965)	Life of Jesus of Nazareth who is the Christ.
Week 7	The Robe (1953)	In the Roman province of Judea during the first century, Roman tribune Marcellus Gallio is ordered to crucify Jesus of Nazareth, but is tormented by his guilty conscience afterwards.
Week 8	Barabbas (1964)	Barabbas, the criminal that Pontius Pilate induced the populace to vote to set free so that Christ could be crucified, is haunted by the image of Jesus for the rest of his life.
Week 9	Jesus Christ Superstar (1973)	Film version of the musical stage play, presenting the last few weeks of Christ's life and his Passion; told in an anachronistic manner.
Week 10	Left Behind (2014)	A small group of survivors are left behind after millions of people suddenly vanish and the world is plunged into chaos and destruction.

The Biblical-Hermeneutic Model

Each of the above scriptural topics allows youth and young adults to further enhance their biblical knowledge while simultaneously enriching their own spirituality and love for the word of God. Immediately following the movie, it is imperative that the youth minister follow-up the film with theological reflection and small group faith-sharing questions. The debriefing process empowers young people to share their feelings, ideas, and insights from the film, and provides a window for the youth minister to situate the film within the tradition of church reflection on biblical narratives. There are many more movie possibilities to use for this strategy. Another possibility is to use the television mini-series *The Bible* (2013), which consists of ten episodes and/or *A.D.* (2015), which comprises twelve episodes. These mini-series could be used in a different way, perhaps in conjunction with a Bible study using the corresponding books of the Bible.

Strategy 5

A fifth implementation strategy is to have a summer weekly youth and young adult gathering that focuses on various biblical themes. The summer could be titled "Uncovering Your Bible Heritage." Each week there would be a lesson and Scripture passages studied in order to thoroughly introduce young people to biblical theology and the Bible. Each lesson could have a twofold emphasis: themes rooted in the Old Testament and in the New Testament. Below is a suggestion of an eight-week or sixteen-week strategy that could be implemented, depending on whether the youth or young adult minister decides to separate Old Testament from New Testament (explained below).[24] Youth and young adult ministers or volunteer catechists could discuss the following various biblical themes:

---

24. This strategy is actually implemented by a former faculty member within the Department of Theology, where I began my collegiate teaching career at Silver Lake College of the Holy Family (Manitowoc, Wisconsin). Professor Francette Riebe, O.S.F., M.A., emeritus, is a friend and former colleague who designed a course titled "Biblical Heritage," which actually investigates and explores the sixteen biblical themes that are mentioned in the biblical-hermeneutical model. The course is adapted for college students and for college credit around two booklets that are now out of print: John Tickle, *Discovering the Bible: 8 Simple Keys for Learning and Praying, Book One* (Liguori, MO: Liguori Publications, 1977); and John Tickle, *Discovering the Bible: 8 Simple Keys for Learning and Praying, Book Two* (Liguori, MO: Liguori Publications, 1980). Reverend Tickle, now deceased, wrote these booklets for the Diocese of El Paso, Texas, and if obtained, permission can be granted by Liguori Publications at (314)464-2500 to make photocopies for religious instruction.

- Week One: Revelation
  » The Old Testament (Deut 5:22–24; Exod 14:15–18; Josh 3:9–13)
  » The New Testament (Matt 3:13–17; John 1:1–17; Acts 3:17–26; 10:36–43; Heb 1:1–4)
- Week Two: Election
  » The Old Testament (Exod 19:6; Deut 7:6; Isa 2:1–4)
  » The New Testament (Matt 19:16–21; Matt 9:9–13; Luke 9:57–62)
- Week Three: Covenant
  » The Old Testament (Gen 6:18; Exod 24:4–8; Deut 7:7–13)
  » The New Testament (Gal 3:15–29; Matt 22:34–40; Heb 9:15)
- Week Four: Law
  » The Old Testament (Ps 1; Exod 20:2–6; Deut 13:2–5)
  » The New Testament (Matt 5:21–48; Matt 12:1–8; Rom 2:17–24)
- Week Five: Sin
  » The Old Testament (Isa 1:2; Job 18:5–21; Wis 1:12–23; 2:23–24)
  » The New Testament (Mark 7:20–23; John 8:46; Rom 6:1–23)
- Week Six: Redemption
  » The Old Testament (Isa 19:20–22; Jer 31:10–12; Isa 43:2–14)
  » The New Testament (Luke 1:76–77; Rom 2:5–11; 1 Cor 6:19–20)
- Week Seven: Messiah
  » The Old Testament (Isa 61:1; 2 Sam 7:8–16; Dan 7:13–28)
  » The New Testament (Acts 2:29–36; Matt 3:13–17; John 5:16–17)
- Week Eight: Love
  » The Old Testament (Gen 22:25–28; 1 Sam 18:1–2; Jer 2:20–37)
  » The New Testament (Luke 10:25–28; 1 Cor 13:1–8; John 17:1–26)

Each of these pericopes or biblical passages would ideally be read, discussed, and explored by young people with their youth or young minister or a qualified adult catechist. It may also be helpful to provide young people with study questions that reflect the content of each pericope being examined. Moreover, a small prayer service could conclude the session that incorporates the biblical theme being discussed. Furthermore, there are another eight themes that can be studied using the same methodology as the above biblical themes: community, hospitality, faith, worship, holiness, justice, suffering, and discipleship. Each of these scriptural themes allows

The Biblical-Hermeneutic Model

young people to further enhance their scriptural knowledge while simultaneously enriching their own spirituality and love for God.

These five pedagogical strategies serve as ways for youth and young adult ministers to further enhance the youth and young adult ministry with the biblical-hermeneutical model. Furthermore, these five pastoral approaches and methodologies engage adolescents and adults in various biblical ideas, themes, and principles. The biblical-hermeneutic model is a tremendous vehicle for young people to experience the Bible as a living reality in their lives, and to see the world around them from new, biblically informed perspectives.

Strengths and Limitations of This Model

The biblical-hermeneutic model, like the other models discussed in this book, has both strengths and limitations. Therefore, it is worth addressing the attributes and concerns of this model for its consideration and contribution to the field of youth and young adult ministry.

Strengths

There are many positive points and respectable values in consideration of the biblical-hermeneutical model that become immediately noticeable upon reflection. The first appeal to the biblical-hermeneutic model is embracing the word of God as a prominent theological and pastoral vehicle that guides and shapes young people's religious experience. Since the word of God is considered the sacred text for Christianity, then this model becomes a paramount symbol and tangible sign of God's interaction between God and young people. The word of God, vis-á-vis the biblical-hermeneutical model, becomes a powerful representation of God's love and compassion for all of humanity, something that is particularly important for youth and young adults to recognize and experience. Beyond being a sign and symbol of God's love, the word of God has the ability to manifest the divine. God communicates to seekers and believers through the written text contained in the word of God, which in turn empower adolescents to reach their fuller potential in God.

A second benefit of the biblical-hermeneutical model is that it is extremely ecumenically friendly. *Sola Scriptura* has been the rallying cry of Protestants since the sixteenth century and this model embraces fully that theology. Sacred Scripture is *norma normas non normata* (the norm-giving norm that is not under any other norm). Consequently, this model transcends denominational boundaries, and in fact, this model should help bridge the gap between neighboring church youth and young adult ministries that are associated with different Christian traditions. Since Jesus the Christ is the centerpiece of the Christian religion and the Bible is predominately and primarily the source that testifies upon Jesus' behalf, then it stands to reason that the Bible is held in the highest esteem. The Bible allows for all Christian denominations to work together as equals, that is, tantamount to one another despite the various theological differences and petty practical grievances. The Bible is God's instrument that "levels" the playing field.

A third effectiveness of this model is its possibility and applicability to engage young people as they become further transformed by the Scriptures and become Christian disciples. The Scriptures consist of real stories about real people; therefore, it becomes paramount that young people quickly realize that the Scriptures are written for their lives. God addresses youth and young adults, in fact, all people, through the transformative pages of the Scriptures. Integrating the Scriptures into young people's lives is critical, especially when the overwhelming majority of adolescent and emerging adult media exposure and literature is written against authority figures, such as parents, church, and God. The biblical-hermeneutical model becomes a benchmark for assisting young people in combating superfluous and negative pop culture, and making the hallowed words in Scripture more meaningful and applicable to their daily life.

A fourth advantage is the Bible's general ideological appeal because of its timeless nature that allows all people, adolescent or adult, to appropriate and experience it as both a classic literary text and as a "living book" that impacts personal piety and communal spirituality. Biblical spirituality can be built upon a limited spirituality or it can be further increased upon an already existing spirituality. Helping young people develop a more encompassing biblical spirituality is part of the process of self-awareness to the conditions that surround youth as becoming mature Christians. Moreover, biblical spirituality is heightened. The heightening of biblical spirituality in a young person's life comes about by self-awareness, a consciousness of one's own personal responsibility toward a given set of circumstances and of appropriation of the Bible that leads toward self-discovery.

A fifth significant point is the flexible character of the sacred Scriptures. In the Scriptures, there is contained a pastoral and theological insight

The Biblical-Hermeneutic Model

that allows youth and young adult ministers to initiate various contemporary topics and themes from both the Old Testament and the New Testament. There is plentiful material within the Scriptures to offer a variety of activities for young people to experience, from once-a-week Scripture studies to entire three- to six-month programs that allow for the correspondence to be felt between God's initiative, as contained in the Scriptures, and God's work in young people's lives as a result of allowing the Scriptures to be utilized and implemented within the ministries.

The biblical-hermeneutic model is a tremendous benefit to be integrated into and implemented in youth and young adult ministries. Moreover, the biblical-hermeneutic model is an awesome resource that gives teenagers, emerging adults, and young adults a strong Scripture-based knowledge and develops personal faith in God. In addition, the model provides youth and young adult ministers, adult catechists, and the adolescents and adults themselves with a solid Bible-centered approach to catechize, and evangelize their faith. Of course, like the other models discussed in this book, the biblical-hermeneutic model *does* present a few weaknesses.

Limitations

The first shortcoming of the biblical-hermeneutic model is the misperception that young people and their respective youth and young adult ministers may have toward the Bible as being too old, too boring, or too narrow-minded for contemporary issues. This mind-set is rather unfortunate and only leads to the verisimilitude and misconception of the Bible being a book only for good or holy people, and not for all people regardless of their personal circumstances.

The Bible must be presented as a timeless book that deserves to be taken off the family room bookshelf, removed from the formal living room table, and be "dusted" off and used as an authentic source of faith. It is imperative that Christians not only become familiar with the Bible, but become immersed in its content in order to become "transformed by the renewing of your mind, that you may discern what is the will of God, what is good, pleasing, and perfect" (Rom 12:2). The Bible can *empower* Christians to search for meaningful and life-applicable lessons that are engaging for everyday life, dilemmas, situations, and issues. This can happen only if young people are exposed to the rich treasures that the Bible offers, and therefore, they actually need to pick it up, read it, and integrate it into their lives.

A second constraint of this model is that youth and young adult ministers themselves may not have adequate training in Scripture studies. From my experience, the majority of Catholic youth and young adult ministers has little or no formal theological education, and therefore, do not understand hermeneutical principles, Scripture exegesis, or biblical criticisms that are taught in most college courses on the Bible. Perhaps this is not true with Protestant or Evangelical youth and young adult ministers. This does not necessarily mean that youth and young adult ministers cannot learn "on the job" by reading Scripture commentaries and by researching and studying on their own. It only makes it all the more challenging. Therefore, it is difficult for youth and young adult ministers to take young people "down a road" that they themselves have not yet traveled or feel comfortable traveling.

This can be eliminated if youth and young adult ministers decide to continue their own study and take Scripture courses at a local college or university, online, or if the diocese or institution they are affiliated with offers courses on the Bible. Moreover, if their congregation is willing to send them to workshops and seminars that foster a deeper understanding and appreciation of the Bible, then that is all the better and part of continuing education.

A third drawback of the model is the various individual and denominational biblical interpretations that each Christian church and each person has regarding the word of God. The main concern is the adoption of a fundamentalist interpretation and literalistic comprehension of the word of God. Typically, such an approach to Scripture is more prevalent in conservative Christians and their traditions. It becomes particularly dangerous if a youth or young adult minister has a misguided understanding of the word of God that tends to be fundamentalist and legalistic; this has the potential of "railroading" young people's faith life.

Fundamentalism can lead to uncritical and unhealthy reading of the word of God and would not take into account biblical criticisms.[25] This lim-

---

25. Biblical criticism refers to that modern search for deeper biblical comprehension of the word of God, a pursuit that offers various scholarly interpretations and approaches for the Bible. Many Scripture scholars highlight six biblical criticisms: *Textual criticism* seeks to establish as closely as possible the original wording of the Scriptures. *Historical criticism* tries to clarify the date, first context, and intention of each biblical book, using evidence from other Scriptures and from such external sources as history, anthropology, archeology, and non-biblical literature. *Form criticism* analyzes and classifies the styles of biblical speech and writing, such as, examining the words (parables) and deeds

itation has direct underpinnings in the previously mentioned constraint, namely, that youth and young adult ministers are typically undereducated in theology and biblical studies.[26] The word of God ideally should be put into practice within a youth and young adult ministry that is consistent with the particular Christian denomination that the youth and/or young adult ministry is associated.

The biblical-hermeneutic model offers both strengths and limitations for parish youth and young adult ministry, as well as college campus ministry and high school campus ministry. However, the limitations are not overbearing and do not constrict the strengths of this model. Youth and young adult ministry in the United States, as well as the rest of North America, can only benefit from this particular model as young people learn about the rich messages contained within the Scriptures and come to a fuller knowledge of biblical principles and ideas that will engage their young lives and empower them for future service and ministry in the church and the world.

Case Study[27]

Francis Zaire Washington is a twenty-seven-year-old African-American male. He has just been appointed young adult pastor of *Pulse Young Adult Ministry* at Bethel African-Methodist Episcopal Church, a lower- to middle-class urban congregation in Philadelphia.

This is his first ministry assignment after graduating from Howard University in Washington, DC, five years prior, with a bachelor's degree in accounting. The position is paid, but part-time; Francis already has a full-time job as one of the accountants at Freedom Financial Bank. It is a twenty-hour per week position and pays approximately $15,000 per year,

---

(miracles) of Jesus. *Traditional criticism* investigates the transmission of the oral tradition and the subsequent written units that entered the books of the Bible as they exist today within the canon of sacred Scripture. *Redaction criticism* studies (1) the motivation and mind-set of the biblical authors, and (2) the meaning and message they wished to convey to their particular audience. *Literary criticism* deals with the value and impact of the biblical texts as pieces of literature. There are brief explanations of each criticism that can be further explained and enhanced by taking an introductory Scripture course and by reading various books on the subject.

26. Canales, "Reality Check," 22.

27. This is an authentic ministry scenario that came to me about fifteen years ago; I have crafted it differently for this particular case study. The names, cities, and institutions listed in this case study are fictional and have been made up to protect their true identities.

with no benefits. Bethel AME has a rich tradition of inner-city youth and young adult ministry (some thirty years) and has seen Francis go through a two-year apprenticeship program (under the mentorship of the previous young adult minister), preparing him for his newly appointed position as director of young adults. His responsibilities are to serve and to lead various theological, biblical, and spiritual initiatives for young adult ministry.

Francis directs a large-sized, young adult ministry of approximately sixty-five college-age students and working young adults, who participate in the Sunday evening young adult gatherings (7–9 p.m.) and a Tuesday night Scripture study called *Stay Plugged* (7:30–8:30 p.m.). The Sunday night activity draws a lot more people than the Tuesday gathering; approximately forty to forty-five as compared to eight. Part of Francis's workload is to provide age-appropriate Bible studies for emerging and young adults.

His dilemma is that he has tried splitting the group into two populations, but this has been unsuccessful because the emerging adults attend more often on Tuesday nights and enjoy hanging around late into the night after ministry activities have ended. Moreover, the young adults enjoy meeting socially at a nearby restaurant or local bar after the Sunday gatherings. However, the working young adults seem to have a more disposable income than the college-aged emerging adults.

Therefore, Francis has decided to blend both ministry activities and have one large Bible study on Sunday evening and two distinct break-out groups that discuss the same passage of Scripture at the appropriate developmental levels. This way, the emerging adults can still feel part of young adults' lives. There has been some "push back" by some of the young adults and not all the volunteer leadership of the young adult ministry is in favor of such a change.

Francis's Plan: Francis wants to try to blend the two groups to be more cohesive and try to do things together as one ministry on the church campus. Francis feels a two-prong Bible study approach is the best course of action to take at this time and in the best interest of Bethel's young adults. Each of the Bible discussions, delivered by Francis, follows a more traditional, catechetical Bible presentation (e.g., read a Scripture passage, preach/teach about the pericope, and have some Q&A about the passage), and then is facilitated by two lay volunteer catechists for large group discussion and discernment. Those lay volunteer catechists are supervised by Francis.

Francis wants to begin a Scripture study that examines healthy respect and dignity for all members of society. Francis's family of origin, his faith-community, and his ethnic community have long supported the rights and roles that minorities and women play in African-American life, and this is part of his worldview. Francis believes that a detailed examination of the Bible can be extremely beneficial for his African-American young adult ministry and can help them approach equality among all people. Francis's approach is to integrate a strong Scripture-based program into a comprehensive young adult ministry, along with specific Bible strategies that will engender a strong theology and spirituality equipping young adults in the ministry to become empowered African-American Christians.

Reflection: Think about the conditions of Francis's ministry. Keep in mind that Francis has full support from his senior pastor and the adult catechists, but not total support from all participants in the young adult ministry. What would you do if you were Francis? How can Francis persuade the majority of young adults to comprehend the fullness of the biblical-hermeneutical model into the ministry? If you were facing Francis's Bible study situation, how would you arrange the format? If you were Francis, which one (or two) of the five implementation strategies would you lean on for use in this situation? How should Francis *begin* to put into motion a more comprehensive biblical-hermeneutic strategy?

Parting Remarks

The biblical-hermeneutical model is one that will benefit everyone associated with youth and young adult ministry. It is a solid model that offers great theological depth and spiritual insight. It is worthy to be implemented in both Catholic and Protestant youth and young adult ministries. Youth and young adult ministers can profit greatly from this model because it facilitates young people's faith-life experience while simultaneously developing strong Scripture-based knowledge and bolstering biblical spirituality.

The model also fosters an environment in which faith can begin to grow and mature, and "yield thirty, sixty, and hundredfold" (Mark 4:1–8). Jesus' simple parable about the Sower and the Seed is precisely an example of the beauty of the biblical-hermeneutical model. This model helps to germinate adolescent and young adult faith through the reading, studying, and praying of sacred Scripture. There are many excellent models available. However, the biblical-hermeneutical model stands as a beacon of light and hope in this current culturally challenged moment of US Christian youth and young adult ministry.

CHAPTER 3

The Servant-Leadership Model

If you seek enlightenment for yourself simply to enhance yourself and your position, you miss the purpose; if you seek enlightenment for yourself to enable you to serve others, you are with purpose.[1]

The Dalai Lama
Spiritual and Temporal Leader of the Tibetans

Preliminary Remarks

This chapter offers a descriptive analysis of one type of approach (model) to leadership that has been used successfully in secular industry and nonprofit work, but is not being fully utilized at present in youth and young adult ministry.[2] Moreover, this chapter demonstrates the various ways that servant-leadership as a model of leadership can be integrated into youth and young ministry on the prescriptive level through various pastoral and pedagogical strategies. Likewise, this chapter is meant to be ecumenical in nature as its aim is to promote a better understanding of the dynamics of servant-leadership for Christian youth and young adult ministry. Finally, the material and insights contained in this chapter are applicable to all Christian youth and young adult ministry and have some applicability beyond Christianity.

---

1. This is a quote taken from the Dalai Lama at one of his numerous lectures while visiting the United States and it can be found in Lad and Luechauer, "On the Path to Servant-Leadership," 54. For similar words see Piburn, *Dalai Lama*, 58, 60, 62–64.

2. Canales, "Models for Adolescent Ministry," 204–232.

The Servant-Leadership Model

A couple of years ago I went out to dinner with a couple of colleagues and a visiting speaker who was presenting to our undergraduate scholars program. Our conversation turned to servant-leadership. The visiting speaker said, "Servant-leadership is dead! No one really uses it or cares about it anymore." My heart dropped when he said this, and I simply replied, "I hope that is not true. If so, about half of the Christian colleges and universities in the country will have to rethink their understanding of the Gospel message."

This chapter contends that servant-leadership is far from dead and that servant-leadership has the potential to be a major model for comprehensive youth and young adult ministry. All Christian youth and young adult ministries, regardless of denomination, will benefit from the usefulness of the servant-leadership model. Moreover, this chapter offers a systematic and intentional approach for the understanding of the ideals, theology, and pedagogical praxis of servant leadership and its integration into Christian youth and young adult ministry.

A Brief Background on Servant-Leadership

Robert K. Greenleaf (1904–90) revolutionized the field of leadership and is considered by leadership studies experts to be the "founder" of servant-leadership. Greenleaf was the first to coin the term "servant-leadership" in his seminal essay "The Servant as Leader" (1970). Servant-leadership became a relatively new methodology for leadership with the groundbreaking work of Greenleaf, *Servant-Leadership: A Journey into the Nature of Legitimate Power and Greatness*.[3] Servant-leadership is a unique style of leadership, one that places the other person's needs and growth as the highest priority.[4] In terms of youth and young adult ministry, that would translate as putting the needs and concerns of young people before the personal agenda of the youth and young adult ministry.

Greenleaf states, "The great leader is seen as servant first, and that simple fact is the key to greatness."[5] Greenleaf's position in the 1970s was not a popular position or even that well-known, especially in the business world, but it is a chief idea whose time has come as pragmatic methodological theory of contemporary leadership.[6]

3. Greenleaf, *Servant-Leadership*.
4. Christenson, "St. Clare of Assisi," 13.
5. Greenleaf, *Servant-Leadership*, 21.
6. Canales, "Models for Adolescent Ministry," 212.

Margaret Kelly has distinguished fifteen traits that characterize servant-leaders:

1. Listens well and seeks to understand the other person
2. Uses language that encourages the imagination of others
3. Accepts the role of "seeker" and "searcher" for truth
4. Withdraws regularly to renew self
5. Uses power of persuasion, not coercion
6. Tries to create opportunity for others
7. Seeks to remediate organizational flaws from the inside
8. Adopts attitude of solution-finding rather than assigning blame in difficult situations
9. Deals with persons as individuals with unique talents, not as functions
10. Accepts others and empathizes with them
11. Senses the unknowable and foresees the foreseeable
12. Practices foresight and has a good sense of right timing
13. Stays aware of the environment both physical and psychological
14. Conceptualizes what "can be" and communicates it well
15. Keeps the vision at the center of all activity[7]

These servant-leadership traits offer a framework to embrace by Christian ministry in a broad sense, and youth and young adult ministry in particular.

What Is Servant-Leadership?

The natural question arises: what is servant-leadership? For the parameters of this chapter, a definition of servant-leadership is as follows: *a process of modeling Jesus' attitude of humility, service, respect, and love, which leads the followers in promoting the mission of the group, organization, or institution.*[8] With respect to youth and young adult ministry, this definition fits

---

7. Kelly, "Leadership," 13.

8. This definition for servant-leadership comes from a course that I have taught several times titled "Models of Christian Leadership." It was a collaborative and collective exercise by the entire class: first, each student wrote their own definition; next, the class was divided into small groups of four and everyone had to contribute part of their

perfectly within the values of Christian youth and young adult ministry. Developing an understanding of servant-leadership values and skills with young people is important, and it is never too early to assist adolescents, emerging adults, and young adults in moving beyond self-absorbed and self-centered existence. Servant-leadership also challenges young people to move beyond themselves and to begin thinking about others' needs first.

Servant-leadership is also a theory and the premise of servant-leadership theory is simple, yet profound: *serve to lead*. Servant-leadership theory is not only uncommon, but deeply reflective because servant-leadership is embedded in the leader functioning in the role of a servant.

The American poet Henry David Thoreau (1817–62) writes his popular prose on the social complaint of humanity: "The mass of [people] lead lives of quiet desperation. What is called resignation is confirmed desperation."[9] Thoreau's essay is the antithesis of Greenleaf's servant-leadership ideals which empower human beings to believe in something greater than themselves. For Greenleaf, dreams are worth pursuing and propel people beyond themselves to try and create something different, new, and meaningful.[10]

Leadership expert Shann Ferch states that "the idea of the leader is rooted in the far-reaching idea that people have inherent worth, a dignity not only to be strived for, but beneath this striving is a dignity irrevocably connected to the reality of being human."[11] Pragmatically, servant-leadership is anchored in empowering the innate integrity and dignity in each person.

Servant-leadership is unique because it implies that the one who serves is the leader. The servant model turns the typical male-dominated, hierarchical, and patriarchal structure, and the coercion approach to leadership, upside-down. Servant-leadership is not coercion. Ethicist Karen Spear maintains that "servant-leadership is a high calling to which to aspire."[12] Servant-leadership is encouraging, edifying, and empowering.

In the Franciscan tradition, albeit appropriate to any Christian denomination, servant-leadership has four foci: (1) it emerges out of our personhood, the person God created us to become; (2) it is always concerned

---

definition to a larger definition; and finally, each group put their definition on the chalkboard and then the entire class selected parts from each group and articulated a common definition for servant-leadership.

9. Thoreau, "Walden," 43. Thoreau's work was originally published in 1865.
10. Greenleaf, *Servant-Leadership*, 30.
11. Ferch, *Servant-Leadership*, 2.
12. Spear, "Contemplating Integrity," 8.

with serving others as distinct from gratifying our egos and ambitions; (3) it seeks to meet, understand, and satisfy the needs of the other person and group; and (4) it is a responsible stewardship in action because it takes seriously the responsibility of seeking the other person's needs.[13] Therefore, by its very nature, servant-leadership puts the subordinate first, the followers first, the employees first, the students first, the children first, the poor first, and the illiterate first.

Two undergirding principles are acceptance and empathy within servant-leadership. The servant *always* accepts and empathizes with people in the moment and never rejects the followers.[14] For Christian youth and young adult ministry this simply means to embody gospel values and practices that help to enhance young people's spiritual, emotional, and intellectual desires. Hence, youth and young adult ministers would be wise to introduce servant-leadership principles and methodologies into their curricula.

The Biblical Foundations and Theology of Servant-Leadership

Greenleaf modeled servant-leadership after the ministry of Jesus of Nazareth. Biblically, there are hundreds of biblical images of servant. The terms "service," "serve," and "servant" appear over 1,300 times in the Bible. Greenleaf was not really inventing a new idea by coining the phrase *servant-leadership*, but he was advocating an approach that is religious and spiritual in nature, which is most appropriate for today's Christian ministries, organizations, and institutions.

Jesus is the ultimate servant-leader![15] The Gospels depict Jesus as a "servant-leader par excellence advocating vision rather than structure, service rather than power, persuasion rather than control, team participation rather than individual performance, and collaboration rather than competition."[16] Jesus called, taught, and modeled to the Twelve to put other's needs before one's own needs.

Greenleaf's analysis of a servant parallels Jesus' message as a servant-leader, "For the Son of Man did not come to be served but to serve and to give his life as a ransom for many" (Mark 10:45; Matt 20:28). This pericope

13. Ibid., 9.
14. Greenleaf, *Servant-Leadership*, 33.
15. Sofield and Juliano, *Principled Ministry*, 79.
16. Kelly, "Leadership," 9.

The Servant-Leadership Model

fuels Greenleaf and his understanding of servant-leadership. For Greenleaf, Jesus is the definitive servant-leader. In another biblical text Jesus states that "whoever wishes to be great among you shall be your servant; whoever wishes to be first among you shall be your slave" (Mark 10:32–35; Matt 20:26–27). From Jesus' own lips we can concur that his leadership style and ministerial ethic was one of servant-leadership.

The classic New Testament text that references the importance of servant-leadership in the ministry of Jesus is the narrative of washing the feet of the Twelve before the Jewish feast-day of Passover.

> "Master, are you going to wash my feet?" Jesus answered and said to him, "What I am doing, you do not understand now, but you will understand later." . . . So when he had washed their feet and put his garments back on and reclined at table again, he said to them, "Do you realize what I have done you? You call me 'teacher' and 'master,' and rightly so, for indeed I am. If I, therefore, the master and teacher, have washed your feet, you ought to wash one another's feet. I have given you a *model* to follow, so that as I have done for you, you should also do" (John 13:6–7, 12–15; emphasis added).

The vision of ministry that Jesus models for the Twelve, and subsequently the Christian church, is servant-leadership. Washing the feet of his friends and followers was the quintessential act of servant-leadership because in Jewish antiquity washing the feet of another person was required of the lowliest of Jewish slaves. The practice of foot-washing that Jesus inaugurated with his disciples is a religious ritual that has been practiced throughout Christianity and continues to be practiced on Maundy Thursday in Christian churches all over the world. Jesus is the original servant-leader, and a person who always led by service.[17]

Theologically, Greenleaf encapsulates the servant-leadership found in the New Testament. He has a passion and desire to move service beyond acts of random kindness and into the workplace of every group, organization, and institution. There is really nothing particularly earth-shattering about Greenleaf's theory; however, moving the concept of service and servant-hood into the reality of corporate and nonprofit leadership *is something innovative and insightful*. Theologically, then, Jesus of Nazareth was the quintessential servant-leader, he was *primus inter pares* or *first among equals*.[18] You might say he is the primordial (first in a sequence) servant-leader.

---

17. Eckert, "Youth Ministry Leadership," 295.
18. MacPhee, "Adoptive Leadership," 276.

Evangelical biblical scholar Efrain Agosto notes that Jesus' theology and leadership style concentrated on the poor and on service. "[He] focused his attention on the poor and the outcast, those suffering the most, those to whom nobody, not even established political and religious leaders who could help, pays attention."[19] All four gospels identify Jesus' leadership with those who suffered, lived marginalized lives, and were disenfranchised by society, which made him a great leader of the *anawim* or those overwhelmed by want and poverty.[20]

Catholic theologian Dennis C. Smolarski maintains that for Christian leadership positions, especially ordained ministers, one must imitate Jesus as servant in order to minister authentically.[21] The servant dimension is fundamental for servant-leadership. Helping young people work toward authentic servanthood is important for youth and young adult ministers to integrate into their ministries regardless of the model they enjoy best. "The servant dimension of Christian leadership is given dramatic expression by the Lord himself who on the night before he died took on the role of a slave and washed the feet of the disciples."[22]

For Smolarski, as well as Greenleaf, the greater the leader, the more one is called to servant-leadership. This is the great attribute of Jesus' approach toward leadership: a style of leadership based on serving rather than being served.

Situating Servant-Leadership in Youth and Young Adult Ministry

The American ecclesial document *RTV* addresses the reality of leadership among young people: "Leadership development *calls forth, affirms,* and *empowers* the diverse gifts, talents, and abilities of adults and young people in our faith communities for comprehensive ministry with adolescents."[23] This is a strong endorsement on developing leadership skills with youth and young adults. Servant-leadership provides a great lens by which youth and young adults are able to understand and interpret leadership.

---

19. Agosto, *Servant-Leadership*, 53.
20. Ibid., 54.
21. Smolarski, *Sacred Mysteries*, 126.
22. Ibid., 127.
23. *RTV*, 40.

The Servant-Leadership Model

The *goal* of integrating servant-leadership is the responsibility of the entire youth and young adult ministry: staff, parents, and teenagers.[24] The *aim* of the youth and young adult minister, within the servant-leadership model, is for each young person in the youth and young adult ministry to eventually become a servant-leader. It is also important to keep in mind that becoming a servant-leader is a journey, not an overnight experience. The *challenge* is to instill servant-leadership principles and skills that will foster adolescent, emerging adult, and young adult Christian disciples and future Christian leaders.[25]

It may be prudent for every phase of youth and young adult ministry to have proper training in leadership development. There are four areas that merit leadership growth: (1) the congregation/parish youth and young adult minister; (2) the coordinating team or volunteer youth and young adult leaders (adult catechists); (3) program leaders;[26] and (4) administrative and support staff.[27] Therefore, youth and young adult ministers may want to do the following to promote servant-leadership:

1. *articulate* the youth and young adult ministry's mission statement and vision statement around servant-leadership principles
2. *develop* servant-leadership systems which invite, train, support, and nourish teenagers, emerging adults, and young adults
3. *cultivate* servant-leadership by experiential learning and praxis-based curriculum
4. *nurture* servant-leadership concepts with adult youth leaders and young adult peer leaders
5. *empower* servant-leadership in young people by training them with advocacy skills to serve in schools, churches, neighborhoods, and civic organizations.[28]

---

24. Canales, "Ten-Year Anniversary of *Renewing the Vision*," 68.
25. Ibid., 68.
26. The term "program leaders" refers to anyone who is charged with a certain area or program that caters to and serves the adolescent population within the youth ministry. Some program leaders in the Catholic youth and young adult ministries are leaders of music and prayer, facilitators of Bible study groups, coordinators of the skit ministry, etc.
27. *RTV*, 41.
28. Ibid., 40–42.

These five points, which foster servant-leadership within youth and young adult ministry, could be integrated rather succinctly into any Christian youth organization.

Another way to help build servant-leadership within youth and young adult ministry is to develop peer ministry.[29] There are four ways to bolster peer ministry with youth and young adult ministry:

1. *provide* leadership training for youth and young adults in peer relationships and peer ministry

2. *utilize* adult education principles (andragogy[30]) in peer leadership development with young adults

3. *select* topics for training peer ministers in diverse areas such as building core teams, planning activities, and/or spiritual initiatives

4. *develop* opportunities for young people to take initiative in larger congregational-life committees and councils[31]

These four approaches to develop peer ministry will also enhance servant-leadership within youth and young adult ministry. Offering servant-leadership training and development is helpful for youth and young adult ministers to identify and encourage young people to become more involved disciples within the community of faith.

Ten Theological Characteristics of Servant-Leadership

Larry C. Spears, executive director of the Greenleaf Center for Servant-Leadership, offers ten characteristics for servant-leadership. These ten characteristics are by no means exhaustive, but they do provide a solid theological and pastoral perspective, which helps to frame servant-leadership development. The ten characteristics of servant-leadership (alphabetically listed) are: (1) awareness, (2) builder of community, (3) commitment to the growth in people, (4) conceptualization, (5) empathy, (6) foresight, (7) healing, (8) listening, (9) persuasion, and (10) stewardship.[32] These ten characteristics are highly applicable to the disciplines of theology and

---

29. *Sons and Daughters*, 27, 34, 37, 40.

30. *Andragogy* is the method and practice of teaching and catechizing adult learners, typically people beyond the "college-age years," in an adult education environment.

31. *Sons and Daughters*, 44.

32. Spears, "Tracing the Growing Impact," 4–7.

pastoral ministry, and they merit attention. Below is a table that I have developed; the chart is *not* part of Spears's schema. However, I think this chart does help to situate servant-leadership and Christian youth and young adult ministry.

Table 3: Ten Theological Characteristics of Servant-Leadership

10 Theological Characteristics of Servant-Leadership	Description of the Servant-Leadership Characteristic	Servant-Leadership's Importance for Youth and Young Adult Ministers
Awareness	Seeing the world with different lenses or with a new mind-set can be awe-inspiring; view situations from an integrated position or holistic position; uses self-discovery, introspection, and self-actualization to understand coming to spiritual awakening.[33]	The adolescent and emerging adult journey is one of self-awareness; helping young people in human growth and development and reaching spiritual maturity; youth and young adult ministers who come to awareness that they are servant-leaders are more likely to help young people become more aware of their self-identity and empower them toward self-discovery.
Builder of Community	The capacity to develop meaningful relationships; the ability to create a circle of trust of the people you know, serve, and work with daily; using solidarity.[34]	Youth and young adult ministers empower young people; youth and young adult ministers must try and build community at various levels: family, school, work, church, neighborhood, and city; one of the key aspects of trying to build community with young people is for the youth and young adult ministry to create an atmosphere of openness, trust, equality, and love, and in doing so will also foster servant-leadership in the process.

---

33. Cunningham and Egan, *Christian Spirituality*.
34. Palmer, *A Hidden Wholeness*.
35. Senge, *The Fifth Discipline*. Also see Joe Batten, "Servant Leadership," 38–53.

Commitment to the Growth in People	Reinforce the conviction that people need one another to live as community; nurture commitment by fostering growth, development, and interdependence within their ministry or organization.[35]	Youth and young adult ministers may discover that commitment to young peoples' growth is fully actualized when personal and communal goals are realized and when separate interests are shaped by shared goals working for the common good.
Conceptualization	Possesses a keen ability to originate and implement ideas, values, and events; the ability to comprehend complex constructs; the aptitude to overcome nuanced thinking; people willing to dream big, create dangerously, and lead with passion.[36]	Youth and young adult ministers who mobilize young people toward transformation through leadership are conceptualizers; youth and young adult ministers are conceptualizing when they are planning and organizing youth-led and peer-led liturgies, when they are integrating and implementing weekend retreats, and when they are creating youth and young adult disciples out of adolescent angst and emerging adult apathy.
Empathy	Understanding a person with sincerity and charity; the empathetic response may be reinforced by my commitment to see Christ in the persons who come into my life; empathy is a feeling from the gut; recognizing the giftedness and uniqueness in others.[37]	Youth and young adult ministers who practice empathy are concerned with experiencing the affect, feelings, and emotions of others with charity and service in mind; youth and young adult ministers would do well to master empathy because it will help to understand young people, and help to move them from anxiety and self-centeredness to awareness and accountability.
Foresight	The ability to project into the future with clarity and accuracy; a kin to the cardinal virtue[38] of prudence; the ability to discern and to make good moral choices; to be intuitive; the skill to act and react in situations as a leader in the *now*—right now—immediately.[39]	The youth and young adult minister with foresight is the one who creatively leads and who passionately initiates ideas and concepts; youth and young adult ministers can develop an understanding of foresight by learning the ways to become multifaceted; youth and young adult ministers will be called to be a teacher, preacher, advocate, and animator; youth and young adult ministers will also be called to be prophetic, wise, and shrewd.

36. Greenleaf, *Servant-Leadership*, 45–82.

37. Gula, *Just Ministry*. Also see Whitehead and Whitehead, *Christian Life Patterns*.

38. The term "cardinal" derives from the Latin word *cardo*, which means "to hinge" and the term "virtue" derives from the Latin word *habitus* meaning "habit." Virtues are

THE SERVANT-LEADERSHIP MODEL

Healing	The capacity to integrate the restorative nature of personal woundedness; to reestablish another person's brokenness; bring self and others to wholeness; able to grasp the theological reality of compassion, and also learn to facilitate a person's experience toward self-discovery of compassion.[40]	Youth and young adult ministers who help to provide young people with understanding and meaning to life's compelling faith issues offer healing; youth and young adult ministers have great potential to be healers because they get the opportunity and privilege of encountering young people in times of brokenness, woundedness, and messiness.
Listening	Listening with intent and purpose; reflection; active listening; concerned about quality dialogue.[41]	The practice of listening allows space for young people's hearts to speak, to make known their fears, hopes, and dreams; facilitates expression of emotion, which is potentially important for youth and young adult ministry; youth and young adult ministers will be more attuned to developing their listening skills and be more likely to practice paying attention and to actively listen.

"hinges" that many other lesser virtues turn upon, while habits may conjure negative images they actually refer to virtuous behavior involving a person's response to doing the good and moral. There are four cardinal virtues: prudence, justice, fortitude, and temperance. The cardinal virtues are synonymously referred to as the "moral" virtues as well. For further information on virtues see Thomas Aquinas's *Summa Theologiae*, Volume II, Part II; and Aristotle's *Nicomachean Ethics*.

39. McBrien, *Ministry*. Also see Cahalan, *Introducing the Practice of Ministry*.

40. Nouwen, *The Wounded Healer*. Also see Also see Cahalan, *Introducing the Practice of Ministry*.

41. Ferch, *Servant-Leadership*, 1–16. Also see White, *Practicing Discernment with Youth*.

Persuasion	Convincing others; build collaboration; the art of influencing others with building consensus; avoids manipulation and coercion; persuasion is part of a leadership style referred to as *purposing*.[42]	Youth and young adult ministers can practice purposing by doing the following: (a) smooth a path for teenage interaction, (b) ease communication between young people and ministers with collaboration, (c) evoke personal piety and devotion in young people, and (d) allay anxiety into emerging adult zeal; youth and young adult ministers are people of persuasion when they teach young people to be counter-cultural and lead them toward virtuous lifestyles and away from consumerism, materialism, and consumptionism.
Stewardship	Acknowledges that all life is sacred and all creation is a gift from God, which emphasizes accountability and respect; trust in the greater good of people; called to respect the environment and encourage awareness of the natural beauty; called to share their time, talent, treasure, and tradition with their community by extending courtesy, demonstrating hospitality, and taking responsibility for creation.[43]	Youth and young adult ministers are also servant-leaders when they function as agents of stewardship by empowering young people with contemporary perspectives which are rooted on four religious beliefs: (a) administrative skills relating to money management, finances, income, and property; (b) responsibility for all others in their life and in the world founded on Jesus' commandment of love; (c) forming a critical judgment to instill gospel values into modern society; and (d) assuming the courage to be prophetic by speaking up for justice and against injustice.[44]

These ten theological characteristics of servant-leadership—awareness, builder of community, commitment to the growth in people, conceptualization, empathy, foresight, healing, listening, persuasion, and stewardship—help to shape a solid understanding of servant-leadership.

The theology of servant-leadership is practical, and can be easily utilized and implemented by youth and young adult ministers. Embracing a theology of servant-leadership within Christian youth and young adult ministry means that churches can develop the necessary young people to become servant-leaders in their congregations, communities, and cities. Practicing servant-leadership, gives certainty and purpose to others and

42. Sergiovanni, *Moral Leadership*.
43. Barrero, Canales, and Mason, *Keeping the Cup Full*.
44. Ibid., 27.

communities who/which may have difficulty in achieving it for themselves.[45] Servant-leadership is a great model for *doing* youth and young adult ministry, and it is legitimate, attainable, and necessary.

Pedagogical and Pastoral Methodologies for Implementation

The method used in this section, like the previous chapter, is prescriptive because it offers concrete examples to be implemented. Before implementing pedagogical and pastoral methodologies for servant-leadership, it may be appropriate and necessary for youth and young adult ministry to do some preliminary work on servant-leadership. For youth and young adult ministers with limited understanding of servant-leadership it may be resourceful to try some of the suggestions listed below before directly moving into implementing the servant-leadership model.

A first recommendation is to purchase Robert K. Greenleaf's book, *Servant-Leadership*. Of course, after purchasing the book, read it cover-to-cover, copiously taking notes and asking self-reflective questions throughout the read.

A second suggestion is to visit the official website of the Greenleaf Center for Servant-Leadership (www.greenleaf.org) located in Indianapolis. Browse through the center's information, order a few books and videos, become familiar with the ideals and philosophy of servant-leadership, and learn from some of the servant-leadership experts.

A third recommendation is to attend a local workshop or seminar on servant-leadership at a local college/university that espouses servant-leadership. Taking a college course or workshop on the topic will definitely broaden one's horizon's on the subject.

All these avenues will help prepare the youth and young adult minister and their coordinating team to become absorbed in servant-leadership. Youth and young adult ministers should not be vexed by the initial preparation; such endeavors are considered continuing education. Studying servant-leadership can also be viewed as learning something worthwhile in order to help facilitate deeper and lasting changes within the lives of the adolescents. Youth and young adult ministers are encouraged to learn about servant-leadership before guiding adult catechists and instructing young people in the principles, ideas, and values of servant-leadership.

---

45. Greenleaf, *Servant-Leadership*, 15.

The Six Strategies

This section will recommend six pedagogical and pastoral strategies that are designed to be pragmatic references that may guide youth and young adult ministers in facilitating a quality servant-leadership curriculum. It is my hope that youth and young adult ministers will find this section practical and useful to their ministry with young people. The implementation strategies below are suggestions that can easily be tweaked to assist youth and young adult ministers in their work of integrating the servant-leadership model.

Strategy 1

A most obvious pedagogical strategy for developing servant-leadership is to organize and implement a servant-leadership project. Such a project could have a positive and effective impact on young people. The servant-leadership project is one that the youth and young adult minister and the youth (and/or young adults) plan together. For high school–age ministry, in order for the servant-leadership project to be successful, recruiting eleventh and twelfth graders in the youth ministry, and those who have already been exposed to service-learning and service projects, is important for the servant-leadership project's success. For emerging adults and young adults, the age or grade of the servant-leadership project is not so imperative. The point is to select young people who are mature enough to handle the responsibility of the project.

Again, to ensure methodological and pedagogical success, the servant-leadership project should start from scratch: brainstorming ideas, developing concepts, planning, conducting meetings, organizing the details, and finally, implementation and execution. A servant-leadership project is one that empowers young people to lead service-learning experiences for their school, sport's team, neighborhood, or parish; this process is known as praxis-based education.[46] Such a project moves youth and young adults

---

46. Canales, "Transforming Teenagers," 83. The term *praxis-based education* refers to a pedagogy that is rooted in experiential learning. Praxis-based education provides young people with a tangible learning experienced based upon service-learning and makes a lasting impact upon their lives as they embark upon this type of education. There are four dimensions of praxis-based education that help to shape and mold Christian identity, spirituality, and faith-formation in young people: (1) academic and pastoral reflection rooted in reality, (2) integrated community learning; (3) recollection and pedagogical accompaniment; and (4) formation of Christocentric imagination. For further discussion on each of these four dimensions see Canales, "Transforming Teenagers," 83–84.

The Servant-Leadership Model

beyond random acts of kindness and leads them toward a theology of social justice and social-systemic change.

Strategy 2

A second pedagogical strategy for developing servant-leadership among adolescents and young adults would be to explore the life of a heroic servant-leader such as Martin Luther King Jr. He was a magnificent servant-leader, not only in the South of the United States, but internationally, receiving global recognition for his role in the Civil Rights Movement.[47]

Martin Luther King Jr. exemplified all the qualities and traits that enable servant-leadership to transform individuals, organizations, and societies. King, like Gandhi before him—and Jesus before him—strongly opposed violence and embraced passive resistance with *agape*, a deep love for all people, an overflowing and redemptive love that asks nothing in return.[48] King proposed that rather than hating the oppressor, we love our oppressor because "love is the key that unlocks the door which leads to ultimate reality."[49]

Such ideals of servant-leadership merit exploration with young people—not just talked about—but also studied and taught. Servant-leadership pedagogy, such as adopting King's message into a curriculum can easily be put into youth and young adult ministry praxis.[50] Here is one example of implementing King's work into a youth or young adult ministry gathering:

- Plan an ecumenical Evening of Reflection. Such an event can be planned with neighboring churches on Martin Luther King Jr. Day.
- The Evening of Reflection could integrate King's writings and key biblical passages that speak of hope and liberation.
- Read Martin Luther King Jr.'s *Letter from Birmingham Jail* to the students.
- Have the students reflect on and react to the content of King's letter.
- Watch a documentary or movie on the life of Martin Luther King Jr., such as *Martin Luther King Jr.: A Historical Perspective* (2002).
- Debrief the movie and the evening (15–20 minutes).

47. Ferch, *Servant-Leadership*, 11.
48. Hill, *8 Spiritual Heroes*, 100–101.
49. King, *Testament of Hope*, 632.
50. Canales, "Transforming Teenagers," 78–81.

Models and Methods for Youth

The task of the youth and young adult minister is to implement Martin Luther King Jr., or others who exemplifies servant-leadership, and to excite, energize, and empower young people within the youth and young adult ministry to become servant-leaders.

Strategy 3

A third pastoral strategy might be to offer a weekend retreat developed around servant-leadership ideas and principles. The theme of the retreat could be "Learning to Lead: Servant-Leadership" or "Leading through Service." Some of the work during the weekend with the young people could be spent exploring the ideas and tenets of servant-leadership. During the retreat, famous servant-leaders—Jesus of Nazareth, Mohandas Gandhi, Cesar Chavez, Thea Bowman, Oscar Romero, Helen Prejean, Robert Greenleaf, and Nelson Mandela—could be studied. Writings from some of them such as Jesus, Gandhi, and Greenleaf could be studied, or possibly acted-out in short skits or in a dramatic reading. Moreover, it may be wise if, during the weekend, young people try to highlight small acts of servant-leadership.[51] Small acts of service help situate the servant-leadership motif throughout the weekend.

During the retreat, servant-leadership themes could be introduced through cinema. Showing a movie that highlights servant-leadership themes can be a powerful tool for youth. Some movies with servant-leadership themes are: *Stand and Deliver* (1988), *Spitfire Grill* (1996), *Les Miserables* (1997), *Patch Adams* (2000), *Pay It Forward* (2002), *The Emperor's Club* (2003), *The Legend of Bagger Vance* (2004), *The Blind Side* (2008), *Soul Suffer* (2010), *The Help* (2012), *Unbroken* (2014), *The Jungle Book* (2016), *Free State of Jones* (2016), and *Wonder* (2017).

After watching the movie, theological reflection should be provided: framing the movie theologically and socially, and breaking into 30–45 minutes of small-group discussion to debrief themes of servant-leadership with the retreat participants. Many youth and young adult ministers show movies, but "are notorious for *not* providing young people with theological

---

51. Examples of small acts of servant-leadership are where the youth and young adult minister and volunteer adult catechists serve the students all their meals, and eat their meals after all the students are served. The same routine could also hold true with taking showers and getting ready for bed; after all the students have taken their showers, and gotten ready for bed then the adults may.

reflection," therefore, programming time for theological reflection is spiritually significant.[52]

The youth and young adult minister may want to prepare some preliminary work before actually introducing the young people to the topic in order to foster a deeper understanding of servant-leadership. This can be accomplished by: (a) previewing the movie and selecting the significant servant-leadership themes that merit discussion; (b) preparing questions based on the movie that highlight servant-leadership moments that the adult catechists may use during small faith-sharing groups; and (c) after the small-group experience, have the young people journal about their perceptions of servant-leadership as portrayed in the movie.

Retreats are a great pastoral tool because a large amount of information can be imparted during the weekend.[53] Moreover, weekend retreats boost a young person's interior life, taking them out of their "comfort zone" and allowing them to concentrate on spiritual matters and experience God's presence.[54] The pedagogical techniques used throughout the retreat will help to facilitate a deeper appreciation and comprehension of servant-leadership within the lives of young people.

Strategy 4

A fourth practical strategy could be to study the life of Jesus of Nazareth as the quintessential servant-leader.[55] Studying Jesus as a servant-leader is good for youth and young adults because Jesus utilized two basic types of servant-leadership behavior: *relational* and *task*. A relational servant-leadership behavior encourages mentoring, supporting, coaching, and developing young people as children of God.[56] A task servant-leadership behavior requires more teaching, guiding, directing, and delegating young people as they grow in confidence and ministry competence.[57] The former (relational) is concerned more with empowering young people with a gentle push, while the latter (task) is more about "pulling up" young people with a strong yank of the hand.

---

52. Canales, "Transforming Teenagers," 78.
53. Canales, *Noble Quest*, 93–94.
54. Ibid., 93.
55. Sofield and Juliano, *Principled Ministry*, 79.
56. MacPhee, "Adoptive Leadership," 280–81.
57. Ibid.

Perhaps a six-week series titled "Jesus the Ultimate Servant-Leader" could be examined, which highlights Jesus' servant-leadership traits in the Gospels. Conceivably, the series could incorporate Franco Zeffirelli's film, a modern-day masterpiece, *Jesus of Nazareth* (1976). The movie could be integrated into a series of curriculum sessions, perhaps during Advent or Lent, with each session focused on various servant-leadership themes within Jesus' ministry. Another resource is Efrain Agosto's book *Servant-Leadership: Jesus & Paul*. Agosto's book can help situate the pericopes about Jesus and servant-leadership.

The six-week series could be used as a springboard to help teenagers connect essential ideas of servant-leadership within Jesus' life and ministry. As a pedagogical tool, this strategy is strong for several reasons: (a) it explores Jesus directly as a model of servant-leadership; (b) it has a strong biblical element in its content; and (c) it captures young people's senses and sensibilities through cinema.

Strategy 5

A fifth pragmatic strategy may be to offer a six-week or eight-week cinema series entitled "The Great Servant-Leaders Series," which showcases the awesome servant-leaders from around the world. The videos could either be documentaries or Hollywood productions that highlight servant-leadership themes. Below is an eight-week ecumenical example.

- Week one: Mohandas Gandhi; watch the movie titled *Gandhi* (1982) produced by Columbia Home Pictures.

- Week two: Dorothy Day; watch the movie titled *Entertaining Angels: The Dorothy Day Story* (1997) produced by Paulist Press (1-800-218-1903).

- Week three: Cesar E. Chavez; watch the documentary titled *Cesar Chavez: Mexican-American Labor Leader* (1995) produced by Schlessinger Video Productions (1-800-843-3620).

- Week four: Dalai Lama; watch the documentary titled *Ocean of Wisdom* (1991) produced by Mediart Films, or *Compassion in Exile* (1992) produced by Direct Cinema Limited (310-396-4774).

- Week five: Oscar Romero; watch the movie titled *Romero* (1989) produced by Paulist Press (1-800-218-1903).

- Week six: Mother Teresa; watch the documentary titled *Mother Teresa* (1986) produced by Red Rose Gallerie (1-800-451-5683).

The Servant-Leadership Model

- Week seven: Nelson Mandela; watch the documentary titled *Mandela the Man* (1996) produced by LDA Videos (1-800-966-5130).

- Week eight: Eleanor Roosevelt; watch the documentary titled *Eleanor Roosevelt: A Restless Spirit* (1994) produced by A&E Home Video (www.aetv.com).

The Great Servant-Leaders Series will provide pragmatic insights and pastoral reflection on an array of lifestyles and people, each with their own unique servant-leadership qualities and abilities. After the youth and young adults watch the particular film, there should be theological reflection and small faith-sharing groups formed, with prewritten questions for either the adult catechists or the youth/young adult peer-leaders to facilitate the small-group process. The servant-leadership experience based on each of the above servant-leaders is an excellent vehicle to provide intensive study and introspection into servant leadership.

Strategy 6

A sixth pedagogical strategy is to invite servant-leadership experts from within the community, from local colleges, organizations, institutions, and businesses to speak to the youth and young adults, and to share their knowledge and experiences as a servant-leader. The youth and young adult minister might enlist input from a local Christian university regarding recruiting servant-leaders within the community. A good place for a youth and young adult minister to begin the quest for enlisting servant-leadership speakers may be to call the departments of theology and education at a Christian university.

The purpose of this scenario is to find out which businesses, organizations, and institutions practice servant leadership and try to bring in servant-leaders to share with the young people about their experience and expertise as a servant-leader. As a pedagogical device, this strategy is strong because if this approach is implemented well, then in all likelihood, the adult catechists, core leaders, and volunteers will learn the essential tenets within servant-leadership alongside the youth and young adults. In subsequent years, the adult catechists and young people themselves can begin to share directly with their peers about their own understanding and experience of servant-leadership. The old adage "you must learn to crawl before you learn to walk" is applicable in learning the skills of servant-leadership.

The potential for young people to grow in knowledge about servant-leadership is fantastic. These six pedagogical and pastoral strategies for implementing servant-leadership within the context of congregational youth and young adult ministry are extremely beneficial. I'm confident that many youth ministers, college campus ministers, and young adult ministers may find these pastoral methodologies equally useful. These types of servant-leadership pedagogical strategies will enhance and empower Christian youth and young adult ministries to recognize that altruism and passion for serving others are the hallmark of a compassionate life.

Strengths and Limitations of This Model

Although this chapter has argued for the priority of the servant-leadership model for youth and young adult ministry and the great impact it can have on young people, it is still important to examine the strengths and limitations of this model.

Strengths

The first important positive feature of the servant-leadership model is its deep biblical roots, particularly in the New Testament (Mark 10:45; Matt 20:26–28). Servant-leadership can be studied from various biblical characters in the Bible such as Moses, Joshua, the prophets, John the Baptist, Jesus, Paul, and John. All have very different styles and traits of servant-leadership, but they all have two attributes in common: (a) they love God, and (b) they have concern for the people of God.

The Apostle Paul is perhaps one of the greatest Christian leaders ever to walk God's earth, and he describes the true worth of a servant-leader when he writes these humble and poignant words:

> Therefore, to keep me from being too elated, a thorn was given to me in the flesh, a messenger of Satan to torment me, to keep me from being too elated. Three times I appealed to the Lord about this, that it would leave me, but he said to me, "My grace is sufficient for you, for power is made perfect in weakness." So, I will boast all the more gladly, so that the power of Christ may dwell in me. Therefore, I am content with weakness, insults, hardships, persecutions, and calamities for the sake of Christ; for whenever I am weak, then I am strong. (2 Cor 12:7–10)

For Paul, authentic servant-leaders refuse to give up, to hide, or to run away in the midst of adversity and calamity. Servant-leaders rise above

The Servant-Leadership Model

and beyond personal weaknesses and move themselves and others to seek strength, security, self-improvement, and self-awareness.

A second quality of this model is that the church only needs to look to the example of Jesus of Nazareth as an authentic servant-leader (John 13:4–17). Jesus is the quintessential servant-leader. Efrain Agosto details Jesus' servant-leadership style. Agosto maintains that Jesus' servant-leadership qualities are numerous, such as humility, affirmation, calling women disciples, commissioning the Twelve for service, and cultivating discipleship.[58]

Servant-leadership is deeply rooted in sacred Scripture and the center of the Christian faith—Jesus the Christ—is the icon for servant-leadership and the primordial servant-leader within the pages on the New Testament. He has been the central figure of Christianity for the past two thousand years. The Bible does not merely present servant-leadership as some sort of lofty ideal to strive for, but as a real and tangible lifestyle to be practiced. Jesus of Nazareth puts the principles of servant-leadership into a fundamental practice and incorporates it into his own spirituality.

A third significant contribution that the servant-leadership model gives the church is the ten attributes that potential servant-leaders may use as a guide toward striving for servant-leadership. The ten servant-leadership characteristics are listening, empathy, healing, awareness, persuasion, conceptualization, foresight, stewardship, commitment to the growth in people, and building community—all of which are crucial for Christian service, discipleship, and ministry.

Servant-leadership is part of a global awareness that is ultimately concerned with helping people achieve transformation from self-centeredness and selfishness to an other-oriented and service-learning lifestyle. Greenleaf states, "The prime requirement of leadership is goal setting or goal finding.... One cannot act on a concept that one cannot articulate."[59] Greenleaf is suggesting here that servant leaders must be people who have goals, set their goals, and put their goals into motion through action. For the servant-leader who is a youth or young adult minister, this means using the resources, talents, and imagination that God has given and put it into practice. Greenleaf reminds all servant-leaders that "nothing much happens without a dream; for something great to happen, there must be a great dream."[60] Therefore, youth and young adult ministers should start dreaming big!

58. Agosto, *Servant-Leadership*, 31–45.
59. Greenleaf, *Servant-Leadership*, 46.
60. Ibid., 74.

A fourth strong point of this model is the overall compassion that this model demonstrates by those in leadership to those not in leadership roles, and the symbiotic association and collaboration that is exercised between leader and follower. This model is particularly important in young adult ministry where relationships are maintained and sustained with peers. The servant-leadership model is crucial because it gives young people the opportunity to become contributing members of the community through service and leadership, two important Christian traits that will help propel them through life. Servant-leadership, although a philosophy for living life, is a way to help young people become empowered to live their lives with altruism at the forefront of their mind. Youth and young adult ministers armed with the ten characteristics of servant-leadership can provide adolescents with enough theoretical and practical substance to help them become effective servant-leaders now and in the future.

Surely there are more benefits to the servant-leadership model, and time and successful implementation will truly help youth and young adult ministers use this model to help influence their ministry to young people. Servant-leadership is a fantastic pastoral model for young people, but it is not without a couple of setbacks, which need to be contemplated.

Limitations

The first drawback that youth and young adult ministers will encounter is not being overly familiar with the philosophy and principles of servant-leadership. Therefore, there will need to be some preliminary work done such as reading Greenleaf's book *Servant-Leadership: A Journey into the Nature of Legitimate Power and Greatness*, and possibly attending a workshop or seminar on servant-leadership.

Servant-leadership is truly enjoying a high point in its history and scores of companies and institutions of higher education are wholeheartedly incorporating its vision and message. Still, there are millions of people who have never heard of servant-leadership or its message. Therefore, if a youth or young adult minister decides to integrate and implement servant-leadership into their curriculum, they should become more familiar with its message and mission. The most obvious downfall is that it will take time for a person, who knows little about servant-leadership, to become competent enough to teach and model it for others to follow, but again, the message is straightforward and simple: serve to lead.

A second disadvantage is that servant-leadership is, at best, a philosophical concept or a leadership construct. It may take a youth and young adult ministry or any church community a few years to begin to operate in the spirit of servant-leadership and a lifetime to perfect. In other words, servant-leadership resembles the old adage: *it is good in theory, but very difficult to put into practice* and even more difficult to measure its effectiveness in people's lives with scientific research and concrete data. Consequently, the appropriation of servant-leadership will not occur overnight or even over the course of several weeks, but over months and years.

The servant-leadership model provides both strengths and limitations for youth and young adult ministers. However, the benefits of integrating servant leadership principles and ideas into youth and young adult ministry far outweigh any concerns regarding this model. Moreover, the pastoral methodologies of this model will be relatively easy to implement once a foundation of servant-leadership is laid.

The Circle of Servant-Leadership

It may be advantageous for Christian youth and young adult ministers to begin to view themselves as servant-leaders. Youth and young adult ministers who envision themselves as servant-leaders will be more likely to integrate the principles of servant-leadership into their ministries and more likely to implement servant-leadership concepts into their pedagogy and catechetical curriculum.

The Circle of Servant-Leadership is a figure that represents servant-leadership. In youth and young adult ministry, the aim is to have the adult catechists and young people become servant-leaders. The Circle of Servant-Leadership helps to illustrate the matrix of possibilities available to Christian youth and young adult ministers to enable them to begin to envision their larger role and responsibilities as a servant-leader within the community.

In a "prefect ministry," the servant-leadership model for youth and young adult ministry would be a community of equals, like the Knights of the Round Table. All participants within the ministry, whether adult or adolescent, can become empowered to be servant-leaders. In this circle diagram, the youth and young adult minister is only *one* person representing servant-leadership, who facilitates the learning experience for young people and adult catechists. Figure 4 below illustrates the Circle of Servant-Leadership for youth and young adult ministry.

Models and Methods for Youth

FIGURE 4

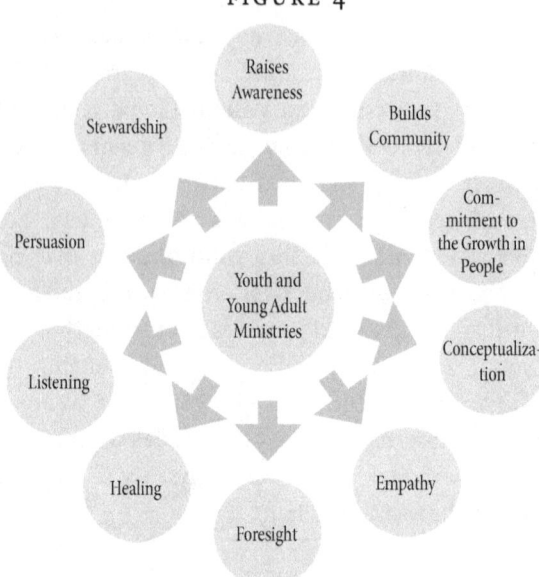

The youth and young adult minister encourages the entire ministry to become servant-leaders. Ideally, everyone will be empowered to become a servant-leader in this model. Some will use the ten characteristics at different times and places within the ministry: at meetings, on retreats, during social outings, etc.

One image of servant-leadership is like a flower petal. When a person acknowledges and becomes a servant-leader, they become a "petal" like on a flower, and they are turned inward, which represents the servant-leader's inward journey. The inward journey, according to Greenleaf, is comprised of both destination and destiny. "*Destination* could be the end of the journey and *destiny* could be the ultimate (therefore unachievable) goal. Paradoxically, at one time one might be at the end and the beginning of one's journey."[61] This flower petal image is a simple reminder of the impact that one servant-leadership-minded individual can have on the entire youth and young adult ministry. Servant-leadership, ideally, should be an "infectious" model that takes hold and moves people out of complacency and into action.

61. Ibid., 335.

The Servant-Leadership Model

Case Study[62]

Rita Rutledge is a thirty-eight year old Caucasian woman who lives in Sturgeon Bay, Wisconsin. Rita has a bachelor's degree from the University of Wisconsin (Madison) in marketing and advertising, but no formal theology training whatsoever. She has worked at various companies over the years.

During college she "dabbled" in serving in campus ministry at a neighboring evangelical church that her boyfriend, and now husband, attended. However, since Rita is Catholic by birth and choice, she was only on the fringes of that college ministry.

Rita is now a successful adult and executive, and she also desires to serve part-time at her parish. After much discernment, she has decided to make a career change, but wants to do it patiently and cautiously. Over the years, Rita has been involved off and on in her parish's campus (college) ministry, but she feels called at this time in her life to become more involved. She notices that there are many emerging adults not involved in the church and wants to reach out and help them, but also serve them as a college minister.

A position opens up for a part-time campus minister at her parish, Ascension Catholic Church, which is not too far from a local university. After some introspection and prayer, and consulting with her husband and two children, she decides to apply. Rita's dream came true and she has been appointed as the new director of college and campus ministry of Connection Point Campus Ministry, the emerging adult ministry that serves Ascension Catholic Church in Sturgeon Bay, Wisconsin.

Rita is thrilled and nervous about her new position. The first thing Rita does on her first day is call the diocesan director of campus ministry for the Diocese of Green Bay. After making contact with the director, they sit down to develop a "plan of action" for her newly acquired ministry position.

First, they decide that since Rita has no theological education or significant ministry experience, she should enroll in the Diocese of Green Bay Commissioned Ministry Leadership Formation Program. The program is a three-year-long, part-time process that empowers her to be a lay ecclesial minister working in the church. It is not youth and young adult ministry

---

62. This is an authentic ministry scenario that came to my about five years ago; I have crafted it differently for this particular case study. The names, cities, and institutions listed in this case study are fictional and have been made up to protect true identities.

specific training that she will receive, but overall theological and ministerial formation. She does just that and begins the process almost immediately.

Second, they decide that she will follow the U.S. Catholic Bishops guidelines for Christian comprehensive youth and young adult ministry and really study the documents that pertain to young people: (1) *Renewing the Vision: A Framework for Catholic Youth Ministry*; (2) *Empowered by the Spirit: Campus Ministry Faces the Future*; and (3) *Sons and Daughters of the Light: A Pastoral Plan for Ministry with Young Adults*. In addition, Rita agrees to have monthly conversations on those documents and her ministry with the diocesan director.

Rita's plan: After reading and studying the three documents Rita discovers that there are two major components for comprehensive youth and young adult ministry that strike her fancy: (1) the ministry of justice and service, and (2) the ministry of leadership development.

Because of her secular experience and the company she works for, John Deere Tractors, she has a basic familiarity with, and has read articles and heard presentations about, servant-leadership. Rita wonders about using servant-leadership with emerging adults: could servant-leadership work in campus ministry? Rita wonders, what does servant-leadership look like in campus ministry?

Rita has an "aha" moment. Rita chooses to integrate servant-leadership into Connection Point Campus Ministry; she purchases copies of Robert K. Greenleaf's book and begins to conduct informal formation sessions with her three volunteer core team leaders and other adult catechists. After four weeks of study, Rita and her catechists design a six-month campus ministry curriculum focusing on servant-leadership.

Reflection: Rita and Connection Point Campus Ministry's situation is unique in being driven by servant-leadership at a time when not many youth and young adult ministers are familiar with its ideas and concepts. The real dilemma is designing a servant-leadership curriculum that meets the theological and catechetical needs of young people. If you were on Rita's core team for developing a servant-leadership curriculum, what input would you give her? If you were in Rita's situation, which one of the five pastoral implementation strategies would you like to integrate? Explain your way of thinking.

Parting Remarks

Over the past eighteen years I have come to learn and deeply respect the insights of servant-leadership as a most appropriate way for organizations, institutions, and ministries to operate. Therefore, it is with strong conviction that I maintain that the ideals and philosophy of servant-leadership will apply quite effectively in a Christian youth ministry, campus ministry, and young adult ministry.

Two fundamental aspects will occur when a youth and young adult ministry shifts its mind-set and perspective into becoming a community driven by servant-leadership: (1) the people involved within the youth and young adult ministry are slowly but surely transformed into servant-leaders who lead by and through service, which permeates through the ministry into the larger parish-community; and (2) the young people themselves begin to emphasize the needs of others above themselves, thus encapsulating Jesus' Golden Rule: love your neighbor as yourself. Ultimately, servant-leadership is realizing that your life is not about you.

CHAPTER 4

The Liberation Model

> *They [the challenging questions about the poor] hammer at the Christian conscience everywhere but are especially acute in Latin America, the only part of the world in which the majority is both poor and Christian. The problem is especially urgent in the pastoral sphere in which the church lives its everyday life; it is therefore a challenge to any theology that endeavors to serve the proclamation of the Gospel.*[1]
>
> Gustavo Gutiérrez
> A Theology of Liberation, 1973

Preliminary Remarks

Adolescent and young adult ministry scholars, as well as youth and young adult ministry educators, are continually examining the ways that Christian youth, young adult ministers, and young people can become more theologically grounded.[2] In other words, youth and young adult ministers need to understand and feel comfortable in a theological framework; they cannot only be satisfied with planning social and spiritual activities and teaching the faith (catechesis).

Here is one of the problems, as I see it, with today's mainline Christian theology of youth and young adult ministry: it is simply incomplete *without*

---

1. Gutiérrez, *Theology of Liberation*, 156. Originally published in Lima, Peru, under the title *Thelogia de la Liberacion* (1971).
2. Root and Creasy Dean, *Theological Turn in Youth Ministry*, 15–18.

liberation theology. My argument is that liberation theology complements and completes a theology of Christian youth and young adult ministry. Certain aspects of liberation theology offer new impulses in the discussions on youth and young adult ministry and methodology.

By introducing liberation theology as an alternative model of youth and young adult ministry it will help adolescents and young adults and their ministers to make a theological turn in their understanding while broadening their ministerial horizons. Moreover, liberation theology will enhance the theological grounding of young people and youth and young adult ministers.

This model is not intended to be a "once and for all" approach that tries to create a fixed *method* for all Christian denominations to utilize in all congregations. The heart and soul of this model lies in creating an inclusive, nonjudgmental, supportive ministry that inspires Christian youth and young adult ministers to think. It will hopefully inspire youth and young adult ministers to think "outside the box" with their young people. Consequently, this chapter is both relevant to the fields of youth and young adult ministry education and practical theology and it breaks new ground as it advances the academic conversation of liberation theology and integrates it into the realm of that ministerial concentration.

Furthermore, this chapter presents a typology of youth and young adult ministry through the parameters of liberation theology, which shapes the pedagogical and catechetical practices of adolescent, emerging adult, and young adult ministers. The intent of this methodology is to demonstrate that the successful integration of *selective* liberation themes into Christian youth and young adult ministry is beneficial.

This different perspective also offers an alternative theological mode of catechizing young people. Like the other models in this book, the methodological context that will undergird this model of liberation theology will be an emphasis on both prescriptive analysis and descriptive design. The prescriptive portion of the chapter will examine the theoretical aspects of liberation theology within the context of Christian youth and young adult ministry and its impact on young people. Particularly, this chapter addresses three themes of liberation which are woven throughout its pages: inculturation, multiculturalism, and interreligious openness. Again, the thrust of these three liberation themes is to promote greater inclusiveness, encourage nonjudgmental attitudes toward others, and to be supportive, open-minded, and affirming of the uniqueness of the holy other. The descriptive section will provide pedagogical methodology for youth and young adult ministers to implement with young people and for youth and young adult ministry educators to discuss with their ministry students.

The methodological considerations of liberation theology are far-reaching for practical theology and for pastoral praxis within Christian youth and young adult ministry. It is my hope that this chapter will empower youth, young adult ministry educators, and youth and young adult ministers with their work with young people.

Liberation Theology in the Context of Youth and Young Adult Ministry

A first question worthy of consideration is: what is liberation theology? A good starting point is to give meaning to the term *liberation theology*. Gustavo Gutiérrez, a Peruvian systematic Catholic theologian and founder of contemporary liberation theology writes, "The theology of liberation offers us not so much a new theme for reflection as a *new way* to do theology. . . . Theology as critical reflection on historical praxis is a liberating theology, a theology of the liberating transformation."[3] Liberation is a theology of reflection and praxis that identifies with the gospel commitment of love, caring, and action.

Liberation theology is not new. Liberation theology has been around for approximately fifty years, with varying degrees of success around the globe. The first time the term *liberation theology* was uttered was by Gustavo Gutiérrez in 1968, in a lecture in Chimbote, Peru.[4] Liberation theology is a theology rooted in a particular socioeconomic and political context, and has for the majority, arisen as a specific Christian theological response to a given lived reality, usually exploitation of the poor and marginalized in Central and South America.[5]

Traditionally, liberation involves several components: fundamental and preferential treatment toward the poor,[6] theological praxis,[7]

---

3. Gutiérrez, *Theology of Liberation*, 12.
4. Hennelly, *Liberation Theology*, 62.
5. Noble, "Liberation Theology Today," 22–23.
6. Boff and Boff, *Introducing Liberation Theology*, 2–3.
7. Erwin, "Youth Ministry Education," 11.

conscientization,[8] spirituality,[9] and tolerance.[10] Albeit these components are important to liberation theology as a whole and perhaps practical theology in part, and they have been expounded upon already in depth within liberation theology circles. The aim in this chapter is to focus the way that liberation theology can enhance Christian youth and young adult ministry.

Another relevant question is: what is liberation theology in the context of Christian youth and young adult ministry? First, liberation theology, if taken seriously, can impact adolescents on a personal, social, and religious level. On a personal level, liberation theology can raise a young person's conscience about human injustice, human rights, and world poverty.[11] On a social level, liberation theology can raise a young person's social awareness concerning collective oppression, ostracizing, and marginalization of various peoples in various cultures and contexts.[12] On a religious level, liberation theology can attune young people to the evils of social sin, corrupt governments, and the ways multinational conglomerates afflict the human dignity of the poor and act against the common good and stewardship.[13]

Second, liberation theology, if taken earnestly, can influence youth and young adults in their attitudes and concerns within the community where they exist. Teenagers and young adults are the *object* of liberation theology; that is to say, they are often oppressed and deserve God's liberation from stereotypes and prejudices against ageism. On the other hand, adolescents are equally encouraged to be *advocates* of liberation theology, on behalf of the Church, where the less fortunate and oppressed are concerned.

Third, in this chapter, liberation theology, within the context of youth and young adult ministry, is *limited* to three dynamics: (1) inculturation, (2) multiculturalism, and (3) interreligious openness. Liberation theology, of course, is much broader than the parameters set within this work. Consequently, these three areas undergird a theology of liberation for Christian youth and young adult ministry that could be the protagonist to counter the hegemonic threat toward exploitation of the powerless.

A third important question is: why try to integrate liberation theology into Christian youth and young adult ministry? The motif of liberation has

8. Freire, *Pedagogy of the Oppressed*, 35, n. 1.
9. Medina, "Transformative Struggle," 217.
10. Ostendorf, "Christian Identity," 34.
11. Ballantyne, "Liberation Theology in Youth Ministry," 2.
12. Ibid.
13. Zalot and Guevin, *Catholic Ethics in Today's Word*, 56–58.

the potential to be an excellent model for Christian youth and young adult ministries to embrace for four significant reasons: (1) it is biblical, and it has its origins in both the Old Testament and the New Testament of sacred Scripture; (2) its foundation is rooted in the ministry of Jesus of Nazareth; (3) it is a theological method that hopes to eradicate poverty, classism, genderism, heterosexism, and racism on a global scale; and (4) the themes of inculturation, multiculturalism, and interreligious openness are important ways to integrate liberation with young people.

Perhaps a word of explanation is necessary when discussing the final significant question: why use the phrase "liberation theology?" Liberation theology has been misinterpreted and misunderstood, and therefore, has not always been seen in a positive light. It has been misperceived by some as advocating Marxism and violence, and this is understandably concerning. However, Marxism, violence, and guerilla warfare are *not* the hallmarks of liberation theology, and therefore, not a Christian enterprise.

Could I label this model without using the term *liberation theology*? Could I raise the consciousness of teenagers, youth ministers, and adolescent ministry scholars without using the term *liberation theology*? The answer is yes to both questions; however, as a Hispanic pastoral theologian, who does his theological work on the margins, the answer is no. Christian youth and young adult ministers, and youth and young adult ministry educators, should not be shy to use the term *liberation theology*.

Adolescence

To focus liberation theology on adolescents and vice-versa is to understand that the institution of adolescence itself is distorted by outside influences that are not always receptive to biblical and Christian contexts. For the most part, common, secular, youth culture today is free of biblical and Christian underpinnings. Youth today have life spaces and social choices that constitute their own culture, including personal styles, choice of clothes, music, television, bedroom decorations, dance, rituals for romance, and subculture styles.[14] Youth culture today is recognized as being present in some form or fashion in every corner of the globe.[15]

---

14. Jacober, *Adolescent Journey*, 82.
15. Ibid.

The Liberation Model

A liberation model of youth ministry will move youth culture "from a culture of entertainment and pleasure" to a culture of grace and mercy.[16] Therefore, youth culture is part of the institution of adolescence, and liberation theology can be one unique way to enhance Christian youth and young adult ministry.

One concern regarding middle adolescence and liberation theology is their lower cognitive development. The majority of middle adolescents do not have the full ability to apply abstractions across the many socially and ethically constructive selves or personas, and therefore, compartmentalize events and areas of life.[17] Although in middle adolescence the brain begins the process of moving from concrete, "first-person" thinking and awareness to abstract abilities, it is just beginning this more mature, formalized type of thinking.[18]

This brings rise to yet another question: does lower cognitive development in middle adolescence shape youth ministers' understanding of liberation theology if adolescents are not fully developed cognitively? One thought is that as an adolescent grows and matures, so will cognitive developmental abilities continue to cultivate and develop, and then middle adolescents are soon able to make connections and comparisons.[19] During adolescence, more mature cognitive functions take place and the brain begins to develop "third-person" abilities and thinking, rationalizing, and awareness.[20] Therefore, middle adolescents are capable of considering in a more objective manner various ideas, philosophies, and theories, and thus are able to discern the merits and importance of liberation theology.

Emerging Adults and Young Adults

To emphasize liberation theology with emerging and young adults is important, but probably not done often in most parishes. Why? Because emerging and young adults typically understand matters of religion, faith, and spirituality as important cognitive assists, but certainly not life-driven tenets.[21] Usually, the driving force of emerging adults and young adults

16. Crosby, "Reformed View of Youth Ministry," 46
17. Bonner, "Understanding the Changing Adolescent," 30.
18. Penner, "Welcoming Wounded and Broken Adolescents," 45.
19. Bonner, "Understanding the Changing Adolescent," 30.
20. Penner, "Welcoming Wounded and Broken Adolescents," 45.
21. Smith, *Souls in Transition*, 154.

has more to do with fun, friends, financial security, family, and jobs, while religious beliefs and spirituality would come next (for the average emerging and young adult). Sociologist Christian Smith notes the conventional mind-set and prevailing voiced views of emerging and young adults concerning religious and spiritual matters fall into the following categories:

(1) Religion is not a very threatening topic

(2) Indifferent toward religion

(3) The shared central principles of religions are good

(4) Religious particulars are peripheral

(5) Religion is for making good people

(6) Religious congregations are elementary schools of morals

(7) Family's faith is associated with dependence and not independence

(8) Religious services are not a place of real belonging

(9) Friends hardly ever talk about their religion

(10) Religion is good and cognitively important, but not a central theme[22]

It would seem that secularization might be creeping its way into religion and into the religious imagination of young people. From my perspective, that is fine; secularization does *not* mean the end of religion. Religion is not leaving anytime soon. Religion and religious beliefs might be changing, but religion is not leaving.

College campus ministers and young adult ministers would seem to have an uphill climb dealing with the typical mentality of today's young person, but there is honesty, hope, and openness for this age group.

In the final analysis, emerging adults and young adults might have little to say regarding liberation theology. However, such a theology might just move emerging and young adults toward a deeper appreciation for ministry and pastoral care *if* it can be proved to be significant in their lives.

Doing Liberation Ministry with Youth and Young Adults

There are probably a dozen or more practical principles to integrate into a liberation model of Christian youth ministry. Nevertheless, this section is limited to: (1) inculturation, (2) multiculturalism, and (3) interreligious

22. Ibid., 144–54.

THE LIBERATION MODEL

openness. Taken together, these areas will help to improve the understanding and overall importance of a liberation model for Christian youth and young adult ministry.

FIGURE 5

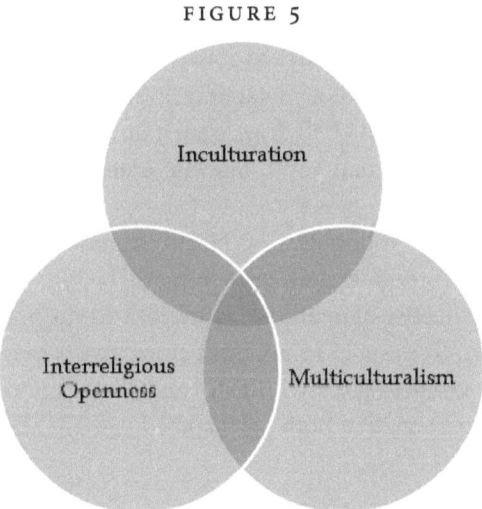

As Figure 5 above shows, all three areas can work interdependently within a liberation framework for youth and young adult ministry. There may be some overlap, but that is perfectly legitimate, and perhaps even necessary.

Evangelical scholar Fernando Arzola Jr. addresses a soteriological motif for urban youth ministers to utilize and employs a liberation perspective to situate holistic youth and young adult ministry.[23] Arzola, whose theology I admire, maintains that liberation theology can be integrated into Christian youth and young adult ministry, particularly into young peoples' spirituality. Liberation is as much a spiritual journey as it is theological mind-set—this is dubbed *prophetic spirituality*. This prophetic spirituality "recognizes salvation as both eschatological and existential reality."[24] For that reason, liberation theology has personal, spiritual, and cosmic dimensions.

Most Christian theologians probably think of social sin and systemic bondage when they think of liberation theology improving a person's status in life. This is totally acceptable.

---

23. Arzola, *Toward a Prophetic Youth Ministry*, 77–79.
24. Ibid., 77.

What about practical theologians such as youth and young adult ministers? How do youth and young adult ministers, especially those who do *not* work in the inner city, help young people galvanize and gravitate toward a better understanding and appreciation for liberation theology? I am especially thinking about white, suburban teenagers and young adults.

Theologically, then, in order to move from the idea and concept of liberation to a practical theology in action (lived praxis), it is essential that there be a context from which to draw, even if one does *not* live in an urban setting. Can those suburban youth likewise enter into a liberation motif and mind-set?

For this reason, especially for North American, white, suburban young people, the three liberation principles will be highlighted in order to help shift the perspective of mainline, white, well-to-do, middle-class youth and young adults. Keeping in mind, this perspective is *only one* avenue for Christian youth and young adult ministry and liberation theology to travel together. It is also a way that both participate *interdependently* in the work of God.

Inculturation[25]

It may be wise to discuss the merits of the following questions: What is inculturation? Why is inculturation important to liberation theology? How is inculturation helpful to youth and young adult ministry? Answering these questions will provide fruitful information for youth and young adult ministers who want to integrate a liberation model of ministry.

What is inculturation? Typically, *inculturation* denotes the presentation of the gospel message and re-expression of the life of Jesus of Nazareth in forms and terms proper to an indigenous culture. Moreover, inculturation, as applied to Christianity, refers to the adaptation of pedagogical

---

25. The term "inculturation" is sometimes mistakenly confused with the social science terms "acculturation" and "enculturation" that have gained popularity. The terms "acculturation" and "enculturation" are two opposite and opposing cultures that are in juxtaposition with each other but operate according to a dynamic of interaction, that is, a delicate balance of un-mutual (dis)respect and tolerance, which is hardly ever successful long-term. An example of acculturation and enculturation, which illustrates the distinction from inculturation, is the South African government's handling of the indigenous black people and its policy known as apartheid. Inculturation is *not* acculturation or enculturation. Ideally, inculturation is a creative and dynamic relationship between the Christian message and various cultures and ethnicities, and is based on mutual respect, dignity, and reciprocity.

methodology that the church imparts and the dissemination of ecclesial dogmas and doctrines to cultures of other religious traditions. Inculturation results in the creative reinterpretation of theology, worship, and charitable works, without being unfaithful to the indigenous population.[26]

Mission work and evangelization are part of inculturation, but the missionary activity of the Christian should always respect indigenous culture as part of the human phenomenon and as a human right.[27] The manipulation or oppression of culture is categorized as abuse.

Why is inculturation important to liberation theology? Inculturation is part of a contextualization process of Christianity. It is an important progression that peacefully and respectfully tries to instill the gospel into a contemporary culture.[28] Inculturation is part of the liberation theology because it expresses the need to relate faith and culture. Inculturation recognizes the presence of God in the plurality of people's customs and experiences, which allows for stimulation of local languages, rituals, and symbols to be encouraged and utilized from a faith perspective.[29] Inculturation is a necessary development in liberation theology. Inculturation tries to blend culture, theology, and life, and it has four dimensions:

> (1) The development of those values of a culture which are compatible with the values of the [Bible]. (2) The transformation of cultural aspects that are opposed to the Gospel through Christian praxis by the members of that culture; the task of the reign of God becomes the principle that moves and guides the people's interpersonal relationships and their active participation in history. (3) The growth and mutual enrichment of people and groups in a particular sociocultural milieu through the following of [God]. (4) The introduction of that culture, with all the gifts that God has given it for the benefit of humanity, into the life of the ecclesial community.[30]

Inculturation is an arduous process, but it is necessary and legitimate because it offers liberation theology vision, content, and methods to help people grow in their faith-life with God.

---

26. John Paul II, *Redemptoria Missio*, n. 52.
27. Ibid., n. 53.
28. Hill, "Authentic Contextualization," 36.
29. Carmen María Cervantes, *Evangelization of Hispanic Young People*, 202–3.
30. Ibid., 205.

How is inculturation helpful to youth and young adult ministry? Inculturation would ideally encompass all areas of life—theological, biblical, liturgical, ethical, catechetical, and spiritual, along with pastoral and ministerial. It seems logical, then, that inculturation is also significant to youth and young adult ministry. The most profound way that suburban youth and young adults in the United States experience a different culture is on a mission or immersion trip, and these trips certainly have their value; however, a mission trip might not always encounter authentic inculturation.[31] Genuine inculturation within youth and young adult ministry is an exercise in liberation. It opens a young person's eyes to another's culture, helps young people discover salvation, extends well beyond personal assurance, and it lives in solidarity with the poor and those on the margins.[32]

Another important way that inculturation is helpful for youth and young adult ministry is that it helps to situate the incarnational message of Jesus to the customs, beliefs, and traditions of indigenous communities. According to Filipino theologian Anscar Chupungco, "Inculturation is stressing the need to keep the Christian message intact throughout the course of cultural exchange."[33] The underlying premise is that the process of inculturating is in no way meant to distort or disrespect an existing culture's components to ratify some quasi-new culture based upon biblical fundamentalism.

For youth and young adult ministry and adolescent/adult catechesis, the process of inculturation means faith-forming young people into the various ways that fluctuate from family to family and culture to culture. Inculturation's purpose in youth and young adult ministry is to cultivate open-minded evangelization and catechesis, never the strict rigidity and narrow-mindedness that lead to tensions and proselytization.

Learning is of particular importance in the inculturation process because it is a significant feature of a young person's faith and life.[34] Moreover, valuing diversity enriches the young people, the youth community, and the larger congregation. Inculturation affirms the diverse experience of culture within civil society and it promotes various expressions of faith-life within the one Christian culture. Inculturation strives for mutual interaction,

---

31. Root and Creasy Dean, *Theological Turn in Youth Ministry*, 185–88.
32. Kilmovitz, "Youth Ministry as an Exercise," 2.
33. Chupungco, *Liturgical Inculturation*, 25.
34. De Kock, "What About Learning in Practical Theological Studies?" 1.

integration, and assimilation of values, customs, and ideas that amalgamate into a dynamic trans-culture that culminates in mutual enrichment.[35]

The inculturation process is also helpful to youth and young adult ministry because it leads to the *principle of interdependence*. Interdependence, in terms of inculturation, brings a better appreciation for diverse cultures. Hispanic theologian Marina Herrera maintains that youth and young adult ministry should celebrate inculturation, multiculturalism, and diversity instead of tearing down those aspects of life that are not identical to personal worldviews.

> Rather than perceiving differences as reasons to stay isolated from other groups, these differences shall be perceived as reasons for growth and complementarily. In keeping with the principle [of interdependence], youth ministers would encourage, plan, and carry out activities which allow young persons from different cultural or racial backgrounds to come together to dialogue around issues which are of importance to them. . . . These opportunities for exchange among [young people] of different cultural or racial backgrounds should be planned by members of all [ministries] concerned and not just by members of the dominant culture who see this dialogue as a *good thing*.[36]

Inculturation and multicultural encounters in ministry will encourage social awareness and responsibility among youth and young adults. The social interaction that takes place is a great testament to a successful cross-cultural exchange.

Inculturation is necessary! It is important to liberation theology and is helpful to youth and young adult ministry. Hopefully young people will recognize that ethnic diversity and racial differences are cultural gifts to be cultivated as distinct from keeping up cultural boundaries or barriers. Young people deserve a faith formation and pastoral care that offers inculturation and that transmits gospel values and positive experiences that are rooted in multiculturalism.

Multiculturalism

Culture is life! Culture is the foundation of society and civility. Culture usually operates on three stages: (1) behaviors that are learned; (2) ideas

---

35. Chupungco, *Liturgical Inculturation*, 29.
36. Herrera, "Toward Multicultural Youth Ministry," 100.

that reinforce beliefs and values; and (3) products that reinforce attitudes.[37] Civil rights activist Martin Luther King Jr. was famous for saying, "Sundays between 11 and 12 is the most segregated hour of the week." Youth and young adult ministry in North America is rarely homogeneous.[38] Ministering with a multicultural mind-set is not an option anymore. Public and private schools are six times more integrated than Christian churches.[39] Today's youth and young adult ministers would be wise to allow culture to influence their context—connecting young people with God in their youth and young adult subcultures and diverse ethnic cultures.

One might argue that multiculturalism is not part of liberation theology. I completely disagree! Since multiculturalism promotes unity, helps to foster tolerance, and fights against prejudice, it is a component of liberation theology. Multiculturalism is a major theme within North American youth and young adult ministry and pastoral practice. According to the U.S. Conference of Catholic Bishops, multiculturalism is to be taken seriously within the context of youth ministry.

> Adolescents today are growing up in a culturally diverse society. The perceived image of the United States has shifted from melting pot to a multihued tapestry. The strength and beauty of the tapestry lie in the diverse colors and textures of its component threads—the values and traditions claimed by the different racial and ethnic groups that constitute the people of the United States. Ministry with adolescents is multicultural when it focuses on a specialized ministry to youth of particular racial and ethnic cultures *and* promotes multicultural awareness among all [young people].[40]

The U.S. Bishops call youth and young adult ministers not only to acknowledge the different racial, cultural, and ethnic groups, but to minister accordingly, to enhance the complexities of cultural diversity, and to foster a deeper awareness of multiculturalism.

There are several important themes worthy of discussion for youth and young adult ministry: serving minorities, immigration status, human development perspectives, ethnic spirtualties, family, and relationships.[41]

37. Rah, *Many Colors*, 24.
38. Doong and Jin, "Thinking Globally," 167.
39. Rah, *Many Colors*, 51.
40. *RTV*, 22.
41. Doong and Jin, "Thinking Globally," 168.

The Liberation Model

There are also two important themes of multiculturalism that merit attention and can bring about awareness and openness within youth ministry, especially a white, suburban youth and young adult ministry: (1) community, and (2) mission.[42]

Community, in this context, refers to the practice of youth and young adult ministry discussing and dialoguing about issues that foster community, and some matters that do not always ensure true community.[43] Authentic community within youth and young adult ministry is not a program to be checked-off on some list to be accomplished. It is a process that is open-ended and ongoing, which stimulates ideas and accountability, and cultivates mutuality and openness with an aim of creating and fostering an intercultural climate.

Mission, in the context of youth and young adult ministry, refers to God already working in the minds and hearts of all peoples and bringing about transformation to all of God's creation. Mission joins up with and enjoys the work of God already in progress within contextualization of multiculturalism.[44] Genuine mission within youth and young adult ministry seeks to observe, learn, and discern adolescents' and young adults' identities in God, and to help young people discover their uniqueness in God as part of a subculture and on the front edge of life.

Mexican theologian Alejandro Aguilera-Titus states, "Striking a balance between the needs and aspirations of adolescents from different cultural and ethnic communities is not an easy task. Equally challenging is accepting each other's differences and confronting each case of prejudice, cultural stereotypes, and expression of racism present in society today."[45] For example, youth and young adult ministers may have to foster a culturally diverse environment for young people to experience the ethnic roots and cultural practices of themselves and others.

There are two pastorally rich ways for ministering to adolescents who come from various racial and ethnic cultures. First, it may be wise when ministering to culturally and ethnically diverse young people to be culturally attuned to address inclusive programming that responds to needs and issues of youth and young adults. Second, it may be sensible when ministering to culturally and ethnically diverse young people to

42. Oestreicher, *Youth Ministry 3.0*, 73.
43. Ibid.
44. Ibid., 75.
45. Aguilera-Titus, "Ministry with Youth in a Culturally Diverse Church," 82.

introduce and integrate ethnic traditions, values, and rituals into ministerial programming.

Aguilera-Titus notes that youth and young adult ministry involves a *spirituality of discipleship* and a human maturity which allows people to grow in welcoming others, embracing them, and journeying with them—leaving behind *we-they* language and moving into *all-of-us-together* language.[46] Much of the work of multiculturalism is being accepting of another's unique heritage and indigenous traditions.

A good reminder for youth and young adult ministers is, "Ministry with [young people] needs to counteract prejudice, racism, and discrimination by example, with youth themselves becoming models of fairness and nondiscrimination."[47] It helps young people develop interpersonal skills for dealing with awkward moments of feeling discrimination onset and for overcoming the social barriers to enhancing self-accomplishment.

Another way to move multiculturalism in youth and young adult ministry even further is through acceptance and openness of others. More specifically, being open and affirming of others' faith experiences beyond Christianity to other world religious traditions.

Interreligious Openness

The importance of interreligious openness cannot be overlooked or overstated today. Unfortunately, it is *unlikely* that many Christian youth and/or young adult ministers have discussed, significantly, the reality and beauty of other religious traditions within the context of youth and young adult ministry.[48] The Second Vatican Council document *Nostra Aetate* addresses the importance and dignity of other world religions.

> The Catholic Church rejects *nothing* of what is true and holy in these [world] religions (primal, Hinduism and Buddhism). It [The Catholic Church] has a high regard for the manner of life and conduct, the precepts and doctrines which, although differing

---

46. Ibid., 83.
47. USCCB, *Renewing the Vision*, 23.
48. This is an anecdotal comment based purely on speculation and personal experience of being involved in Christian youth and young adult ministry for the past thirty years. From my experience, most youth and young adult ministers are too busy with their own curricula and agenda and do not entertain other world religious traditions. Christian youth and young adult ministers are usually caught up in "bringing young people to Christ," instead of addressing the similarities between major world religious traditions.

The Liberation Model

> in many ways from its own teaching, nevertheless often reflect a ray of that truth which enlightens all men and women.... The [Catholic] Church, therefore, urges its sons and daughters to *enter with* prudence and charity into discussion and collaboration with members of other religions. Let Christians, while witnessing to their own faith and way of life, *acknowledge, preserve* and *encourage* the spiritual and moral truths found among non-Christians, together with their social life and culture.[49]

At the time this was written, it was considered vanguard; in many ways, it still is progressive and open-minded. The significant point for youth and young adult ministers to grasp is that it is good for Christians to be in dialogue with people from other religions. Christian youth and young adult ministry would be wise to attempt to interact positively with an incredible variety of religious views because it is a reality in contemporary society.

Shantra D. Premawardhana, director of the National Council of Churches Interfaith Relations, argues that there are two affirmations for Christian ministries to be more interreligious. First, Christianity alone does not have the resources to resolve the entire world's problems, and that religious communities cannot afford to do our work for peace in isolation from each other anymore.[50] Second, Christianity needs to listen to the voices of the world's poor, oppressed, indigenous people, women, disabled refugees, homosexuals, the displaced, and the silenced.[51]

Working for justice is a priority for interreligious openness because oppressive governments and authoritarian powers have a vested interest in keeping world religions from common and collaborative dialogue. Traditionally, negative or distant views toward other world religions will not help to develop meaningful relationships nor will it help toward adopting a new attitude aimed at interreligious dialogue and openness.

Feminist theologian Alison Downie likens interreligious openness to a certain type of spirituality: a *spirituality of openness*. Downie states, "Interreligious dialogue is [called] to investigate a spirituality of openness. Exploring this spirituality of openness across intra-Christian diversity contributes to interreligious dialogue because themes and values in this spirituality are also present in other feminisms and religious traditions."[52]

---

49. *Nostra Aetate*, 739n2. Emphasis added.
50. Premawardhana, "Christian Openness," 1.
51. Ibid., 2.
52 Downie, "Spirituality of Openness," 56.

Downie's schemata for interreligious openness touches on several developmental themes for youth and young adult ministry: (1) rationality of the self, (2) relational ways of knowing, (3) cultivating the ability to be open-minded, (4) learning the ethic of discernment, (5) learning the ways to take calculated risks, and (6) understanding the power of divine beauty.[53] The ability to allow these six points to be addressed in a youth and young adult ministry demonstrates the facets of true hospitality. It is in embracing the holy other person that authentic hospitality is extended and received.

Feminist theologian Marianne Moyaert explains that every religious tradition is open to an individual's inner response to the Divine, which should be enough reason for interreligious openness. Moyaert claims, "The Transcendent is often experienced in events such as birth, love, grief, pain, suffering, disaster, sexuality, death, and the like."[54] These are tangible and every day events, pastoral elements of life to which youth and young adult ministries cater. Interreligious openness would be a new ministerial horizon for most Christian youth and young adult ministries in North America to integrate into their curricula, but one that could be cause for joy and celebration.

One cause for celebration is catechizing young people that all religious people are actually committed to the *same religious object*. The phrase "the same religious object" is taken to mean God. All religions share the same God. In some sense, I am trying to get away from the dangerous exclusivist position that maintains all other religions are false and misleading, and that Christianity is the best and only way to God. The hard-line position of exclusivism cannot thrive in an ever-changing, pluralistic world. The way forward for interreligious openness is to look beyond the particular to the various areas that unite and transcend all religious perspectives and traditions.[55] There are no strangers in God's house (John 14:2).[56]

In a recent study of Muslim youth workers, American adolescent ministry scholar Len Kageler addresses the reality that not all youth [and young adult] ministry takes place within the context of Christianity. Other world religious traditions also care for and love their own young people! Kageler

---

53. Ibid., 60–66.
54. Moyaert, "Interreligious Dialogue," 731.
55. Ibid., 737.
56. Ibid.

notes, "It seems to me that the presence of *religious other* forces the issue of reflection on personal faith."[57]

There is a genuine concern for young people understanding the similarities and differences between Christianity and other world religions. There is much to gain from interreligious openness, and Christian youth and young adult ministries are ripe for such fruitful exchanges. Canadian and U.S. young people are submersed in a multicultural and a multi-faith society. Today's young people, perhaps more than ever, are steeped in tolerance, subjectivism, pluralism, and postmodernism, which is really good for Christian youth and young adult ministry.[58]

The three liberation principles for integration—inculturation, multiculturalism, and interreligious openness—are legitimate ways in which youth and young adult ministers may better serve the adolescent, emerging adult, and young adult populations within church-communities. These integration practices are part of a larger liberation model that tries to make meaning out of that which is ethically subjective from the dominant culture's perspective. No theology or ministry can be socially or politically uncommitted because that which is true for the poor, marginalized, and oppressed is equally true for the wealthy and powerful.

Perhaps the challenge is to work for organizational change within Christian youth and young adult ministry. Simple, linear thinking that produces a typical, play-it-safe, approach to youth and young adult ministry may not be the best way to be in contact with the rest of the world. Youth and young adult ministers may need encouragement to begin to think about liberation as inculturation, multiculturalism, and interreligious openness, because there will be natural resistance while trying to build a model of youth and young adult ministry from the margins, which is constructed on multiethnic and multicultural principles.

Pedagogical and Pastoral Methodologies for Implementation

The method used in this section is prescriptive because it provides tangible examples to be implemented. Andrew Root reminds us that practical theological method "cannot be reduced to only immanent/empirically observed

---

57. Kageler, "Foundations and Models," 84.

58. Ibid. Although interreligious dialogue is not exactly the intent of Kageler's article, and he was not necessarily supporting interreligious openness, his thoughts were helpful.

realities."⁵⁹ In this case, the method seeks to say something particular and something practical about integrating liberation theology into Christian youth ministry.⁶⁰ Today's young people live in a rich multicultural and multi-religious world, and youth and young adult ministry practices would be wise to seek out lived and concrete experiences within a faith and spiritual context.⁶¹

Contextualization

Contextualization is the *sine qua non* (absolutely necessary) process for fully understanding and properly engaging in pastoral formation, practical theology, youth and young adult ministry, multiculturalism, and/or interreligious dialogue.⁶² Practical theologian Stephen B. Bevans maintains that there is only one way to truly participate in theology, that is, contextually. "As a theological method, the praxis is by its very nature wedded to a particular *context*. It will never be a theology that does not have its 'feet on the ground.'"⁶³ Contextualization is an enterprise different from traditional theology because it is rooted in a particular context and culture in some implied or tangible way. Therefore, "there is no such thing as *theology*, there is only *contextual* theology. . . . The contextualization of theology—the attempt to understand faith in terms of a particular context—is really a theological imperative."⁶⁴ This is the focus of the liberation model: to understand practical and pastoral theology from a youth and young adult ministry perspective and to help extend young peoples' theological worldview.

Important to contextualization and youth and young adult ministry is the way young people view the church and perhaps the way the church sees young people. German practical theologian Tobias Faix reminds the church's theologians to reflect on these poignant questions: "How can we understand this generation? How can we take them more seriously? How can we learn from them?"⁶⁵ As one young person put it, "If the church

---

59. Root, "Regulating the Empirical in Practical Theology," 54.
60. Ibid., 48.
61. Ibid., 54.
62. Arzola, *Toward a Prophetic Youth Ministry*, 72.
63. Bevans, *Models of Contextual Theology*, 77.
64. Ibid., 3.
65. Faix, "Hybrid Identity," 77.

wanted to get in touch with me, [the church] would need to come to me—and not just with a pearl of bells on Sunday morning. Only when the church engages with me, starts to enter into critical and humorous dialogue with me, can it win me back."[66]

Contextualization is critical to youth and young adult ministry and is not some passing fad. Contextualization, like inculturation, is vital to youth and young adult ministries understanding of the self-revelation of God.

The Four Strategies

It is always advisable to give a few preliminary suggestions before discussing the four methodological strategies for implementation of the liberation model. First, a youth and young adult minister may want to purchase and read (and reread) carefully the book by Gustavo Gutiérrez titled *A Theology of Liberation* to begin to comprehend the scope and nature of liberation theology from its inception.

Second, a youth and young adult minister might want to select a book or two from this chapter's bibliography to further enhance one's familiarity with the complexity of liberation theology, and its implications and ramifications for youth ministry.

Third, a youth and young adult minister might want to coordinate a half-day workshop on liberation theology for the adult volunteer catechists and the student peer-leaders within the youth and young adult ministry to help them understand the aim of integrating the liberation model into the youth and young adult curriculum and ministry.

Within this half-day (4–5 hours) workshop, several aspects concerning liberation theology could be discussed: (1) a liberation theologian from a local Christian college could catechize the group about essentials of liberation theology; (2) a video could be shown that addresses pertinent ideals pertaining to liberation theology, such as preferential option for the poor, tolerance, and multiculturalism; and (3) a discussion centering on significant liberation theological ideas could help launch the liberation model into motion within the youth and young adult ministry.

Youth and young adult ministers certainly are highly expected to learn as much as possible about liberation theology and its key concepts before introducing the liberation model to a larger spectrum of the youth and young adult population within the ministry.

66. Ibid.

In order to formulate new pedagogical approaches and pastoral strategies for Christian youth and young adult ministers to implement is to acknowledge that something *new* needs to be asserted. The assertion here is to offer four inculturation, multicultural, and interreligious strategies for youth and young adult ministries. The possibilities are far-reaching.

Strategy 1

One pedagogical strategy is outlined in Mexican theologian Lara Medina's scheme of multicultural awareness and liberating theological praxis of storytelling with female Hispanics. Medina insists that *Las Hermanas* (The Sisters) expresses the spirituality of liberation of women, rooted in personal experience of being Mexican, Puerto Rican, or Cuban, who are shaped religiously by the Christian faith-life.[67] To comprehend the sociohistorical context of any cultural minority, especially from a dominate culture, it is prudent to learn about liberation theology.

Feminist Hispanics "rely on the voices of the subjects 'to tell their stories' and to enrich one's interpretive analysis is vital to representing Latino(a) theology and religions."[68] Through telling our stories, female adolescents and young adults engage in self-reflection that gives purpose to their encounters, reveals shared experiences, and leads to the recognition that their personal-ideological worldview is significant to communal living.[69] Through the sharing of personal narratives (this is also called auto-theme biography) young people will be able to reflect on the quintessential questions of life: Who am I? Where did I come from? Why do I look different than others? Who loves me? What do I want to do with my life? This practical methodology of small faith-sharing groups and sharing personal narratives is also used by other ethnicities.

Vietnamese theologian Peter C. Phan acknowledges that storytelling among young Asians is a fundamental methodology: "it is the cumulative unresolved feeling that arises out of people's experience of injustice . . . and reveals itself in the *telling* of tragic stories."[70]

Faith-sharing groups can be formed around various populations: age, minority, gender, and interests. Young people are invited to share their personal narratives, regrets, fears, mishaps, joys, hopes, and dreams. Sharing

---

67. Medina, "Transformative Struggle," 218.
68. Ibid., 219.
69. Ibid., 231.
70. Phan, "Method in Liberation Theologies," 59.

personal narratives provides for personal witness and communal shared stories, and can be powerful liberation and transformation experiences for young people. Helping youth and young adults experience their own spirituality through ethnicity and cultural heritage may lead to more open-mindedness and less racially motivated misperceptions.

Strategy 2

A second pastoral strategy involves inculturation, interreligious openness, and Asian Christology. This liberation approach to ministry has two foci: religiousness and poverty.[71] In teaching about Asian minorities, such as the Hmong (minority people of Laos), Vietnamese, Burmese, and Koreans, it would seem reasonable to make Jesus' life relevant and appealing to their ethnicity. For instance, a youth and/or young adult minister may teach low ascending Christology[72] to a group of Asian students by situating Christ in an Asian context, one that unifies Asian religious poverty and the poor religiousness[73] of liberation. Below is an example of a six-session catechetical series for a youth and young adult ministry that meets once a week:

---

71. Phan, "Jesus the Christ with an Asian Face," 406–7.

72. "Low ascending" Christology is a contemporary approach to Christology, and it is distinct from "high descending" Christology, or classical Christology. Low ascending Christology focuses on Jesus of Nazareth as a human person first, functioning as a first-century Palestine Jew, and investigates the words, actions, and deeds of Jesus and that which he was capable of doing as a Jewish person living in the first century. Particularly, low ascending Christology tries to investigate the humanness and Jewishness of Jesus in terms of his earthly human experiences: faith, hope, love, fear, sadness, sexual desire, pain, laughter, trust in God, and a myriad of fundamental encounters that constitute the human condition. The low ascending approach begins with Jesus' earthly ministry and focuses primary on the information gleaned from the Synoptic Gospels as distinct from the Gospel of John because the fourth gospel favors a high descending approach to Christology. Finally, low ascending Christology *does not* begin with asserting the two classical dogmas attesting to Christ's divineness: (1) the Dogma on the Divinity of Christ (Council of Nicea in 325 CE) and (2) the Dogma on Hypostatic Union (Council of Chalcedon in 451 CE). Low ascending Christology does not deny or negate these two dogmas, but gets its starting point from humanness and Jewishness of Jesus. The difficulty with the classic Christology has always been in explaining the genuine human experiences that Jesus encountered without automatically jumping to the conclusion that "Jesus is God."

73. Pieris, *Asian Theology of Liberation*, 21. The term "poor religiousness" within an Asian liberation schemata is chiefly concerned with the fact that Christian churches directly and Christian theology indirectly have remained in Asia, but have not inculturated as part of Asia. Christian churches and theologies have failed to join together other world religious traditions' religiousness (Buddhism, Hinduism, Taoism, and Confucianism)

- Week 1: Examine briefly the history of Christianity in Asia, its beginnings, its struggles, and its advancements.

- Week 2: Study the similarities between Jesus the Christ and Gotama the Buddha, addressing Jesus' Sermon on the Mount and the Buddha's teachings on the Four Noble Truths.[74]

- Week 3: Identify Jesus as the *poor monk*, linking Christ between religion and liberation and asceticism with liberation religiousness.[75]

- Week 4: Recognize Jesus the Christ as *I Ching* (perfect realization of Change), discussing the Taoist concept of *yin/yang* philosophy, demonstrating its effectiveness and its applicableness within Christianity.[76]

- Week 5: Teach Christian stories with an Asian "twist," utilizing a hermeneutic of a crucified people, a proletariat hermeneutic if you will, one that resonates Jesus who was poor and people who are now poor, outcasts, and socially and politically oppressed.[77]

- Week 6: Associate Jesus as the *minjung* (Korean term, literally "the popular mass") or Suffering Servant motif that enables Asians to see meaning in their own suffering and to accept suffering and service as part of their option for emancipation.[78]

This strategy is an excellent way for welcoming an Asian population into Christian youth and young adult ministry. It does not matter if the youth

---

and material poverty or, to use Pieris' own metaphors, "because they have refused the *double baptism* of the 'Jordan of Asian religion' and the 'Calvary of Asian poverty'" (Pieris, *Asian Theology of Liberation*, 21). Pieris' play on words is an excellent point that reinforces the separation between Christianity and culture in Asian countries.

74. The Four Noble Truths are as follows: (1) the truth of *dukha*, which is the conditional or temporal experiences are not ultimately satisfying, and therefore, lead to suffering and frustration; (2) the truth of desire, which is clinging to or craving sensory pleasures, whether for fame or fortune, or for things to stay the same or to become different, either way it is an attachment that leads to dissatisfaction; (3) the truth of cessation, which attempts to put an end to or to cease all earthly desires, and only live in the present moment, and free from all self-centeredness and selfishness; (4) the truth of liberation, which realizes that only a life of morality, concentration, wisdom, and compassion can put an end to suffering, and this leads to the Eightfold Path of Enlightenment and Liberation. For more Buddhism beliefs and practices see Fischer, "Buddhism," 129–75.

75. Phan, "Jesus the Christ with an Asian Face," 407–8.

76. Ibid., 411–12.

77. Ibid., 418–19.

78. Ibid., 422–23.

or young adult population is Hispanic or black because all ethnicities can benefit from the Asian culture. This is one way to connect Christianity and Asian religious traditions.

Strategy 3

A third pragmatic strategy in developing tolerance is to empower young people to overcome their anxieties, fears, and prejudices concerning people of different lifestyles and who have a different color of skin. This strategy tries to foster a spirit of multiculturalism and tolerance. There are two videos that will cause young people to reflect on their own prejudices and intolerance toward minorities.

- Scenario 1: Have students watch the movie titled *Live to Tell* (1995), a short (forty-minute documentary), touching, and brave film regarding the life experiences of LGBTQ high school students who attend their first openly gay and lesbian senior prom. After viewing the film, theological reflection is encouraged: break into small groups, ask pertinent questions about the movie and "break down" any barriers that young people have regarding intolerance toward homosexual people.

- Scenario 2: Have students watch the gripping film titled *4 Little Girls* (1998), a lengthy documentary about bigotry and racism in the U.S. South. The story revolves around four teenage girls who died during a bombing at Sixteenth Street Baptist Church in Birmingham, Alabama on November 15, 1963. The bombing is a direct result of racism and hatred. The girls died innocently and unjustly at the hands of one bitter man. Once the film has been shown, the youth or young adult minister may want to stimulate discussion. Questions concerning the film may be raised. What is something new you learned watching this movie? Do you know of anyone who has been persecuted against because of their race or ethnicity? Do you have any good friends that are African-American? Such questions help to eliminate barriers that adolescents may have regarding intolerance toward black people.

These movies will allow youth and young adults to feel empathy and foster compassion for minority groups. Moreover, these movies will cause lively discussion surrounding racism, intolerance, and multiculturalism.

Strategy 4

A fourth practical strategy is to expose Christian young people to interreligious openness, multiculturalism, and tolerance. One approach is to examine and discuss Islam.[79] A month-long series on Islam could be designed like this:

- Week 1: The Core Teaching of Islam. There are five central teachings of Islam, which can be discussed in general or at great length: (a) the oneness of God and humanity, (b) the prophet-hood and the completeness of Islam, (c) the human relationship to the divine, (d) the unseen life, and (e) the last judgment.[80]

- Week 2: The Five Pillars and Jihad. There are five vital tenets of Islam that every Muslim should follow: (a) belief and witness, (b) daily prayers, (c) *Zakat* (almsgiving or tithing), (d) fasting, and (e) *hajj* (the once in a lifetime journey to Mecca).[81] *Jihad*, commonly mistranslated as "holy war," actually means "striving," that is striving for internal and external peace. Technically, *Jihad* is not one of the Five Pillars of Islam, but it is an integral and daily part of Muslim life.[82]

- Week 3: Cinema Night on Islam. There are several movies and documentaries to choose from to help Christian young people learn more about Islam. Here are a few: *The Message* (1977), the quintessential Muslim film about the birth of Islam and the Prophet Mohammed; *Malcom X* (1990), a movie about the 1960s American born and religiously converted Malcom X Little; *Islam: Empire of Faith* (2000), a documentary about the rise of Islam and Islamic culture and practices; *Mooz-lum* (2010), which examines the daily life of a troubled young American Muslim man coming to terms with his religious faith and identity; *Innocence of Muslims* (2012) portrays the increasing persecution and poor human rights of Muslims in modern-day Egypt. All five of these movies are acceptable for youth and young adults to

---

79. The term *Islam* is a multifaceted Arabic word that means peace, purity, acceptance, and commitment. A Muslim is a person who freely and willingly accepts the supreme power of God (*Allah* in Arabic) and earnestly strives to arrange her/his life in full submission or total accord with the teachings of God and the Qur'an, or the sacred readings for Muslims.

80. Fisher, "Islam," 372–76.

81. Ibid., 381–84.

82. Ibid., 386.

The Liberation Model

watch and will help young people to understand religious diversity and tolerance.

- Week 4: Field Trip to a Mosque. Visit a local Muslim mosque with the youth and/or young adult ministry on a day that the Muslim community is not gathering for worship (Friday afternoon is the main weekly religious day for most Muslims). This is a practical way to introduce Christian youth and young adults to the worship life of Muslims. An *Imam* (Muslim minister) can help the young people understand the various elements of Muslim worship and symbolism within the mosque.

A series on Islam is a wonderful way to expose young people to the truth and misnomers regarding Islam. The series will also generate much discussion among young people. The series is a way to help Christian young people to encounter other world religious traditions, contribute to interreligious dialogue, and experience firsthand interreligious openness.

As a pedagogical approach a youth and young adult minister may want to prepare for inculturation, multiculturalism, and interreligious dialogue to flourish by integrating a few catechetical techniques.

- First, *teaching* about the rich ethnic heritages that shape the Christian landscape in various countries where one ministers.
- Second, *providing* and *encouraging* cross-cultural experiences that facilitate opportunities for personal growth and introspection.
- Third, *fostering* an atmosphere of acceptance of cultural diversity and respect for other races and nationalities is an enriching practice.
- Fourth, *dialoguing* about the similarities and fruitfulness of other world religions and their beliefs.

Netherlands Protestant theologian Jos de Kock calls this type of catechetical learning environment "developmental" learning because "the [young person] learns from the catechist [or youth and young adult minister] who may engage in questioning, contradicting, or even challenging the [young person's] personal theories."[83] These four catechetical techniques are wonderful ways to help youth and young adult ministers to prepare the way for young people to learn and experience something new.

---

83. De Kock, "Typology of Catechetical Learning Environments," 277.

As a whole, these four pedagogical and pastoral implementation strategies will provide spiritual growth and produce self-awareness in young people regarding their own prejudice, intolerance, and lack of openness.

These four methodological strategies are mere *suggestions* for using within a liberation model of youth and young adult ministry. There are countless more that can be integrated into this model, such as book clubs or taking a pilgrimage to another world religion's sacred space. I am confident that a younger and more creative youth and young adult minister (than I), or cluster of youth and young adult ministers, could design several pastoral strategies and integrate a different one each year. It would be wonderful if a youth and young adult ministry selected one world religion each year and spent four-to-six weeks studying and learning about that religion, comparing and contrasting it to Christianity.

The Strengths and Limitations of This Model

Evaluating the strengths and limitations of the liberation model is admitting that there are both positive points and concerns for this model, like all other models. The liberation model will appeal to some youth and young adult ministers and not appeal as strongly to others. The approach to evaluating whether or not a community should utilize the liberation model in their youth and young adult ministry should not only take into account the information gleaned from this particular chapter, but also the general consensus of the youth and young adult ministry staffs, volunteers, and paid ministers. And of course, prayer and the needs of the young people are paramount to its success.

Strengths

There are many fine qualities that youth and young adult ministers will find appealing in the liberation model. First, the most obvious strength is that the liberation motif is deeply rooted in sacred Scripture. Both the Old Testament and the New Testament offer liberation as a reality toward which Jews and Christians are to strive. Second, liberation was modeled on the ministry of Jesus of Nazareth and he always championed the poor; and a careful reading of the New Testament makes this quite evident. Third, liberation has its own flavor, distinct in theology and rich in pastoral praxis, and is a major movement within Latin America, as well as with minority groups within the world's Catholic, Protestant, and Evangelical churches, which try to create equality for all God's people.

Fourth, the practice of liberation in the church earnestly tries to eradicate poverty, prejudice, racism, and violence that are perpetuated upon the marginalized and disenfranchised. Fifth, liberation is not only theologically relevant; it is also pastorally relevant, and can be studied and learned in various ministry venues. This is precisely the reason that the three components are key within liberation (inculturation, multiculturalism, and interreligious openness) and make the liberation model exciting and appealing to develop. Sixth, beyond theology and pastoral ministry, liberation reminds United States citizens of their civic responsibility, because liberation corresponds to the firm foundation laid forth by the Civil Rights Movement in helping eradicate bigotry and hatred toward others, and maintaining peace through nonviolence.

These points offer a pragmatic approach for developing this model and integrating it into youth and young adult ministry, and that alone is sufficient reason to pursue the liberation model.

Limitations

There are a few drawbacks to the liberation model. However, the limitations should not detract from the exciting possibilities of developing a strong liberation model within a comprehensive youth and young adult ministry.

First, liberation is often confused with revolutionary movements, violence, or religious fundamentalism, and that is a shame. Latin American liberation theologians have received their fair share of "bad press" over the years, which may have youth and young adult ministers (and their pastors) apprehensive about adopting this model for youth and young adult ministries.

Second, for some, this model might appear to be too reductionistic. Liberation theology can be complex, and simplifying it into three main themes may not appeal to all pastoral ministers. Nevertheless, liberation motifs tend to focus on the future in temporal terms of social, political, and economic, rather than integrating the future in spiritual terms of religious, divine, and mystical. Perhaps there needs to be a both/and focus for pastoral ministers to galvanize toward.

Third, and this is a major weakness with the liberation model, is the applicability of integrating and implementing liberation. What exactly does liberation look like? How will American churchgoing young people experience liberation in the youth and young adult ministry? How will a youth or young adult ministry financially afford the outreach to ensure that liberation takes place? These are tough questions that will need to be addressed by youth and young adult ministers in the field.

There are several strengths and limitations to the liberation model, but as previously mentioned, the limitations should not sway a youth or young adult minister away from developing this model. From a practical standpoint, even discussing liberation in a youth and young adult ministry setting will help young people to overcome personal prejudices and destroy class distinctions. Liberation is a paradigm within the Christian experience and it offers a comprehensive youth and young adult ministry an authentic avenue to help alleviate the suffering in the community while simultaneously transforming hearts and minds of young people.

Case Study[84]

Gloria Catalina Sanchez is a thirty-three-year-old youth minister of *Get Loud Youth Ministry* at Saint Edward's Episcopal Church in southeastern Los Angeles, California. Saint Edward's is an urban congregation and is predominately a Latino/Hispanic parish. All of St. Ed's staff and members are bilingual.

Gloria is working in her third youth ministry position; she began work as a youth minister immediately upon graduating from Portland University in Portland, Oregon, with a degree in theology and a minor in psychology. She also has a Master of Pastoral Studies degree from Pacific Theological Union. Gloria was an excellent student in college and graduate school, with great interpersonal abilities and pastoral care and counseling skills. Gloria is also married and has two small children of her own.

Gloria has only been working at Saint Edward's in this position for one year. She has a rather large youth ministry that meets several times a week for various events: Tuesday night Bible study, Thursday night is feeding the homeless, and Friday night is game night. However, her most significant night of the week is Wednesday. There are approximately 135 high school students who participate in the Wednesday night youth gatherings, which

---

84. This is an authentic ministry scenario that came to me about seven years ago; I have crafted it differently for this particular case study. The names, cities, and institutions listed in this case study are fictional and have been made up to protect their true identities.

tend to be a mixture of fun activities, socializing, and catechetical presentation, followed by small group discussions.

After several months into her new ministry position, Gloria began to realize that many of the Hispanic male youth were ridiculing and making derogatory remarks while referring to homosexual males. She often heard them using terms such as "homo," "fag," "queer," and the phrase "that's gay." Gloria did not think much of it at first, but as the disparaging remarks continued, she became concerned. Gloria's main concern was about the male adolescents within the ministry, with regard to using ridiculing language and negative humor with respect to homosexual people.

Moreover, Gloria was also well aware that other students heard these remarks coming out of the boys' mouths. Through her private conversations with this one young person, Gloria was also privy to one member of the youth community who was questioning his/her sexuality and sexual identity.

Gloria's Plan: Gloria decided to create a brief questionnaire that addressed concerns about intolerance within the Get Loud Youth Ministry. The questionnaire accomplished three important things. First, it provided a backdrop against which to discuss issues of prejudice and tolerance. Second, it gave her valuable information to evaluate all her students' understanding of issues surrounding homosexuality and Christianity's teaching on *imago Dei*. Third, it gave her measurable data that she could begin teaching from as she continued to assess her youth ministry.

Reflection: Do you think a questionnaire is a good idea? Would you have gone with this approach? Think about the circumstances of Gloria's ministry for a minute. If you were in Gloria's position, what would you do? Again, if you were in Gloria's shoes, in which ways would you to try to rectify this situation? Which one of the four implementation strategies do you think Gloria should put into practice in the youth ministry? Although the four strategies might not fit exactly with Gloria's situation, with a little alteration a youth minister could come up with a great strategy.

Parting Remarks

The liberation model for youth and young adult ministry is an attempt to blend three complex and important ideas, and bring them to the fore of adolescent and young adult practice. A central idea of this model is engendering hope and justice to the minorities within a dominant culture. The thrust of this chapter has been to integrate two areas: (1) providing three practical components of liberation—inculturation, multiculturalism, and interreligious openness—and (2) proposing four pedagogical methodologies for implementation. It is my argument that these two areas are beneficial for Christian youth and young adult ministry.

Cuban-American theologian Miguel A. De La Torre passionately insists, "The hope of the marginalized is not a utopian dream based on the fantasy world of imagination; rather, it is usually a feet-on-the ground utopianism anchored in the realism of the disenfranchised."[85] The desired pastoral reality and practice of youth and young adult ministry is to allow for adolescents and young adults to express themselves freely, as well as explore the cultural dimensions of other cultures and ethnicities. Minorities, in this case, also mean sexual minorities.

The ultimate questions that young people should be asking themselves are: what does liberation feel like? What will tolerance do for me? What does diversity and multiculturalism look like? What are my own unique prejudices? How the young people in the youth and young adult ministry reflect and answer these questions will determine the intrinsic relationship between liberation theology and the pastoral practice that develops as a direct result of cultivating people's experience, especially the experience of the poor.

Argentina theologian Ivan Petralla notes, "Liberation theology cannot wish to solve [traditional theologies] impasse by means of analysis and/or deductions of the concept of God . . . but by starting with experiences of God in the center of history and with critical analysis of the concepts we use to interpret such experiences."[86]

In other words, the liberation model and its methodology, as described here in this chapter, are an integrative approach to youth and young adult ministry. This pastoral approach to youth and young adult ministry is rooted in: (1) the experience, service, and defense of the life and dignity of the poor, marginalized, and victimized; and (2) the evangelization and catechesis of the dominant culture about the minority and in most cases, poorer culture.

Finally, the liberation model involves growth, learning, maturing, and conscious development; and adolescents and young adults, as with all

---

85. De La Torre, *Doing Christian Ethics*, 54–55.
86. Petrella, *Latin American Liberation Theology*, 2.

The Liberation Model

people, must continue to struggle toward transformation and authentic liberation.

If liberation is going to occur with young people, then adults would be wise to become aware of the reality of one's not only existing in the world, but being responsible for the world's needs. Self-awareness is a gradual process in young people, and often two steps forward and one step backward. Nevertheless, youth and young adults are capable of thinking critically, analyzing a situation, becoming more open-minded, and engaging in transformative action to build a more sane and humane world.[87] Those who minister to youth and young adults recognize the raw potential and the awesome capability that young people possess to be Christian liberators.

---

87. Cervantes, *Hispanic Young People*, 98.

CHAPTER 5

The Christian Discipleship Model

> *Christianity without the living Christ is inevitably Christianity without discipleship; and Christianity without discipleship is always Christianity without Christ.*[1]
>
> Dietrich Bonhoeffer
> *The Cost of Discipleship*, 1937

Preliminary Remarks

This chapter maintains that Christian discipleship is *the* primordial model for comprehensive Christian youth and young adult ministry.[2] It presents a systematic approach for understanding discipleship and integrating it into comprehensive youth and young adult ministry. This chapter addresses eight theological categories for the youth and young adult ministry community and provides six pedagogical and pastoral strategies (methods) for implementation into a youth and young adult ministry. The teleological (end) goal of the Christian discipleship model is to chal-

---

1. Bonhoeffer, *Cost of Discipleship*, 59.

2. In 2006, I wrote an article entitled "Models for Adolescent Ministry: Exploring Eight Ecumenical Examples," which appeared in the journal *Religious Education*. This article has been quite influential and popular over the past decade. I am proud to state that has resulted in at least three other scholarly articles written by other theologians and practitioners and has been the impetus of two MA theses in the United States. Moreover, at an IASYM Conference in Europe, I was told this past year by a colleague that he uses this article is his doctoral class on youth ministry and catechesis at the Protestant University of Netherlands in Amsterdam.

The Christian Discipleship Model

lenge, empower, engage, and inspire young people on their faith journey. Christian discipleship is a model to be cultivated and sustained within Christian youth and young adult ministry—really it is the standard for all Christian ministries.

Situating Christian Discipleship in Youth and Young Adult Ministry

It may be worthwhile to articulate terminology. The title of this chapter implores the term "primordial." Why is the term *primordial* used? This is the case because it's defined as "the first in a sequence" or "the first to be created." The presupposition is that Christian discipleship is the foundation for all other models of youth and young adult ministry. Another way of looking at it is Christian discipleship model is the pinnacle of youth and young adult ministry models.

For example, in liturgical churches and in sacramental theology it is often stated that "Jesus Christ is the primordial sacrament of God." What does this mean? It means that Jesus Christ is the first among many or the first in a sequence of all the other sacraments. Before there was an institution called "the church" and before there were seven (or five or two) sacraments, there was Jesus Christ. Therefore, for our purposes, I am merely claiming that the Christian discipleship model is the primordial model for youth and young adult ministry.

Another word that is often used in this chapter (and others) is the word "comprehensive." The term comprehensive is used to describe the systematic and intentional approach to ministry with Christian young people, and is a holistic synthesis articulated by ecclesial documents.[3] I like to tell my students and youth and young adult ministers in the field that the word "comprehensive" simply means ministry from A to Z. These guidelines

---

3. There are five guidelines for ministering to Christian youth set by the US Catholic Bishops: (1) utilize each of the church's ministries—advocacy, catechesis, community life, evangelization, justice and service, leadership development—with adolescents; (2) provide developmentally appropriate programs and activities that promote personal pastoral care, prayer, and worship—in an integrated approach to achieving the three goals for ministry and spiritual growth for young and older adolescents; (3) enrich family life and promote the faith growth of families of adolescents; (4) incorporate young people fully into all aspects of church life and engage them in ministry and leadership in the faith community; and (5) create partnerships among families, schools, churches, and community organizations in a common effort to promote positive youth development (*RTV*, 20).

for comprehensive youth and young adult ministry are an important dimension for Christian ministry to youth and young adults, and provide a framework for engaging young people.

Another generic phrase that is used is "Christian discipleship," and it is meant to encompass several outcomes. Regarding Christian discipleship, several points emerge for youth and young adult ministry. Throughout the centuries, discipleship has been continuously affirmed and held in high esteem as being the predominant paradigm for devout and dedicated Christians. The phrase is biblically relevant and is repeated over 250 times in the Bible. The Greek term *mathetes*, meaning "disciple" or "pupil," is used 260 times in the New Testament.[4] Predominately, the term "discipleship" is found in all four Gospels and in Acts of the Apostles.[5] The disciple is the one who "follows" Jesus and becomes his "apprentice" or "understudy." Today, within Christian circles, the word being used instead of apprenticeship is *mentoring*.

In a youth and young adult ministry sense, Christian discipleship is treated as the "learner" and "teacher" model. In adolescent ministry specifically, the learner is the youth and is treated as the disciple; the one who follows the instruction of others who are more knowledgeable and experienced in the faith. They are considered to be the teacher(s)—usually the youth minister and adult youth leaders.[6] In young adult ministry, discipleship is more likened to peer-ministry, but there still may be a power dynamic at play between the young adult minister and the young adult.

In a Christological sense, Christian discipleship is identification with the Paschal Mystery—the life, ministry, suffering, dying, and rising of Jesus the Christ—and the issues of imitating Christ that are initiated in the waters of baptism, sealed with oil at confirmation, and nourished at the Eucharistic table.[7]

It is natural that youth and young adult ministers and religious educators desire young people to understand and embrace discipleship. Catholic young people are exposed to discipleship in various ways: participating in Sunday worship, faith formation, informal conversations with ministry leaders, religious education classes, Bible studies, retreats, and service projects. Perhaps the best way that Catholic youth and young adults are exposed to discipleship is through Christian living in their homes.

---

4. Cahalan, *Introducing the Practice of Ministry*, 3.
5. Segovia, "Introduction: Call and Discipleship," 2.
6. Webber, Singleton, Joyce, and Dorissa, "Models of Youth Ministry in Action," 209.
7. Camp, *Mere Discipleship*, 119, 137, 165.

The Christian Discipleship Model

One Australian study noted that Christian discipleship is an essential part of all youth and young adult ministry activities and programs.[8] Exposing young people to Christian discipleship varies from ministry to ministry and it can be accomplished in myriad ways: Bible studies, prayer meetings, retreats, worship, athletic activities, and social endeavors.

Lex vivendi (law of Christian living) is in actuality the essence of Christian discipleship. Living the Christian faith is experiencing discipleship and part of God's vision.[9] Inevitably, the church wants young people not only to know about God and Jesus intellectually and theoretically, but also desires that Catholic teens know God intuitively and experientially.

Christian discipleship is important to youth and young adult ministry because it allows young people to experience God in a tangible and profound sense. The US Catholic Bishops' document for youth ministry, which is also applicable to young adult ministry, maintains that Christian discipleship is a major goal of youth ministry. The document iterates the significance of discipleship for comprehensive youth ministry is "to empower young people to live as disciples of Jesus Christ in our world today."[10] The challenge of ministering to adolescents and young adults is empowering them toward *lex vivendi*. The bishops further note, "All ministries with adolescents must be directed toward presenting young people with the Good News of Jesus Christ and inviting and challenging them to become his disciple."[11] Therefore, discipleship, *lex vivendi*, and catechesis maintain a symbiotic association.

In the US Conference of Catholic Bishops ecclesial document *Sons and Daughters* there is nothing specific about cultivating Christian discipleship in young adults, but it is implied. The document identifies four major goals that young adult ministers may want to integrate into their activities and programs with emerging adults and young adults.

- Goal One: Connecting young adults with Jesus Christ.
- Goal Two: Connecting young adults with the church.
- Goal Three: Connecting young adults with the mission of the church in the world.
- Goal Four: Connecting young adults with a peer community.[12]

8. Ibid., 209.
9. Canales, "Models for Adolescent Ministry," 220.
10. *RTV*, 9.
11. Ibid., 10.
12. *Sons and Daughters*, 27, 34, 37, 40.

These goals are not exhaustive, but they do provide a basic vision and framework for young adult ministers to follow and utilize for specific ministry objectives and strategies.

Christian discipleship is really at the heart of all ministries! The real task, however, is integrating Christian discipleship into youth and young adult activities, adolescent and adult catechesis, evangelization initiatives, and the congregations' mission. The *Catechism of the Catholic Church* states, "At the heart of catechesis we find, in essence, a person, the Person of Jesus of Nazareth, the only Son from the Father. . . . To catechize is to reveal in the Person of Christ, the whole of God's eternal design reaching fulfillment in that Person."[13] Christian catechesis is *sine qua non* (absolutely indispensable) for Christian discipleship. Both are interdependent—discipleship echoes the Christian faith (catechesis) through the process of teaching (pedagogy) and experiential living (*lex vivendi*).

Developing a Theology of Christian Discipleship

A theology of Christian discipleship for youth and young adult ministry illuminates adolescent pedagogy and praxis. There are five areas that are salubrious of exploration: (1) heeding God's call, (2) having a deep abiding commitment for God, (3) experiencing God, (4) changing one's horizon, and (5) living the call of holiness.

Heeding God's Call

First and foremost, the call from God is the invitation that every baptized Christian receives to live a life of discipleship.[14] This invitation from God to serve God and to help usher in the kinship of God.[15] Adolescents and adults alike are encouraged to heed God's call upon their lives. It is the responsibility of parents and pastors to help young people discern and heed that call. The call is one that can easily be avoided by saying, "No, not me, God" or "I am not a religious person." Whatever the excuse young people make, the simple truth is that baptism is the entrance into the Christian community

---

13. Interdicasterial Commission, *Catechism of the Catholic Church*, no. 426. This document will be referred to henceforth as *CCC*.

14. Cahalan, *Introducing the Practice of Ministry*, 1.

15. Canales, "Christian Discipleship: How Do Christians Accept Discipleship," A9.

The Christian Discipleship Model

and the *initial* calling to serve neighbor as a disciple.[16] Baptism calls youth and young adults to live a life of discipleship. "Jesus calls . . . Christians in whatever state or age to the fullness of Christian life."[17] God calls us all and it is up to us—young or old—to heed God's call upon our life. The famous Scripture that emphasizes God's call on our lives is, "For all are called, but few are chosen" (Matt 22:14). It reflects a choice to the invitation given by God to "come follow me" (Matt 4:19), because many might hear God calling but few decide to consciously, actively, and willingly heed God's call.

The *ways* Christians individually, and collectively in community, respond to that call from God and community is an entirely different matter. It is paramount that youth and young adult ministers help young people discern God's call upon their lives.

Having a Deep Abiding Commitment for God

Second, God requires a certain standard of commitment that perhaps differs from the secular world. The deep and abiding commitment of the Christian disciple is one that turns the *status quo* upside down and may appear radical at times.[18] It is a commitment to God which puts people first, despite religious affiliation, ethnicity, or the color of skin. Commitment to God is seeing Jesus in the other person, it is "walking" in their shoes, and the call to "love your enemy as your neighbor" (Lev 19:18; Mark 5:44).[19]

Young people, just as older people, are to be emboldened to commit themselves to God in a deep abiding way through the process of discipleship. By participating in God's plan—living a life of faith—we demonstrate our abiding commitment to God. Youth and young adult ministers, along with adult catechists, can support this commitment to God by helping young people view themselves positively and in their fuller potential, twenty, thirty, forty years from now.

This deep abiding commitment for God usually implies a cost. A cost; what does that mean? The term *cost* conjures up the old adage, "What's in for me?" or "What's it going to cost me?" The term "cost" within the parameters of Christian discipleship means that in order to live discipleship

---

16. Cahalan, *Introducing the Practice of Ministry*, 2.

17. USCCB, *Co-Workers in the Vineyard of the Lord*, 7. This document will be referred to henceforth as *Co-Workers*.

18. Camp, *Mere Discipleship*, 23–24.

19. Canales, "Christian Discipleship: Discipleship Requires 'Attachment,'" D1.

authentically, there must be a complete detachment from old ties and a total attachment to Jesus the Christ. A complete submission to the will and purpose of God is usually a scary proposition for the average young person. Spanish theologian Fernando F. Segovia argues,

> This new allegiance involves two interrelated and interacting dimensions: on the one hand, discipleship means being molded by a tradition, being empowered by an experience, and being a participant in a community; at the same time, each of these essential components involves two others: a way to walk and a mission to fulfill.[20]

Discipleship clearly involves a cost, one that cannot be ignored for those who earnestly desire to pattern and condition their lives on the true dimensions of discipleship. The archetype of discipleship in the Christian tradition is one that is marked by an *inner* and *outer* change in one's character and disposition. As a direct result of following God in Christ, the interior disposition of a young person is altered, this reflects an exterior transformation.[21]

For the famous German Lutheran pastor and martyr, Dietrich Bonhoeffer (1906–45), the obedience shown to God is both the grace and the cost of being a disciple of Christ.[22] Youth and young adult ministers help young people to see the cost of following God by sharing in obedience of God during times of personal slackness and spiritual drought.

Experiencing God

Third, experiencing God is different for each person, but it is a cornerstone of discipleship. It is in the experiencing of God's self-communication to each believer that engages and empowers a person into a deeper and more meaningful relationship with God.[23] God is available to everyone; however, it is the responsibility of the Christian believer to discover and experience the absolute mystery (God), the Transcendent One, a mystery that pervades daily life.

---

20. Segovia, "Introduction: Call and Discipleship," 8.
21. Canales, "Rebirth of Being *'Born-Again*,'" 105.
22. Bonhoeffer, *Cost of Discipleship*, 57–58.
23. Canales, "Rebirth of Being *'Born-Again*,'" 105.

The Christian Discipleship Model

The great German Jesuit priest Karl Rahner (1904–84) maintains that it is inescapable and quite impossible for a person *not* to have at least a rudimentary experience of God, "whether consciously or unconsciously, whether suppressed or accepted, whether rightly or wrongly interpreted, or whatever the way in which it is present."[24] Creating meaningful experiences of God for young people is one of the quintessential elements of youth and young adult ministry.

Parents and youth and young adult ministers working collaboratively can strengthen and shape experiences of God for young people by helping them to become increasingly *attuned* to the presence of God in their lives. As Rahner poignantly states, "In everyday life this transcendental experience of God in the Holy Spirit remains anonymous, implicit, un-thematic, like the widely and diffusely spread light of a sun that we do not directly see, while we turn only to the individual objects visible in this light in our sense-experience."[25]

Therefore, a young person's experience of God—especially in church or during ministry—cannot be aloof or so completely distant that it becomes ignored or misinterpreted. God can be experienced because God is ubiquitous, and at times clandestine, but never uninvolved.[26]

Changing One's Horizon

Fourth, the experience of God can lead young people to change their horizon and make a paradigm shift in their own lives.

> Christian disciples must move beyond their world-view, sphere of influence, or comfort zone. As their horizon expands so does their world-view, and a change of horizon can occur depending on different interests, converging points of view, protection of certain customs and traditions, and by the limits that people place upon themselves.[27]

Discipleship is a process that expands and contracts, as does a person's field of vision and worldview. According to the Canadian Jesuit Bernard J. F. Lonergan (1904–84), a change in one's theological horizon

---

24. Rahner, "Experience of the Holy Spirit," 195.
25. Ibid., 199.
26. Canales, "Models for Adolescent Ministry," 220.
27. Canales, "Rebirth of Being 'Born-Again,'" 105–6.

> denotes the bounding circle, the line at which earth and sky appear to meet. This line is the limit of one's field of vision. As one moves about, it recedes in front and closes in behind so that, for different standpoints, there are different horizons. Moreover, for each different standpoint and horizon, there are different divisions of the totality of visible objects. Beyond the horizon lie the objects that, at least for the moment, cannot be seen. Within the horizon lie the objects that can now be seen.[28]

Therefore, a change in a young person's religious and spiritual horizon can occur depending on different interests, converging points of view, protection, and the loosening of certain customs and traditions, and by the limits that people place upon themselves. Empowering youth and young adults to change their theological horizons is integral to youth and young adult ministry because it is a time in their life when young people are becoming more open-minded and exposed to new ideas. Youth and young adult ministers can empower a change in theological horizon by providing platforms for youth and young adults to shift their outlook on life, thinking, behaving, and spiritualizing. This change in horizon leads a young person to deeper holiness.

Living the Call of Holiness

A final responsibility of Christian discipleship is living the universal call to holiness. All the way through the Acts of the Apostles, the term *disciple* is referenced as synonymous with and tantamount to the word *believer* (Acts 6:1–2, 7; 11:26; 14:20; 15:10). Faith in Jesus as the Christ is indispensable and undeniable in the life of a Christian disciple. Holiness is living out the call of discipleship with conviction and commitment in an extraordinary way that builds Christian character and leads to being transformed into "a chosen race, a royal priesthood, a holy nation, and a redeemed people" (1 Pet 2:4–5, 9) for the glory of God.

Pope John Paul II notes that the universal call to holiness *is* a Christian mandate, not only to live a virtuous life for God, but a passion-filled life for God, one that leads the believer to experience the risen Christ.[29] It is imperative that Christian discipleship is an *experience* in the risen Christ, not an *experiment* in Christianity.[30]

28. Lonergan, *Method in Theology*, 235–36.
29. John Paul II, *Church in America*, n. 30.
30. Canales, "Rebirth of Being 'Born-Again,'" 106.

The Christian Discipleship Model

Catholic religious education expert Michael Carotta articulates developmental theories for catechizing young people for Christian discipleship through three dimensions:

> (1) the way one relates to God through prayer, worship, and religious practices (vertical); (2) the way one relates to God through moral interactions with others (horizontal); and (3) the way one experiences God's ability to help deal with internal pain, stress, loneliness, fear, sadness, anger, and other emotions (internal).[31]

Part of the young person's journey toward Christian discipleship is one that strengthens, shapes, and challenges the adolescent and young adult in the above three dimensions. These dimensions—vertical, horizontal, internal—will aid youth and young adult ministers and religious educators in developing a well-balanced discipleship program that empowers adolescents and adults to exercise Christian faith, ethical living, and emotional management.[32] Understanding the journey and the complexity of discipleship will allow parents and pastors the ability to discern the faith life and spirituality of their youth and young adult population.

Finally, it may be worth noting that Christian disciples are not born, they are made, through time, dedication, and spiritual energy. Therefore, disciples of Jesus need help to become aware of, comprehend, and acknowledge their own transcendent experiences and feel comfortable claiming these encounters.

These five criteria— heeding God's call, having a deep abiding commitment to God, an experience of God, a change of horizon, and the call to holiness—are necessary and indispensable to Christian discipleship. These five areas of Christian are not merely about *accepting* Jesus, or *believing* in Jesus, or *worshipping* Jesus. They are all about *following* Jesus the Christ (*mission Dei*), and having "boots on the ground" or *walking the talk!* Christian discipleship is a practical and lived theology.

The Integration of Eight Theological Categories

All that Christian discipleship entails is at the core of the Gospel. Christianity is fundamentally a *lived human endeavor* and discipleship is essentially a *lived reality*, in which there is really no comparable substitute.[33]

---

31. Michael Carotta, "Revisiting Adolescent Catechesis," 43.
32. Ibid., 44.
33. Jones, "It's a Matter of Time," 215.

Christian discipleship has many components. However, only eight categories will be addressed here: (1) community, (2) conversion, (3) faith, (4) leadership, (5) morality, (6) prayer, (7) service, and (8) spirituality.[34] These eight categories—listed alphabetically and not by importance—are by no means exhaustive.[35] Taken together they represent a practical theology and model of praxis for Christian discipleship in relation to comprehensive youth and young adult ministry.

Community

Youth and young adults are the present and future of each community. The old adage, "young people are to be seen, but not heard," is *not* applicable to youth and young adult ministry. It is imperative that youth and young adult ministry facilitate and strengthen the relationship between young people in the parish and the adults in the community.[36] Young people contribute to the community by simply being themselves! Building, fostering, and maintaining a strong community with young people has several advantages.

Community creates an atmosphere characterized by gospel values that nurture meaningful relationships among young people, values that enhance the quality of adolescent and adult life.[37] Creating a community on biblical values and gospel principles (*koinonia* in the Greek) is important for youth and young adults to experience God. "For an increasing number of [young people] today, the church is not just *another* place to receive biblical guidance and instruction; it is the *only* place to receive biblical guidance and instruction."[38] Therefore, the Christian community can be an important dynamic in a young person's faith life.

Community is important because it helps develop youth and young adults by enhancing relationship-making and friendship-maintaining

---

34. Canales, "Integrating Christian Discipleship," 34. In the article I give a fuller description of each category and its integration into Catholic undergraduate education; however, the methodology is applicable to youth ministry, emerging adult ministry, and young adult ministry.

35. Camp, in *Mere Discipleship*, offers five categories of discipleship: worship, baptism, prayer, communion, and evangelization; while Cahalan, in *Introducing the Practice of Ministry*, provides six categories of discipleship: teaching, preaching, care, prayer and worship, social mercy and justice, and leadership and administration.

36. Canales, "Models for Adolescent Ministry," 222.

37. *RTV*, 35.

38. Cosby, "Reformed View of Youth Ministry," 50.

skills of youth and young adults, which are grounded in Christian values. "Forming faith communities of peers provides opportunities for young [people] to find among their peers the necessary support and encouragement as they journey through life and fulfill their mission to the world."[39] Community also fosters human growth and development.

Community also has the real potential to enrich relationships and foster family-friendships within the *domus ecclesia*, Latin for "domestic church," or the family unit itself through various programs, activities, and faith initiatives supported by the youth and young adult ministries. It is easy to discern that community plays an integral role in adolescent, emerging adult, and young adult life, culture, and spirituality, and thus, discipleship.

Conversion

Conversion is particularly important with regard to adolescents and emerging adults because their lives are in constant flux between the demands of teenage life, emerging adulthood, and young adulthood. Conversion is usually referred to as a journey—a journey with God, with self, and with community. Conversion is a journey of self-discovery and self-actualization. Conversion entails an assent for discovering truths about God and about human life. Conversion is a process that is absolutely necessary for all who accept the Gospel and live as Christian disciples.

> This is crucial: we must be converted—and we must continue to be converted! We must let the Holy Spirit change our lives! And we must be open to the transforming power of the Holy Spirit who will continue to convert us as we follow Christ. If our faith is alive, it will be aroused again and again as we mature as disciples.[40]

Youth and young adult ministers would be wise to have concrete steps in place to empower young people to identify with the conversion process: (1) turning to or seeking God, (2) desiring to be with God, (3) struggling with God, sin, and identity, (4) surrendering to God, and (5) living a life for God.[41] Moreover, youth and young adult ministers may notice that young people may need help in articulating conversion in their own lives,

---

39. *Sons and Daughters*, 40.

40. USCCB and the Committee on Evangelization, *Go and Make Disciples*, n. 14. This document will be referred to henceforth as *Go and Make Disciples*.

41. Canales, "Rebirth of Being 'Born-Again,'" 103.

but there are ample stories of conversion within the Christian tradition to demonstrate to young people the necessity for the conversion process in fostering Christian discipleship.

Lonergan maintains that there are fundamentally three levels or types of conversion that a person can experience: (1) intellectual conversion; (2) moral conversion; and (3) religious conversion. *Intellectual conversion* occurs when the human person experiences liberation from stubborn, false, misguided, and deceptive myths about reality, objectivity, and knowledge.[42] *Moral conversion* is an affective change that shapes human decision-making through symbols, images, and rituals that eradicate hatred, jealousy, prejudice, and racism through new images and authentic moral decision-making.[43] *Religious conversion* is the denial of worldly pleasures, pursuits, and realities that hinder the relationship from turning totally toward the transcendent God.[44] Lonergan's theory of conversion is important for youth and young adult ministers to understand because developmentally, adolescents and emerging adults will wax and wane in their understanding of beliefs and their ethical behavior might become less conventional as well.

Faith

Teaching about faith or catechizing the faith to young people is only one aspect of youth and young adult ministry. Perhaps a more important aspect of youth and young adult ministry is fostering faith within the lives of young people. Youth and young adult ministers are called to "foster the total personal and spiritual growth of each young person."[45]

Christian youth and young adult ministry are *always* concerned with nurturing and strengthening faith within a young person, which aims to achieve Christian identity and discipleship. Adolescent and young adult catechesis would be wise to strive toward empowering young people to develop personal faith in Jesus Christ, which in turn will be directly applicable to their Christian faith and daily experiences. To help young people "confess faith in Jesus Christ is to believe that we live within the context

---

42. Lonergan, *Method in Theology*, 238.
43. Ibid., 240.
44. Ibid., 242–43.
45. *RTV*, 15.

The Christian Discipleship Model

of a divine decision."[46] A decision that leads young people to partner with Christ.

Protestant theologian Paul Tillich refers to this partnership of faith in Christ as "the state of being ultimately concerned."[47] Faith is a way that most people make sense of their lives and existence; lest we forget that faith is a gift from God (Rom 5:1; 1 Cor 12:9; and Gal 5:5). Learning the faith is a living reality that engages and inspires young people toward God. Faith is the foundation that the fountain of Christian life flows; it is the building block for furthering adolescent and young adult growth, gifts, and spirituality.[48]

Leadership

Youth and young adult ministry are ripe for training young people to become Christian leaders. Christian adolescents, emerging adults, and young adults are usually yearning for ways in which they might lead in their faith communities.[49]

Leadership is a rather nebulous term because it can have a multitude of meanings. A contemporary understanding of leadership is defined as "a process whereby an individual influences a group of individuals to achieve a common goal."[50] Therefore, understanding leadership involves two crucial components—process and influence—and both help to move a group or individuals toward a common purpose and goal.

Typically, leadership skills within Christian ministry need to be developed and nurtured in a person. As a ministry, leadership involves development and "*calls forth, affirms,* and *empowers* the diverse gifts, talents, and abilities of . . . young people in our faith communities."[51] A leading youth and young adult ministry strategy in Christian circles is to try and infuse five operational principles of leadership development into ministry practice: (1) rooted in ministerial relationships; (2) integrate faith and prayer; (3) respect, support, and encourage other activities; (4) build meaningful roles; and (5) build upon existing strengths and assets.[52]

---

46. Johnson, *Theology as Discipleship*, 61.
47. Tillich, *Dynamics of Faith*, 1.
48. Canales, "Integrating Christian Discipleship," 37.
49. Canales, "Models of Christian Leadership," 27.
50. Northouse, *Leadership*, 3.
51. *RTV*, 40.
52. Moser, "Youth Ministry," 136–38.

There are four predominate prototypes of leadership within Christianity—servant-leadership, moral leadership, spiritual leadership, and transformational leadership—and all four of these approaches can be traced back to Jesus of Nazareth's public ministry.[53]

Youth and young adult ministers would be prudent to seek out these leadership archetypes, see which one resonates best with their spirituality, and then try to promote them within their respective ministries. The usual way that youth and young adult ministers train teenagers and young adults in leadership is by learning and performing roles within the congregation and community. This type of experiential leadership development has merit and it can be accomplished in various settings: peer-leaders for faith-sharing talks, small group facilitators to be used on retreats and Bible studies, helping with religious education classes, and liturgical ministries for specialized youth and young adult–led liturgies.

The goal with leadership is to motivate and empower youth and young adults to create pastoral environments for young people to thrive as authentic Christian leaders.[54]

Morality

The Christian moral life is about grounding one's self in God. What constitutes Christian morality? From a Christian perspective, morality cannot be separated from God, it cannot be freestanding. Morality must be expressed in the Christian's total view of life, as well as being part of God's purpose and plan for an individual's life. Moral instruction is highly encouraged in a comprehensive youth and young adult ministry. Morality is the art of Christian living, which, of course, thoroughly entails discipleship. Moral behavior becomes a determining device for living a characteristically Christian life.[55]

Teaching moral principles such as conscience, character, making good choices, and living a virtuous life is ethically advantageous for Catholic young people.[56] Cultivating adolescent and young adult discipleship is to aid in the moral development of young people based on Christian principles, sacred Scripture, and holy tradition.

---

53. Canales, "Models of Christian Leadership," 29–41.
54. Ibid., 29–42.
55. Ibid., 38.
56. *RTV*, 31.

The Christian Discipleship Model

The knack of living Christian discipleship, coupled with morality, and navigating through a morally complex world looms large with youth, emerging adults, and young adults. There is a theological axiom to this effect: *Deus impossibilia non iubet* (Latin for "God does not command the impossible"). The adage is applicable in describing moral growth and development.

The medieval Dominican theologian Thomas Aquinas (1224–74) reminds us that all artists love that which they create: parents love their children, poets love their poems, craftsmen love their handiwork. Therefore, God could not hate a single thing since God is the artist of everything.[57] Consequently, one aim of the discipleship is to become an artist of moral living.

Prayer

Prayer is *language of the heart*. Prayer is absolutely essential in cultivating Christian discipleship in all people: adolescents and adults alike.[58] Youth and young adult ministers may want to adapt a strong prayer regiment within their ministries, one that introduces young people to a large spectrum of prayer forms and styles that enhance an encounter with God. Both liturgical (public) and non-liturgical (personal) prayer forms are to be explored and fostered in Christian youth and young adult ministry. Most youth and young adult ministries provide plenty of opportunities for young people to learn and experience different forms of personal and group prayer.[59] Exposing young people to all types of prayer forms is critical to faith and spiritual development.

It is important to encourage young people to pray. Youth and young adult ministers would be wise to have plenty of opportunities for prayer built into their ministry programs and activities. "Providing an array of opportunities for [young people] to pray will allow them to encounter a 'smorgasbord' of meaningful spiritual activities."[60] Guiding young people in their prayer-life is an important dynamic of discipleship and will enhance other areas of the Christian life.

---

57. Aquinas, *Summa Theologica*, vol. 1, 328–30, q. 66, a. 1.
58. Canales, "Noble Quest," 70.
59. *Sons and Daughters*, 28.
60. Canales, "Noble Quest," 71.

Worship is an important element of prayer. In fact, worship is the highest expression of prayer. Catholics and Protestants have a long tradition of celebrating Sunday worship, which constitutes several areas of prayer: (1) blessings and adoration, (2) petition, (3) intercession, (4) thanksgiving, and (5) praise.[61] The variety of prayer strengthens youth and young adult faith-life, helps to cultivate spirituality, and integrates Sunday worship experiences with Christian identity.[62] There are many forms of prayer for young people to encounter God; the task is to help youth and young adults with the disciple and desire to pray.

Today's youth and young adult culture represents a distinctive expression that needs to be understood and appreciated in order for young people to feel incorporated into the Christian community. Prayer is an important dynamic of adolescent discipleship; it fosters faith and spiritual wholeness.[63] Teenagers and young adults, just like adults, approach God differently and pray according to their personality, interior disposition, culture, and tradition, and this represents a wide spectrum of styles.

Service

Service is a major component of Christian discipleship. The majority of adolescents, emerging adults, and young adults enjoy participating in outreach activities and service projects that empower others to transform their lives.[64] It is good for young people to be involved in service activities and outreach initiatives. In the Christian tradition, service comes from the Greek word *diakonoia*, which means "to minister" or "to serve." Performing acts of random kindness or serving other people (Christian or not) has always been constitutive of the church's mission. Christian service occurs at three distinct levels: (1) serving God and community, (2) serving friends and family, and (3) serving neighbors and strangers.[65]

It is reported that young people who participate in religious activities sponsored by church ministries tend to be involved in a variety of social

---

61. *CCC*, no. 2626–42.
62. Canales, "Strengthening Eucharistic Spirituality," 9–10.
63. White, *Practicing Discernment with Youth*, 141.
64. Canales, "Transforming Teenagers," 73.
65. Ibid., "Integrating Christian Discipleship," 43.

THE CHRISTIAN DISCIPLESHIP MODEL

service projects.[66] Service and outreach are part of social justice and are integral to ministry with young people.

The US Bishops state, "Service *nurtures* in young people a social consciousness and a commitment to a life of justice and service rooted in their faith in Jesus Christ, in the Scriptures, and in the Catholic social teaching."[67] The affirmation that youth and young adults glean from serving others through outreach initiatives will help them to recognize that they are working for justice and living as Christian disciples. The benefits of service for young people are that it provides social justice learning opportunities,[68] theological reflection on the ministry experience,[69] and praxis-based education.[70] Service has a simple yet profound message for young people to respond to, and service is also social; therefore, service rewards both the servicer and service.

---

66. Smith, *Soul Searching*, 115.

67. *RTV*, 38.

68. The term *social justice learning* refers to the attempt to bridge the gap from a purely cerebral education to one that encourages students to learn through serving others with social justice in mind. In comprehensive Catholic youth ministry, the object of social justice learning is to empower students to move beyond merely engaging in acts of service and charity and move into the realm of social justice, which is rooted in human dignity, empathy, and compassion (Canales, "Integrating Christian Discipleship," 48). Social justice learning refers to the experiential learner that is specific to enhancing adolescent's knowledge about social justice issues and is committed to expanding their comprehension of the Catholic Church's social justice teachings and principles. Social justice learning is *not* tantamount to service learning, since not all service learning is focused on social justice issues and concerns or the root systemic problem of unjust systems (Canales, "Transforming Teenagers," 91).

69. Theological reflection is a contemporary method of discernment and discussion of a ministry experience or pastoral encounter. It is a pastoral tool used by ministry educators and ministers in the field to evaluate, debrief, critique, and inform pastoral action. Theological reflection is usually influenced by a person's religious tradition, cultural background, family of origin, and the personal experience or ministry encounter that is being reflected upon.

70. Praxis-based education has tangible and lasting impact upon young people. Praxis-based education has four ways that help to shape Christian identity, spirituality, and faith in young people: (1) academic and pastoral reflection rooted in reality, (2) integrated community learning and group process, (3) recollection and pedagogical accompaniment, and (4) formation of Christocentric imagination. See Canales, "Transforming Teenagers," 81, 83–85.

Spirituality

Young people *are* spiritual![71] Adolescents and young adults are on the path of learning and becoming spiritual people despite their age.[72] Since baptized young people are Christians, they are already infused with the power and presence of the Holy Spirit. It is an aim of Christian youth and young adult ministry to facilitate a deeper sense of awe and spirituality within young people. Enhancing spirituality is extremely important to Christian discipleship and spiritual formation.

Ecclesial documents note the significance of spirituality for young people. "To foster the total person and spiritual growth of each young person,"[73] is a major goal for ministry with young people, and "to help young adults develop their spiritual life rooted in a personal relationship with Jesus Christ as their Redeemer and Savior" is part of a young person's overall spiritual formation.[74] However, spirituality does not simply happen, like turning the water faucet on and off. Spirituality involves a great deal of time, dedication, discipline, energy, and patience. Spirituality, rightly understood, is rooted in the total person: mind, body, and spirit.

Adolescent and young adult spirituality embraces young people in their present issues and needs, as well as leading them to the source of life, which is found in Jesus Christ.[75]

Christian juvenile, emerging adult, and young adult spirituality ought to allow for free expression of personal abilities, gender, sexual orientation, limitations, and personalities, because a person's spirituality is a reflection of one's values and attitudes within a social and historical context.[76] A young person's individual spirituality is uniquely and intimately connected with their sexuality and identity.

Christian discipleship and the spiritual life are to make us not simply better people—ethically upright and morally aware—but to make us divine, to conform us to a participation in the life of the Trinity in and through Jesus the Christ.[77] The path to becoming spiritual means taking risks and

---

71. Tacey, *Spirituality Revolution*, 30.
72. Meehan, "Belonging, Being, and Becoming," 39.
73. *RTV*, 15.
74. *Sons and Daughters*, 27.
75. Canales, "Reality Check," 11.
76. Cervantes, *Hispanic Young People*, 96.
77. Barron, *Strangest Way*, 29.

THE CHRISTIAN DISCIPLESHIP MODEL

demands courage because becoming spiritual is a lengthy process.[78] Youth and young adult ministers would be demonstrating their spiritual savviness if they adopted activities and appropriated initiatives that empowered spirituality among young people. The possibilities for enhancing a young person's spirituality are endless.

Summary of the Eight Theological Categories

Christian discipleship is a process and for most people an arduous process filled with highs and lows. Christian youth and young adults are like adults, they experience peaks and valleys in their journey with God. This process and journey of Christian discipleship is a noble quest.[79] These eight integrated theological categories within Christian discipleship—community, conversion, faith, leadership, morality, prayer, service, and spirituality—will help youth and young adult ministers better comprehend the dynamics of Christian living.[80] Below, Figure 6 illustrates the movement and interconnectedness between God's call on people's lives, the theology of discipleship that accompanies a person's call, and the eight theological components or categories that Christian disciples manifest throughout their lives.

FIGURE 6

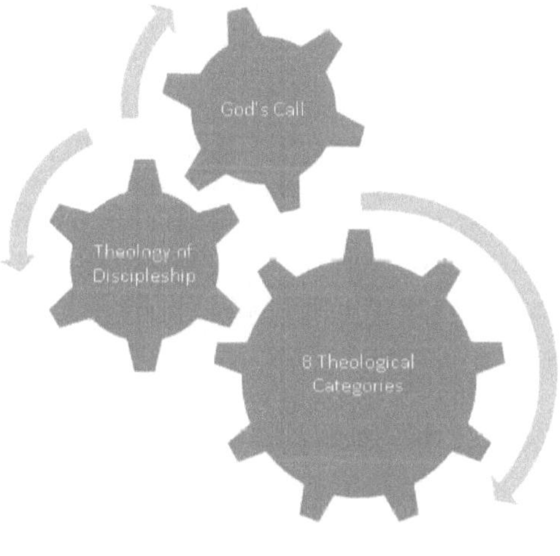

78. Daloz-Parks, *Big Questions, Worthy Dreams*, 42–43.
79. Canales, "Noble Quest," 63.
80. Canales, "Models for Adolescent Ministry," 221.

This is the great challenge of Christian discipleship: hear the word, follow Christ, and participate in the church's mission.[81] Pastoral ministers would be wise to recognize that all ministries with adolescents, emerging adults, and young adults must be directed toward presenting young people with the liberation of Jesus Christ, inviting them to become his disciples, and challenging them to be imitators of his life. Living authentic discipleship is difficult and demanding; nevertheless, the Gospel invites young people to an authentic adventure into living a life of discipleship. The real challenge is to *integrate* Christian discipleship with contemporary pedagogy that will penetrate and impact young people in their schools, churches, and society.[82]

Pedagogical and Pastoral Methodologies for Implementation

The method used in this section, as in the other chapters, is prescriptive because it delivers real and solid examples to be implemented.

A primary goal of youth and young adult ministry is "to *empower* young people to live as *disciples* of Jesus Christ in our world today."[83] This goal has always been part of Christianity's 2,000-plus year tradition. It is good that Christian churches actually desire to foster discipleship in young people. Good ministry with young people always involves and is concerned with biblical values, catechesis, evangelization, family dynamics, pastoral care, relationships, sexuality, and stewardship, which are also the elements of Christian discipleship.

Before implementation of the Christian discipleship model, it may be advisable for the youth and/or young adult minister to do some preliminary reading and studying on the subject, which will enhance pedagogical and pastoral success. Youth and young adult ministers are encouraged to purchase and read books on Christian discipleship.

Some good books include: *The Strangest Way: Walking the Christian Path* by Robert Barron; *The Cost of Discipleship* by Dietrich Bonhoeffer; *Mere Discipleship: Radical Christianity in a Rebellious World* by Lee C. Camp; and *Francis of Assisi: Performing the Gospel Life* by Lawrence S. Cunningham. These books are insightful and inspirational and will impact and influence youth and young adult ministers on Christian discipleship.

81. Johnson, *Theology as Discipleship*, 61, 73, 85.
82. Canales, "Models for Adolescent Ministry," 221.
83. *RTV*, 9.

The Christian Discipleship Model

Moreover, it may be advantageous for youth and young adult ministers to take a class on Christology or Soteriology, or perhaps read books on Christology to situate Jesus' earthly ministry and its impact for discipleship today.

It may also be prudent for youth and young adult ministers to become familiar with the lives of extraordinary holy people or saints, especially the young saints that are positive role models for young people such as Joan of Arc (1412–31), Aloysius Gonzaga (1568–91), John Bosco (1815–88), Dominic Savio (1842–57), Maria Goretti (1890–1902), Pier Giorgio Fassati (1901–25), and Mary Faustina Kowalska (1905–38). Knowing about the lives of these holy young people will allow today's youth and young adults to fully comprehend the history of discipleship and the ways that holy people lived their own discipleship.

In reality, all youth and young adult ministry initiatives generate an atmosphere for Christian discipleship. Youth and young adult ministers would be judicious to assist young people to become sagacious disciples through knowledge of the Christian faith, the practice of morality, participating in social justice learning and service projects, celebrating various types of prayer and worship and Sunday Eucharist, and developing Christian spirituality and identity. Such honorable practices are encouraged since youth and young adult ministry is primarily concerned with Christian discipleship.

The Six Strategies

This section provides six pedagogical and pastoral implementation strategies to support the advancement of the Christian discipleship model within Christian youth and young adult ministry. The strategies presented are suggestions to contribute in fostering and sustaining youth and young adult Christian disciples, but they are by no means exhaustive.

Strategy 1

One pastoral approach might be loosely following an academic calendar, in which these eight areas could be broken down into four parts, discussing one-quarter (25 percent) of each area once a month. Each month would represent a specific area within Christian discipleship. For example: September introduces students to Jesus of Nazareth; October addresses the conversion process; November studies the dynamics of faith; December investigates morality and ethical behavior; January examines the many facets of prayer; February explores the reality of community; March practices various types of Christian spirituality, April discovers service and social justice through hands-on experience; and May discusses styles of Christian leadership.

Another pastoral overture using the same strategy of implementation could be to discuss the eight themes of discipleship in any particular order; therefore, March might be the month to spend discussing morality issues with teenagers. For example, each week within the month of March, a different topic is explored:

- Week one: an overview on Christian morality
- Week two: the process of conscience and decision-making
- Week three: morality and human sexuality
- Week four: human dignity and human rights

There are numerous possibilities for implementation and discussion. Limiting each area to three or four weeks allows for the youth and young adult minister to select different topics in the forthcoming years, ensuring that young people do not hear the same presentation each year.

Strategy 2

A second pedagogical method is to empower young people to live the Gospels and learn experiential ways to become advocates of change through action-reflection and social justice learning.[84] Youth and young adult ministers may want to host catechetical workshops for adolescents, young adults, and the ministry's adult volunteers to further enhance their understanding of discipleship. One suggestion is to offer a day of reflection focusing on prayer, which is an area of growth in discipleship. The day could provide

---

84. The term *action-reflection* refers to the "critical investigation and assessment of a theological enterprise, coupled with the identification of a pragmatic praxis of ministry. Action in and of itself lacks intellectual inquiry; therefore, action-reflection facilitates student learning through critical introspection and personal reflection on a particular experience. Through action-reflection students move beyond their personal *status quo* and come to a different place, ideally a better place, through serious introspection and self-awareness, which leads to self-discovery and transformation" (Canales, "Integrating Christian Discipleship," 48). The integration of action-reflection within youth ministry has many rewarding benefits, but most especially incorporating theology with a teenager's life experience, and empowering young people to become self-actualizers.

The Christian Discipleship Model

four presentations followed by small faith-sharing groups, and resemble and focus on these topics:

- Presentation 1: Jesus and Prayer: the centrality of Christian prayer
- Presentation 2: Public Prayer: celebrating various types of communal prayer
- Presentation 3: Private Prayer: meditations, journaling and the Rosary
- Presentation 4: Sunday Eucharist: the week's pinnacle worship experience

It may be beneficial if each presentation did *not* focus exclusively on the catechesis, albeit important, but also on "doing" prayer and the pragmatic implications of prayer for discipleship. The aim of the day is not only reflection on prayer, but also teaching and modeling to young people the diverse ways to pray and to approach prayer with new awareness.

Strategy 3

As a third ministry proposition, the youth and young adult minister may want to have a mid-week Bible study. The Bible study theme could be "Discipleship and the Scriptures." Each Bible course could highlight a different biblical book and the study of discipleship. Below are suggestions for coupling discipleship and Scripture. This strategy covers five biblical books and discipleship themes, and realistically lasts several weeks.

- Bible Course 1: Uncertain Faith: The Gospel of Matthew's Portrait of the Disciples
- Bible Course 2: Historical Accounts of Discipleship in the New Testament: Discipleship in Luke and Acts of the Apostles
- Bible Course 3: "Peace I Leave With You—My Peace I Give to You": Discipleship in the Gospel of John
- Bible Course 4: "Be Imitators of God": Discipleship in the Book of Ephesians
- Bible Course 5: Friendship with God: Discipleship in the Book of James[85]

---

85. The five suggested Bible courses come directly from Segovia, *Discipleship in the New Testament*. The recommendations I offer reflect only five of the nine chapters within the book.

The above suggested Bible courses could be as in-depth or as cursory as the youth or young adult minister deems beneficial.

It is highly recommended that a youth or young adult minister who wants to embark on a biblical exploration of Christian discipleship should first read diligently Fernando F. Segovia's book *Discipleship in the New Testament*. The book is a serious investigation of discipleship in the New Testament, but it is quite accessible for a lay person to read and retain valuable information. This strategy will take quite an effort by the youth and young adult ministry staff, but the results will be fantastic!

Strategy 4

A fourth practical procedure could utilize the summer months. Summer is a great time to accomplish faith-formation and pedagogical success in young people. Two areas within youth and young adult discipleship connect well during the summer months: service and leadership. Engaging in service opportunities and developing leadership skills are necessary in creating adolescent, emerging adult, and young adult peer and/or core team leaders within the youth and young adult ministry. There are three summer scenarios that are worth considering.

- Scenario A: Take a group of young people on a one-week, work-camp trip. The trip could be scheduled during the early summer. The work-camp provides young people with a great service opportunity away from their comfortable surroundings and usually takes place in a region of the country that is poor and depressed. The work-camp endeavor usually helps a poor neighborhood rebuild houses through construction work, under the supervision of professional contractors and builders. Young people benefit from such an experiential learning activity, and it is both physically and spiritually edifying. There are work-camp organizations for Protestant and Catholic youth and young adults.[86] Summer work-camps are a great way for privileged, educated, suburban young people to see the way less fortunate peoples' lives.

---

86. As a former youth minister, campus minister, and young adult minister I have had great success with work-camps over the years. The two most popular work-camp organizations in the United States are: Catholic Heart Workcamps (Catholic), P.O. Box 2226, Goldenrod, FL 32733, or call (407)678-0073, or visit www. heartworkcamp.com; and Group Workcamps (Protestant), P.O. Box 485, Loveland, CO 80539, or call (970)669-3636, or visit www.groupworkcamps.com.

The Christian Discipleship Model

- Scenario B: Take a group of young people on a two-week immersion trip, which could be scheduled for mid-summer. The immersion trip, also known as a "mission trip," provides an opportunity for students to experience a third-world country in the Caribbean Islands, Central America, South America, or Africa, to help a poor and remote village with daily labor or to build new construction. Such a trip is usually in conjunction with a mission relief organization.[87] Immersion trips are powerful Christian discipleship tools because they "plop" young people directly into the gritty realities of social poverty and personal despair, which is typically a startling contrast to the way the majority of American, white, middle-class young people live.[88] It is critically important that youth and young adult ministers do not make a mission trip into an adventure in tourism: going shopping, visiting museums, or sipping cocktails.[89] The immersion experience is an opportunity to live and interact with another culture and in a cultural way of being/mode of existence, and a chance to experience a new culture through another culture's worldview.[90] Barring the tourism trap, immersion trips are good, and allow youth and young adults to serve countries and people beyond their borders and limited worldview, while embracing other cultures and ethnicities.

- Scenario C: Take a group of young people on a one-week Christian outdoor wilderness course, which could be scheduled in late summer.[91] The course is constructed around regional outdoor activities such as hiking, canoeing, camping, ropes courses,[92] and rock

---

87. For further information regarding immersion trips contact Jesuit Volunteers International, P.O. Box 3756, Washington, DC 20027, or call (202)687-1132, or visit www.jesuitvolunters.org.

88. Canales, *Noble Quest*, 8.

89. Root and Creasy Dean, *Theological Turn in Youth Ministry*, 185–87.

90. Ibid., 185.

91. I have taken a variety of groups on wilderness trips in my ministry career: middle school youth, high school seniors, college students, adolescent male juvenile criminals, and law students. It is a positive experience for all involved. For Christian wilderness trips in the US, contact Blueridge Backcountry, a wildlife and wilderness subsidiary of Montreat College (Presbyterian, USA) P.O. Box 1267, Montreat, NC 28757, or call (828)669-8012, ext. 3406, or visit www.montreat.edu.

92. Ropes courses are obstacle courses constructed out of rope securely fastened to either telephone poles or large sturdy trees and they usually are about thirty feet in the air.

climbing,[93] which includes traveling to a destination that has real crag formations. Throughout the week, youth and young adults will also learn about the four major models of Christian leadership: servant, moral, spiritual, and transformational.[94] Throughout the week, young people also participate in Bible studies, hear brief presentations, and contribute to discussion groups. The purpose of the course is to foster Christian discipleship through leadership initiatives, which creates individual trust, reliability in others, and develops self-confidence. The ropes and climbing experiences allow a young person to conquer their personal fears: fear of heights, fear of falling, fear of failure, and the fear of embarrassment. The goal is to demonstrate that life is full of opportunities and oppositions, as well as uncomfortable situations, and dealing with life's stressfulness often takes courage and overcoming obstacles.

Throughout each scenario, the youth and young adult minister should debrief and facilitate the experiences shortly after they happen. The facilitation session should not only check whether or not young people enjoyed the experiences (because not all will), but to name and claim the feelings they experienced and grappled with while in the midst of these initiatives.

The various experiences within the week-long wilderness trip, along with its discernment, debriefing, and discussion are known as *praxis-based education*, and they provide young people with a "Christocentric formation that points to the trust that young people must go through as they put their faith in Christ and hope in God."[95] Taken together, these three summer scenarios will create marvelous memories that last a lifetime, as well as form social justice-oriented young people. These three summer trips also develop valuable leadership knowledge and Christian disciples.

Strategy 5

A fifth pedagogical strategy is to have a Christian leadership institute that specifically focuses on developing young people as Christian leaders to serve in their communities. The Christian leadership institute could offer regular courses perhaps once or twice a year. The institute could offer a

---

93. Rock climbing services always have professional rock climbing staff to give mandatory safety lessons to beginner climbers as well as introductory courses through advanced courses for experienced climbers.

94. Canales, "Models of Christian Leadership," 29–41.

95. Canales, *Noble Quest*, 84.

The Christian Discipleship Model

series of presentations on Christian discipleship. The course could be titled "The Christian Discipleship and Leadership Challenge" and provide adolescents with five sessions, each about forty-five minutes in length.[96] Youth and young adult ministers may want to read the work by Marilyn Kielbasa, *The Challenge of Discipleship*, who uses these topics:

- Session 1: The Call to Conversion—"Come Follow Me"
- Session 2: A Christian Disciple is a Person of Faith, Hope, and Love
- Session 3: A Christian Disciple is a Person of Commitment and Action
- Session 4: Christian Discipleship and Christian Leadership
- Session 5: Discerning your Gifts as a Leader.

Ideally, a Christian leadership institute should cover Christian discipleship and other leadership themes, styles, traits, and models. This strategy can be easily integrated into any youth and young adult ministry curriculum.

Strategy 6

A sixth pragmatic approach is to formulate and offer Christian discipleship weekend retreats. Retreats increase discipleship, particularly in the areas of faith and spirituality, and have the ability to captivate, inspire, and motivate adolescents into a more meaningful relationship with God.[97]

The best retreat that I have seen successfully stimulate discipleship in young people is the "One-on-One Retreat." The retreat name recalls and reaffirms the personal commitment that every baptized Christian must undertake in their lives. The One-on-One Retreat is demanding in terms of format and content, but it focuses on following Jesus as a Christian disciple. It addresses the personal assent of faith based upon individual free will. Although the retreat's title suggests a privatized or personal spiritual experience ("me and Jesus"), the retreat is meant to subsist as a communal immersion experience over the course of a weekend ("we and Jesus").

A description of the retreat is as follows: The One-on-One Retreat is designed to empower youth and young adults to experience the risen Christ in their lives through a series of presentations, small group sharing, Bible study, and community and peer interaction. The ultimate goal is for the young people to personally articulate and commit and/or recommit

---

96. The Christian discipleship course could loosely follow Kielbasa, *Challenge of Discipleship*.

97. Canales, "Christian Discipleship: The Primordial Model," 42.

their lives to the Christ of faith—the present Lord and Savior of the church and world, and the Second Person of the Blessed Trinity. Finally, the retreat objectives are as follows: The One-on-One Retreat will offer youth and young adults the opportunity to encounter God, community, and self as they experience various activities that direct them toward a personal relationship with Jesus the Christ.

The One-on-One Retreat will encourage young people in the following five ways: (1) to gain deeper insight about themselves as a person living in the world and society; (2) to begin to reflect upon their relationship with God, self, and others; (3) to be encouraged to cultivate a more meaningful relationship with Jesus the Christ; (4) to be afforded the opportunities to commit and recommit their lives to God through Jesus the Christ in a nonthreatening and age-appropriate way; and (5) to start to foster a Christocentric spirituality that is rooted in solid contemporary theology and ecclesiology. The retreat is ideally implemented during a weekend format: Friday night through Sunday afternoon. This retreat has a great potential for transforming teenagers and calling them more deeply into Christian discipleship.[98]

These six pastoral implementation strategies are pedagogical recommendations and can be easily integrated into a youth and young adult ministry curriculum. Many of the suggestions are inexpensive, but like most youth and young adult ministry initiatives, fundraising may be a prerequisite.

There are many other pedagogical strategies that could be used, such as a film series or a book discussion group. Again, the possibilities of implementing pastoral strategies concerning Christian discipleship with youth and young adult ministry are vast. Comprehensive youth and young adult ministry will always be concerned with cultivating Christian discipleship, and it is the primordial model for developing Catholic faith, identity, and spirituality.

These eight categories and six methodological strategies of Christian discipleship help to give pastoral clarity, theological explanation, pedagogical rationale, and experiential praxis to Christian discipleship and all its wonderful nuances within youth and young adult ministry.

---

98. Ibid.

The Christian Discipleship Model

Strengths and Limitations of This Model

The strengths and limitations of the Christian discipleship model can be critiqued like any other model in this book. Christian discipleship is perhaps beyond being a model, and is instead a paradigm and measuring-stick of Christian living for two thousand years. Moreover, Christian discipleship has rarely been completely studied in a systematic way within theological circles, and has rarely, if ever, been studied analytically and completely for youth and young adult ministry. Nevertheless, despite the longevity and success of Christian discipleship it still has both positive attributes and a couple of concerns worth considering.

Strengths

The first and obvious advantage of the Christian discipleship model is that it already is a major paradigm for Christian living. It is reasonable that comprehensive youth and young adult ministries investigate the possibilities that Christian discipleship offers. Youth and young adult ministers can always reenvision Christian discipleship so it is age-appropriate and applicable to young people in such a way that they are discovering and rediscovering the benefits of being a follower of Christ.

Reenvisioning discipleship in the Christian tradition could be developing workshops, courses, concepts, and ideas that can help young people learn and resonate with Christian service, or a deeper discerning of the various ministry vocations within each denomination, and specifically, to heed the call of God in their lives. The possibilities of integrating and implementing Christian discipleship into youth and young adult ministry are limitless, as long as there are creative Christians in the world, then, this model will be constantly used, over and over again.

A second important benefit to this model is that it will help develop adolescents into authentic Christian disciples in the overall framework that discipleship demands: heeding God's call, having a deep abiding commitment, an allegiance that implies cost, the experience of God, a change of horizon, and the universal call to holiness. Good Christians are not born, they are made! Through much desire, dedication, and discipline, Christian disciples are being formed apart from the crowd, but are part of the crowd; that is, Christians are called to thrive in discipleship in the midst of culture and society and not run away from them. Comprehensive youth and young adult ministry can help young people become authentic Christian disciples through evangelization, formation, and catechesis.

A third positive feature of the Christian discipleship model, as presented in this study, is the eight theological categories that merit discussion and discernment by youth and young adult ministers, pastors, and parents. The topics of conversion, faith, morality, prayer, community, spirituality, service, and leadership are applicable to all Christians. These various facets within Christian discipleship are the fruits and the challenges that will help youth and young adult ministers relate to young people the essential *kernels* of Christian living, without overly focusing on the *husk* of Christianity's dogmas and doctrines. It is crucial that young people understand exactly the things that Christian disciples do—worship God weekly in community, get baptized at an appropriate age, pray in private and in public—are parts of a larger faith-community, and share their faith with others in a non-threatening way.

A fourth merit to this model is one that might appeal to some adolescents and young adults is that Christian discipleship is a "radical" call to follow Jesus Christ. Christian discipleship should be a radical embrace of living the Gospel life and following Jesus the Christ, and even a counter-cultural endeavor. Following Jesus is not merely some fad, but an authentic call to experience him in union with God the Father and God the Spirit.[99] Christian discipleship is concerned not only with following Jesus, but with learning about him, and ultimately becoming more and more intimately connected to Jesus.[100] Youth and young adult ministers are in a unique position to empower and encourage young people to come to know more about Jesus.

These four strengths are significant and will help guide youth and young adult ministers in discerning Christian discipleship as a model for youth and young adult ministry. However, there are a couple of confines for this model that also need deciphering.

Limitations

One of the most pressing drawbacks of the Christian discipleship model is that it is an expansive area of inquiry. Although this study has restricted discipleship to eight theological categories there could be several more

---

99. Hahnenberg, *Theology for Ministry*, 47.
100. Ibid.

added, such as preferential option for the poor, human sexuality, pastoral care, evangelization, preaching, and stewardship, to name and few. Such an expansive field of inquiry deserves to have educated and/or properly certified youth and young adult ministers lead young people down the transformative path of Christian discipleship. The availability of having youth and young adult ministers that are theologically educated and pastorally trained is vital. These eight theological categories of discipleship could be overwhelming for less experienced youth and young adult ministers.

A second concern for this model is that Christian discipleship should be a distinctive characteristic within any comprehensive youth and young adult ministry. Unfortunately, the cold hard reality is that only a few components of discipleship are usually stressed—faith, prayer, morality, and service—while other components are left out of the equation altogether. Many Christian youth and young adult programs try to integrate Christian discipleship, but few are intentionally and systematically introducing teenagers to the crucial attributes, which are demanded in following Christ as an authentic disciple.

Despite these two objections, the Christian discipleship model is one of the strongest models presented in this book. Youth ministers, campus ministers, and young adult ministers can readily integrate the eight theological categories and easily implement the six pastoral strategies into a comprehensive youth and young adult ministry.

Case Study[101]

Layla Kim is a twenty-three-year-old Korean-American who is director of *Powerline Youth Ministry* at Emmanuel Lutheran Church in Hartford, Connecticut. Layla is extremely excited because she has recently graduated from Hunt College with a bachelor's degree in youth ministry, but her only real experience of youth ministry since graduating from high school is limited to two semesters of internship while in college. Therefore, Layla has *not* been extensively involved in adolescent ministry since she was seventeen years old. Despite her lack of experience, the search committee and the pastor really liked her enthusiasm and her practical theology.

---

101. This is a genuine ministry scenario that came to me about ten years ago; I have crafted it differently for this particular case study. The names, cities, and institutions listed in this case study are fictional and have been made up to protect their true identities.

She has just been employed as the director of youth ministry and is beginning her first year as a full-time youth minister for Emmanuel Lutheran, which is part of the ELCA Synod (Evangelical Lutheran Church of America).

Layla directs a mega-youth ministry within a large, suburban, multicultural, and wealthy church of approximately 4,000 households. There are approximately 330 high school students registered in Powerline Youth Ministry. The pastor, parents, and youth expect a lot from their youth minister because it is a long-standing ministry within the church. Powerline Youth Ministry has been serving and catering to needs of adolescents for over thirty years old at Emmanuel Lutheran.

Immediately, Layla notices the magnitude of this ministry. There are plenty of volunteer adults (catechists) and parents who want to help out in any way they are asked, and there are also great resources in the youth ministry office. There are more pluses to this position: Layla has a full-time administrative assistant, a full-time assistant youth minister, an advisory board and two part-time youth ministry interns (college students) working with her in the youth department.

Layla's Plan: After a couple of months working at Emmanuel church, Layla decides to integrate a two-year curriculum on Christian discipleship that will be geared to reach the majority of students in Powerline who are sophomores and juniors in high school. After much planning and preparation, Layla meets with her adult leaders, some parents, the Youth Ministry Advisory Board to discuss her Christian discipleship curriculum. Everyone who hears Layla's proposal is excited and enthusiastic about the model. All parties involved agree that the Christian discipleship model should be put into motion.

However, the current dilemma for Layla is where to begin and how to start. She has a firm grasp of Christian discipleship from her studies at Hunt College, yet is unsure of the best way to begin implementing a Christian discipleship model. Layla, again, decides to consult with some of her adult catechists. Layla and the selected adult leaders decide to begin the new model in mid-January, after Christmas break and once students are back in school. Since everyone is in total support of the Christian discipleship model, it only needs to be integrated and implemented into the youth ministry. All of Powerline's initial groups and gatherings in January will begin to stress Christian discipleship: Bible studies, weekly catechetical sessions, core meetings, winter ski retreat, spring lock-in, and summer mission trip planning committees.

Reflection: Think about the Layla's ministry and the tremendous resources that she has available to her, including adult leaders, parents, and the advisory board. If you were in Layla's position, which steps would you begin to take to integrate a two-year curriculum on Christian discipleship? Which one of the six pastoral implementation strategies do you think Layla should put into practice at Powerline Youth Ministry? Explain your rationale.

Parting Remarks

Christian discipleship as the primordial model for youth and young adult ministry is rather encompassing because it involves many components of Christian living. Fostering Christian discipleship in young people is not an easy enterprise! Nevertheless, it is a priority for all Christian youth and young adult ministry. The Christian discipleship model makes good theological and pastoral sense because learning the ways of discipleship can benefit all ages of young people and can easily be integrated into a congregation's youth and young adult ministry curriculum. Although the specific formats may vary, discipleship does merit exploration and integration into Christian youth and young adult ministry.

The Christian discipleship model for comprehensive youth and young adult ministry can be one of the most challenging but rewarding models within the youth ministry. It is challenging because the youth and young adult minister must study and learn the various components of Christian discipleship. It is rewarding because it creates an atmosphere for young people to learn the ways to live and grow as Christians.

The task to create Christian disciples does *not* rest exclusively on the shoulders of the parish youth and young adult minister, or on the volunteer catechists. The task of raising-up Christian disciples is the responsibility of the entire community of faith, which must seek to draw adolescents and young adults into the life of love, faith, and service.[102] Youth and young adults are not alone in becoming Christian disciples; they have their parents who foster their faith, the community that calls them forth, the congregational youth and young adult ministry that cultivates their spirituality, and Christ who guides them in wisdom and prudence.

102. Canales, "Transforming Teenagers," 81–82.

Conclusion:
The Journey of Youth and Young Adult Ministry

> *People were bringing [young people] to [Jesus] that he might touch them, but the disciples rebuked them. When Jesus saw this he became indignant and said to them, "Let the [young people] come to me; do not prevent them, for the kingdom of God belongs to such as these."*
>
> Jesus of Nazareth
Gospel of Mark 10:13-14

Preliminary Remarks

Hopefully, *Models and Methods for Youth and Young Adult Ministry: Ecumenical Examples and Pastoral Approaches for the Christian Church* has been theologically stimulating and pastorally relevant. Equally, I hope that the book was a rich discovery for those who have a passion to serve and walk the journey with young people.

The four Christian and ecumenical models presented in this book represent only some of the models that can be used in youth and young adult ministry. There are potentially many more that could be addressed and used within comprehensive youth and young adult ministry. The four models described and examined in this study are intended to: (1) *increase* youth and young adult ministers' knowledge and wisdom of a particular ministry model; (2) *enhance* youth and young adult ministers' way of doing youth and young adult ministry; and (3) *boost* youth and young adult ministers' breadth and depth of comprehensive youth and young adult ministry.

Each of the four models presented—the biblical-hermeneutic, the servant-leadership, the liberation, and the Christian discipleship—will improve youth and young adult ministers' concepts and ideas for planning, developing, amalgamating, and implementing ministry with young people. The chief aim of this book has been to provide various theologically engaging, spiritually enriching, and pastorally relevant interconnected models that, when implemented either separately or in relation to one another, can be mutually satisfying for young people, and for youth and young adult ministers.

One of the benefits of these four models is that they can all be integrated into a comprehensive youth and young adult ministry because all the models "*empower* young people to live as disciples of Jesus Christ in our world today; *draw* young people to responsible participation in the life, mission, and work of the Catholic faith community; and *foster* the total personal and spiritual growth of each young person."[1]

The importance of *empowering*, *drawing*, and *fostering* young people in the church's mission is that it provides youth and young adult ministers with a broad understanding of the direction of youth and young adult ministry. The significance of the four models presented in this book is that it gives youth and young adult ministers, whether Catholic, Protestant, Evangelical, or Orthodox, a compass to follow in order to help situate theologically, spiritually, and pastorally youth and young adult ministry in a direction in which adolescents and adults can learn, grow, and blossom as healthy and mature Christians.

The journey of youth and young adult ministry is not complicated, but at times it can be arduous and can take detours along the way as youth and young adult ministers leave parishes, as pastors change assignments, and as bishops retire. The challenge is to keep comprehensive youth and young adult ministry at the forefront of every Christian congregation. Youth and young adult ministry is integral to the life of the Christian church, and integrating and implementing the four models prescribed in this book will help foster adolescent and young adult Christian disciples and future leaders.

Lex vivendi ("law of living") is the basis for living the Christian life in a way that motivates youth and young adult ministers to move beyond programming events and activities, and to move young people to experience a deep and rich theological and spiritual life. Youth and young adult ministry is most definitely the work of the Holy Spirit and is best accomplished when

---

1. *RTV*, iii.

it utilizes the five facets of ministry: (1) comprehensive, (2) unitive, (3) collaborative, (4) ecumenical, and (5) culturally diverse.

The Five Facets of Ministry

The future of Christian youth and/or young adult ministry in the United States should ideally represent each of these areas to the fullest:

1. **Comprehensive.** Christian youth and young adult ministry must be comprehensive; that is, it must try to accomplish ministry with young people from A to Z. Comprehensive youth and young adult ministry is: (a) Christ-centered, (b) biblically based, (c) prayerful and spiritual, (d) relational, (e) moral and ethical, (f) ministerial and pastoral, (g) goal-centered, (h) multidimensional and multicultural, (i) holistic and developmental, and (j) family-centered.[2]

Moreover, comprehensive youth and young adult ministry requires being faithful to the various components of youth and young adult ministry: (a) advocacy, (b) catechesis, (c) community life, (d) evangelization, (e) justice and service, (f) leadership development, (g) pastoral care, and (h) prayer and worship.[3]

Finally, comprehensive youth and young adult ministry maintains that youth and young adult ministers are not merely doing ministry off the "top of their heads." They must be rooted in the teachings of the Christian Church, grounded in sacred Scripture, and firmly solid about their personal identity, psychology, and spirituality.[4]

2. **Unitive.** Christian youth and young adult ministry must be unitive; that is, a single youth or young adult ministry cannot be an island unto itself or standing in isolation. The parish youth and/or young adult ministry must be connected to the larger church infrastructure and support, which means that youth and young adult ministers must be allied to other youth and young adult ministers in their region or deanery (a cluster of churches in a geographical area in a Catholic diocese), and the diocese or state in which they reside.

Unitive maintains that individual, Christian community, youth and young adult ministries must be part of the overall vision of their denomination's mission and vision, which means supporting and participating in

2. Ibid., 3–4.
3. Ibid., 26–44.
4. *Co-Workers*, 36–37.

regional, state, and national events and activities. It should make bishops, pastors, and diocesan directors of youth and young adult ministry nervous if a group of youth and young adult ministers is "boycotting" regional events arguing that "we can do it better ourselves," instead of allowing young people to experience the larger Christian community or diocese.

Being unitive implies that it is *not* about doing youth and young adult ministry as a "lone-ranger," but being part of the bigger picture of youth and young adult ministry. Good ministry with young people is *not* silo-ministry or solo-ministry; ministry with young people cannot be self-absorbed.[5] Being unitive also implies that each congregation is joined to the larger universal church worldwide and participates, if applicable and age-appropriate, to universal events such as North American Christian Convention, Global Leadership Summit, or World Youth Day.

In addition, unitive requires that parishes and dioceses are in relationship with the national directives and programs provided by national offices such as the National Federation for Catholic Youth Ministry (Washington DC) and the National Catholic Young Adult Ministry Association (Washington DC). Such national offices provide national sponsored retreats, workshops, and conferences for youth and young adult ministers.

Being unitive calls every parish youth and young adult ministry into accountability and reliability, because there may be times when the diocese or certain denominational office needs the support of several youth and young adult ministers to plan, organize, and implement some regional or state multi-ministry event, such as a youth conference, a day of prayer, or a mission trip.

The bottom line is that being unitive requires that youth and young adult ministries be united to the larger church. In some cases, the larger church's vision and continual guidance, training, and leadership serves a need for a congregation's young people.

3. **Collaborative.** Christian youth and young adult ministry must be collaborative; that is, parish youth and young adult ministers would be wise to be involved in the life of the congregation and helping young people assimilate into the different ministries in the community. It is part of each person's baptismal rights, roles, and responsibilities that young people, too, become involved in the life of their congregation.

Collaborative means that youth and young adult ministers are diligently trying to link their ministry efforts with other efforts within the

---

5. Sofield and Juliano, *Collaboration*, 150.

Conclusion: The Journey of Youth and Young Adult Ministry

congregation. Therefore, if there is a parish mission or church revival during the liturgical season of Lent, it is the responsibility of the youth and young adult minister to help plan and organize young people to be part of that effort, or have an age-appropriate adolescent and young adult mission or revival simultaneously with the adults. The point is, young people need to experience the larger life of the parish and not *only* be part of the youth and/or young adult ministry.

Each congregational minister or parish priest should be familiar with and know the names of the core young people within the youth and young adult ministry. I have always maintained the approach with my youth (while I was a youth minister) and with my students (as a college professor) that it is a good idea to have young people become involved in two ministries within the church and outside of youth and young adult ministry: (1) one liturgical (worship) ministry (liturgical server, lector, greeter, usher, Eucharistic minister, sacristan, prayer writer, choir member, cantor, musician, organist, etc.); and (2) one service-type ministry (coaching, homeless ministry, tutoring children, teaching religious education, grounds and maintenance crew, Bible study, soup kitchen, food pantry, etc.).

It is imperative that young people be associated with the larger life of the congregation. It is a major task and goal of the youth and young adult minister to integrate young people into the larger life of the community. Teenagers, emerging adults, and young adults should never be disconnected from their family of faith.

4. *Ecumenical.* Christian youth and young adult ministry must be ecumenical; that is, it should *always* be open to the spirit of unity and oneness with all Christian denominations.[6] The call to Christian unity is the call to openness and to love other Christians and their churches. The call to Christian unity is also the call to conversion and transformation, and to foster a sense of belonging and community, not one of separation and isolation.[7]

I get nervous and feel sad when I hear of congregations that bring in a renowned "Christian apologist" because it usually "smacks" in the face of ecumenism and tries to "fix," correct, or put-down other denominations' worldviews. Today, Christians live in an ecumenical world, not an apologetic world. Youth and young adult ministry cannot afford to have an

---

6. Gros, McManus, and Riggs, *Introduction to Ecumenism*, 1–3.
7. *Co-Workers*, 44–45.

attitude of alienation that leads to division.[8] Today's world is too small to be closed-minded and to take a defensive posture regarding other Christian denominations.

Being an ecumenical youth and young adult ministry means to live with the tensions and common hopes and joys of other Christian denominations and communities. An ecumenical youth and young adult ministry requires leaving behind denominational bigotry, tearing down denominational walls, and developing associations and partnerships with churches from various denominations. Being an ecumenical youth and young adult ministry implies reflecting on Christian unity and dialoguing and discussing common theological and ministry interests, not tearing down doctrinal differences. Collaboration is an important dynamic to ecumenism and collaboration is a fundamental response to God's invitation and call to Christian unity.[9]

5. ***Culturally Diverse.*** Christian youth and young adult ministry must be culturally diverse; that is, it promotes mutual awareness of unity among all young people.[10] The Christian Church is extremely diverse today and being attuned to that reality is part of good ecclesiology.

All Christian denominations embrace *ecclesial integration* as a fundamental principle of growth, tolerance, and unity in diversity. Ecclesial integration is part of a culturally diverse and rich ministry, which welcomes people from all countries, cultures, and ethnicities, and embraces them for their own gifts, talents, rituals, and traditions. A youth and young adult ministry that emphasizes and embraces cultural diversity is affirming and valuing the traditions and customs of other ethnicities is witnessing ecclesial integration.[11]

Today's youth and young adult ministers live and work in a multicultural and multi-faith world. Because our world is so plural and ethnically and culturally diverse it places ministry within the context of *intercultural ministry*.

Intercultural youth and/or young adult ministry is a pastoral outlook and approach that invites and successfully unites young people around common issues, interests, and needs from two or more culturally diverse groups (e.g., Hispanic/Latino(a) teens, Asian youth, and/or black

---

8. Gros, McManus, and Riggs, *Introduction to Ecumenism*, 16.
9. Sofield and Juliano, *Collaboration*, 18–29.
10. Aguilera-Titus, "Ministry with Youth," 72.
11. Ibid., 77.

Conclusion: The Journey of Youth and Young Adult Ministry

adolescents). Being a culturally diverse youth and young adult ministry means to welcome all strangers (God's children) into ministry, and such a ministry embraces unity in diversity. To do otherwise or to not be a culturally diverse ministry would be a living contradiction and tantamount to racism.[12]

If these five areas—comprehensive, unitive, collaborative, ecumenical, and culturally diverse—are firmly in place, then Christian youth and young adult ministry will flourish for years to come. The task of youth and young adult ministry specialists and adolescent and young adult ministry scholars is to continually work toward training and catechizing youth and young adult ministers, directors of religious education, and parish priests and congregational ministers in these areas.

This book tries to offer insight and inspiration for youth and young adults ministers to learn from and utilize in their ministries. It also tries to provide youth and young adult ministers with a way to grow in their understanding and knowledge of the four different theological areas and various pastoral and pedagogical methodologies.

These four models hopefully will empower youth ministers to think and do ministry "outside the box," and will equip them with the foundational theology to utilize these models. The danger will be if youth and young adult ministers merely read the pastoral implementation strategies of each chapter and *foolishly* ignore the pages leading up to the methodological sections.

Christian youth and young adult ministry is concerned about bringing adolescents, emerging adults, and young adults to a personal relationship with God through Jesus the Christ, and these four models will help encourage youth and young adult ministers on that awesome journey. In the final analysis, the purpose of Christian youth and young adult ministry is not to "wow!" teenagers, or to have the biggest or best youth or young adult ministry in the city or state. The purpose of Christian youth and young adult ministry is to help adolescents and young adults discern for themselves (with guidance) their faith-life in the church and to become the best they can be in Jesus the Christ.

---

12. USCCB, *Brothers and Sisters*, 3.

Bibliography

Agosto, Efrain. *Servant-Leadership: Jesus & Paul*. St. Louis, MO: Chalice, 2005.

Aguilera-Titus, Alejandro. "Ministry with Youth in a Culturally Diverse Church." In *Leadership for Catholic Youth Ministry: A Comprehensive Resource*, edited by Thomas East, 71–98. New London, CT: Twenty-Third, 2014.

Anderson, Ray S. *The Shape of Practical Theology: Empowering Ministry with Theological Praxis*. Downers Grove, IL: IVP Academic, 2001.

Angel, Maria. "Vineyards and Landscapes: *Lectio Divina* in Secular Age." *Nova et Vetera* 11 (2013) 19–38.

Aquinas, Thomas. *Summa Theologica*. 5 vols. Translated by Fathers of the English Dominican Province. Westminster, MD: Christian Classics, 1981.

Aristotle. *The Nicomachean Ethics*. Oxford World Classics. Oxford: Oxford University Press, 1980.

Arnett, Jeffrey J. *Emerging Adulthood: The Winding Road from the Late Teens through the Twenties*. New York: Oxford University Press, 2004.

Arzola, Fernando, Jr. *Toward a Prophetic Youth Ministry: Theory and Praxis in Urban Context*. Downers Grove, IL: IVP Academic, 2008.

Ballantyne, James. "Liberation Theology in Youth Ministry: An Inconvenient Truth?" *Detached Youthworker*, September 25, 2015. https://jamesballantyneyouthworker.wordpress.com/2015/09/25/liberation-theology-in-youth-ministry-an-inconvenient-truth/.

Barrero, Joseph F., Arthur David Canales, and Seth P. Mason. *Keeping the Cup Full: Financial Stewardship for Teens and Young Adults*. Austin: Cornerstone Financial Education, 2009.

Barron, Robert. *The Strangest Way: Walking the Christian Path*. Maryknoll, NY: Orbis, 2002.

Batten, Joe. "Servant Leadership: A Passion to Serve." In *Insights on Leadership: Service, Stewardship, Spirit, and Servant-Leadership*, edited by Larry C. Spears, 38–53. New York: John Wiley & Sons, 1998.

Benedict XVI, Pope. *Verbum Domini*. Vatican City: Libreri Editrice Vaticana, 2010. http://w2.vatican.va/content/benedict-xvi/en/apost_exhortations/documents/hf_ben-xvi_exh_20100930_verbum-domini.html.

Bergler, Thomas E. *From Here to Maturity: Overcoming the Juvenilization of American Christianity*. Grand Rapids, MI: Eerdmans, 2014.

———. "Mapping the Missional Landscape of Emerging Adults." *Journal of Youth & Theology* 15 (2017) 64–96.

Bibliography

Bevans, Stephen B. *Models of Contextual Theology: Faith and Cultures.* Rev. and exp. ed. Maryknoll, NY: Orbis, 2001.

Bishops' Committee on the Liturgy. *Rite of Christian Initiation of Adults: Study Edition.* Chicago: Liturgical, 1988.

Boff, Leonardo, and Clodovis Boff. *Introducing Liberation Theology.* Maryknoll, NY: Orbis, 1992.

Bonhoeffer, Dietrich. *The Cost of Discipleship.* New York: Simon & Schuster, 1937.

Bonner, Steven. "Understanding the Changing Adolescent." In *Adoptive Youth Ministry: Integrating Emerging Generations into the Family of Faith*, edited by Chap Clark, 22–38. Grand Rapids, MI: Baker Academic, 2016.

Borgman, Dean. *Foundations for Youth Ministry: Theological Engagement with Teen Life and Culture.* 2nd ed. Grand Rapids, MI: Baker Academic, 2013.

Brewster, Melanie E., Bonnie Moradi, Cirleen DeBlaere, and Brandon L. Velez. "Navigating the Borderlands: The Roles of Minority Stressors, Bicultural Self-Efficacy, and Cognitive Flexibility in Mental Health of Bisexual Individuals." *Journal of Counseling Psychology* 60 (2013) 543–56.

Cahalan, Kathleen A. *Introducing the Practice of Ministry.* Collegeville, MN: Liturgical, 2010.

Camp, Lee C. *Mere Discipleship: Radical Christianity in a Rebellious World.* Grand Rapids, MI: Brazos, 2004.

Canales, Arthur David. "The Biblical-Hermeneutical Model for Youth Ministry: Four Scriptural and Pedagogical Approaches for Youth Workers." *The Bible Today* 51 (2013) 237–47.

———. "Christian Discipleship: Discipleship Calls Christians to Better Life." *Herald Times Reporter*, May 3, 2003, A9–A10.

———. "Christian Discipleship: Discipleship Requires 'Attachment' to Jesus." *Herald Times Reporter*, April 26, 2003, D1–D2.

———. "Christian Discipleship: How Do Christians Accept Discipleship? *Herald Times Reporter*, April 19, 2003, A9–A10.

———. "Christian Discipleship: The Primordial Model for Comprehensive Catholic Youth Ministry." *Journal of Religious Education* 60 (2012) 35–45.

———. "Integrating Christian Discipleship *Is* Franciscanism." *The Journal of the Association of Franciscan Colleges and Universities* 1 (2004) 34–53.

———. "Models for Adolescent Ministry: Exploring Eight Ecumenical Examples." *Religious Education* 101 (2006) 204–32.

———. "Models of Christian Leadership in Youth Ministry." *Religious Education* 109 (2014) 24–44.

———. *A Noble Quest: Cultivating Spirituality in Catholic Adolescents.* Waco, TX: PCG Legacy, 2011.

———. "A Noble Quest: Cultivating Christian Spirituality in Catholic Adolescents and the Usefulness of 12 Pastoral Practices." *International Journal of Children's Spirituality* 14 (2009) 63–77.

———. "A Reality Check: Addressing Catholic Hispanic Youth Ministry in the United States of America (Part 1)." *Apuntes: Reflexíones Teológicas desde el Contexto Hispano-Latino* 25 (2005) 4–23.

———. "Reaping What We Sow: Addressing Catholic Hispanic Youth Ministry in the United States of America (Part 2)." *Apuntes: Reflexíones Teológicas desde el Contexto Hispano-Latino* 25 (2005) 44–74.

BIBLIOGRAPHY

———. "A Rebirth of Being '*Born-Again*': Theological, Sacramental, and Pastoral Reflections from a Roman Catholic Perspective." *The Journal of Pentecostal Theology* 11 (2002) 89–119.

———. "Servant-Leadership: A Model for Youth Ministry." *Journal of Youth & Theology* 13 (2015) 42–62.

———. "The Spiritual Significance of the Nicodemus Narrative to Youth Ministry." *The Living Light* 38 (2002) 23–32.

———. "Strengthening Eucharistic Spirituality in Adolescents." *Emmanuel, Eucharistic Spirituality* 115 (2009) 9–23.

———. "The Ten-Year Anniversary of *Renewing the Vision*: Reflection on Its Impact for Catholic Youth Ministry." *New Theology Review* 20 (2007) 58–69.

———. "Transforming Teenagers: Integrating Social Justice into Catholic Youth Ministry or Catholic Education." *Verbum Incarnatum* 4 (2011) 69–91.

Carotta, Michael. "Revisiting Adolescent Catechesis." *The Living Light* 38 (2002) 40–48.

Cervantes, Carmen M. *Evangelization of Hispanic Young People*. Vol. 2, *Prophets of Hope*. Winona, MN: Saint Mary's, 1995.

———. *Hispanic Young People and the Church's Pastoral Response*. Vol. 1, *Prophets of Hope*. Winona, MN: Saint Mary's, 1994.

Christenson, Georgia. "St. Clare of Assisi: A Servant-Leader." *The Journal of Association of Franciscan Colleges and Universities* 10 (2013) 13–25.

Chum, Kirstyn Y. S., and Anneliese A. Singh. "The Bisexual Youth of Color Intersecting Identities Development Model: A Contextual Approach to Understanding Multiple Marginalization Experiences." *Journal of Bisexuality* 10 (2010) 429–51.

Chupungco, Anscar J. *Liturgical Inculturation: Sacramentals, Religiosity, and Catechesis*. Collegeville, MN: Liturgical, 1992.

Cone, James H. *A Black Theology of Liberation*. 20th anniversary ed. Maryknoll, NY: Orbis, 1992.

Cosby, Brian. "The Reformed View of Youth Ministry." In *Youth Ministry in the 21st Century*, edited by Chap Clark, 37–72. Grand Rapids: Baker Academic, 2015.

Cousins, Ewert H. "Models and the Future of Ministry." *Continuum* 7 (1969) 78–91.

Crosby, Michael. *Spirituality of the Beatitudes: Matthew's Challenge for First World Christians*. Maryknoll, NY: Orbis, 1981.

Cunningham, Lawrence S. *Francis of Assisi: Performing the Gospel of Life*. Grand Rapids, MI: Eerdmans, 2004.

Cunningham, Lawrence S., and Keith J. Egan. *Christian Spirituality: Themes from the Tradition*. Mahwah, NJ: Paulist, 1996.

Daloz-Parks, Sharon. *Big Questions, Worthy Dreams: Mentoring Young Adults in Their Search for Meaning, Purpose, and Faith*. San Francisco: Jossey-Bass, 2000.

Dei Verbum. In *Vatican Council II: Constitutions, Decrees, Declarations*, edited by Austin P. Flannery, 97–115. Northport, NY: Costello, 1992.

De Kock, A. Jos. "A Typology of Catechetical Learning Environments." *International Journal of Practical Theology* 18 (2014) 264–86.

———. "What About Learning in Practical Theological Studies? Toward More Conceptual Clarity." *SAGE* 5 (2015) 1–12.

De La Torre, Miguel A. *Doing Christian Ethics from the Margins*. Maryknoll, NY: Orbis, 2004.

———. *Reading the Bible from the Margins*. Maryknoll, NY: Orbis, 2002.

Bibliography

De La Torre, Miguel A., and E. D. Aponte. *Introducing Latino/a Theologies.* Maryknoll, NY: Orbis, 2001.

Department of [Catholic] Education. *A Vision of Youth Ministry.* Washington, DC: United States Catholic Conference, 1976.

Doong, David J. H., and Jinna Sil Lo Jin. "Thinking Globally: An Asian American Case Study Approach." In *Adoptive Youth Ministry: Integrating Emerging Generations into the Family of Faith,* edited by Chap Clark, 165–79. Grand Rapids, MI: Baker Academic, 2016.

Downie, Allison. "A Spirituality of Openness: Christian Ecofeminist Perspectives and Interreligious Dialogue." *Feminist Theology* 23 (2014) 55–70.

Dulles, Avery. *Models of the Church.* Expanded ed. New York: Image, 1987.

———. *Models of Revelation.* Garden City, NY: Image, 1985.

Dunn Richard R., and Jana L. Sundene. *Shaping the Journey of Emerging Adults: Life-Giving Rhythms for Spiritual Transformation.* Downers Grove, IL: IVP, 2012.

Eckert, Ann M. "Youth Ministry Leadership." In *Leadership for Catholic Youth Ministry: A Comprehensive Resource,* edited by Thomas East, 294–321. New London, CT: Twenty-Third, 2009.

Erwin, Pamela. "Youth Ministry Education: Where Practice, Theology, and Social Sciences Intersect." *The Journal of Youth Ministry* 4 (2006) 9–18.

Faix, Tobias. "Hybrid Identity: Youth in Digital Networks: A Model of Contextualization for Christian Youth Ministry." *Journal of Youth & Theology* 15 (2016) 65–87.

Ferch, Shann R. *Servant-Leadership, Forgiveness, and Social Justice.* Voices of Servant-Leadership Series 9. Indianapolis: Greenleaf Center for Servant Leadership, 2004.

Fields, Doug. *Your First Two Years in Youth Ministry: A Personal and Practical Guide to Starting Right.* Grand Rapids, MI: Zondervan, 2002.

Fisher, Mary P. "Buddhism." In *Living Religions,* by Mark P. Fisher, 129–75. 6th ed. Upper Saddle River, NJ: Prentice-Hall, 2007.

———. "Islam." In *Living Religions,* by Mary P. Fisher, 362–416. 6th ed. Upper Saddle River, NJ: Prentice-Hall, 2007.

Freire, Paulo. "Conscientizing as a Way of Liberating." In *Liberation Theology: A Documentary History,* edited by Alfred T. Hennelly, 5–13. Maryknoll, NY: Orbis, 1990.

———. *Pedagogy of the Oppressed.* 30th anniversary ed. New York: Continuum, 2002.

Greenleaf, Robert K. *Servant-Leadership: A Journey into the Nature of Legitimate Power and Greatness.* 25th anniversary ed. New York: Paulist, 2002.

Greytak, Emily A., Joseph G. Kosciw, and Madelyn J. Boesen. "Putting the 'T' in 'Resource': The Benefits of LGBT-Related School Resources for Transgender Youth." *Journal of LGBT Youth* 10 (2013) 45–63.

Gros, Jeffrey, Eamon McManus, and Ann Riggs. *Introduction to Ecumenism.* Mahwah, NJ: Paulist, 1998.

Gula, Richard M. *Just Ministry: Professional Ethics for Pastoral Ministers.* Mahwah, NJ: Paulist, 2010.

Gutiérrez, Gustavo. *A Theology of Liberation.* 15th anniversary ed. Maryknoll, NY: Orbis, 1992.

Hahnenberg, Edward P. *Theology for Ministry: An Introduction for Lay Ministers.* Collegeville, MN: Liturgical, 2014.

Hennelly, Alfred T. *Liberation Theology: A Documentary History.* Maryknoll, NY: 1990.

Bibliography

Herrera, Maria. "Toward Multicultural Youth Ministry." In *Readings in Youth Ministry*. Vol. 1, *Foundations*, edited by John Roberto, 89–103. Washington, DC: National Federation for Catholic Youth Ministry, 1986.

Hill, Brennan R. *8 Spiritual Heroes: Their Search for God*. Cincinnati: Saint Anthony Messenger, 2002.

Hill, Graham. "Authentic Contextualization of Theology and Practice in Youth Ministry." *Journal of Youth and Theology* 1 (2002) 36–46.

Interdicasterial Commission. *Catechism of the Catholic Church*. 2nd ed. Vatican City: Libreria Editrice Vaticana, 1997.

Irwin, Kevin W. *Models of the Eucharist*. New York: Paulist, 2005.

Isasi-Diaz, Ada M., and Yolanda Tarango. *Hispanic Women: Prophetic Voice in the Church*. San Francisco: Harper & Row, 1998.

Jacober, Amy E. *The Adolescent Journey: An Interdisciplinary Approach to Practical Youth Ministry*. Downers Grove, IL: IVP 2011.

John Paul II, Pope. *The Church in America: On the Encounter with the Living Christ—the Way to Conversion, Communion, and Solidarity in America*. Washington, DC: USCCB, 2000.

———. *Redemptoria Missio*. Rome: Liberria Editrice Vaticana, 2000.

Johnson, Keith L. *Theology as Discipleship*. Downers Grove, IL: IVP Academic, 2015.

Jones, Tony. "It's a Matter of Time." In *Adoptive Youth Ministry: Integrating Emerging Generations into the Family of Faith*, edited by Chap Clark, 212–20. Grand Rapids, MI: Baker Academic, 2016.

Kageler, Len. "Foundations and Models of Muslim to Muslim Youth Work." *Journal of Youth & Theology* 12 (2013) 64–84.

Kaplan, Abraham. "Equality." In *Bigotry, Prejudice, and Hatred: Definitions, Causes, and Solutions*, edited by Robert M. Baird and Stuart E. Rosenbaum, 81–90. Buffalo, NY: Prometheus, 1992.

Kelly, Margret J. "Leadership." In *Catholic Church Management: A Concise Guide*, edited by Kevin E. McKenna, 5–22. Notre Dame, IN: Ave Maria, 2010.

Kielbasa, Marilyn. *The Challenge of Discipleship*. Winona, MN: Saint Mary's, 1997.

Kilmovitz, Greg. "Youth Ministry as an Exercise in Liberation Theology: Reflections on Gustavo Gutierrez." *Unfinished* (blog), June 28, 2011. http://gregklimovitz.blogspot.com/2011/06/youth-ministry-as-excercise-in.html.

King, Martin Luther, Jr. *A Testament of Hope*. San Francisco: HarperCollins, 1986.

Kuhn, Thomas S. *The Structure of Scientific Revolutions*. 2nd ed. Chicago: University of Chicago Press, 1970.

Lad, Lawrence J., and David Luechauer. "On the Path to Servant-Leadership." In *Insights on Leadership: Service, Stewardship, Spirit, and Servant-Leadership*, edited by Larry C. Spears, 54–67. New York: John Wiley & Sons, 1998.

Lonergan, Bernard J. F. *Method in Theology*. Toronto: University of Toronto Press, 1994.

Lorenzen, Thorwald. *Resurrection and Discipleship: Interpretive Models, Biblical Reflections, and Theological Consequences*. Maryknoll, NY: Orbis, 1995.

MacPhee, Bill. "Adoptive Leadership." In *Youth Ministry in the 21st Century: Five Views*, edited by Chap Clark, 273–87. Grand Rapids, MI: Baker Academic, 2015.

McBrien, Richard P. *Ministry: A Theological, Pastoral Handbook*. San Francisco: Harper & Row, 1987.

McFague, Sallie. *Models of God: Theology for an Ecological, Nuclear Age*. Philadelphia: Fortress, 1987.

Bibliography

Medina, Lara. "Transformative Struggle: The Spirituality of *Las Hermanas*." In *New Horizons in Hispanic/Lation(a) Theology*, edited by Benjamin Valentin, 217–37. Cleveland: Pilgrim, 2003.

Meehan, Catherine. "Belonging, Being, and Becoming: The Importance of Understanding Beliefs and Practices in the Teaching of Religious Education in the Early Years." *Journal of Religious Education* 59 (2011) 36–49.

Moser, Greg. "Youth Ministry: The Component of Leadership Development." In *The Vision of Catholic Youth Ministry: Fundamentals, Theory, and Practice*, edited by Robert J. McCarty, 134–43. Winona, MN: Saint Mary's, 2005.

Moyaert, Marianne. "Interreligious Dialogue and the Value of Openness: Taking the Vulnerability of Religious Attachments into Account." *The Heythrop Journal* 50 (2010) 730–40.

Mueller, Walt. *Youth Culture 101*. Grand Rapids, MI: Zondervan, 2007.

National Federation for Catholic Youth Ministry. *The Challenge of Adolescent Catechesis: Maturing in Faith*. Washington, DC: United States Catholic Conference, 1986.

Noble, Tim. "Liberation Theology Today: Challenges and Changes." In *Mezinárodi Symposium O Teolgii Osvobození: Sborník Příspevků*, edited by Michal Cáb, Roman Míčka, and Marek Pelech, 22–36. České, Budějovice: Teologická Fakulta Jihočeské University, 2007.

Northouse, Peter G. *Leadership: Practice and Theory*. Thousand Oaks, CA: SAGE, 2007.

Nostra Aetate. In *Vatican Council II: The Conciliar and Post-Conciliar Documents*, edited by Flannery Austin, 738–42. Northport, NY: Costello, 1992.

Nouwen, Henri J. M. *The Wounded Healer*. New York: Image, 1979.

Oestreicher, Mark *Youth Ministry 3.0: A Manifesto*. Grand Rapids, MI: Youth Specialties, 2008.

O'Grady, John F. *Models of Jesus, Revisited*. New York: Paulist, 1994.

Ostendorf, David. "Christian Identity: An American Heresy." *Journal of Hate Studies* 1 (2012) 23–55.

Palmer, Parker J. *A Hidden Wholeness: The Journey Toward an Undivided Life*. San Francisco: Jossey-Bass, 2004.

Penner, Marv. "Welcoming Wounded and Broken Adolescents into the Family of God." In *Adoptive Youth Ministry: Integrating Emerging Generations into the Family of Faith*, edited by Chap Clark, 39–51. Grand Rapids, MI: Baker Academic, 2016.

Petrella, Ivan. *Latin American Liberation Theology: The Next Generation*. Maryknoll, NY: Orbis, 2005.

Phan, Peter C. "Jesus the Christ with an Asian Face." *Theological Studies* 57 (1996) 399–430.

———. "Method in Liberation Theologies." *Theological Studies* 61 (2000) 40–63.

Piburn, Sidney. *The Dalai Lama, a Policy of Kindness: An Anthology of Writings By and About the Dalai Lama*. Ithaca, NY: Snow Lion, 1991.

Pieris, Aloysius. *An Asian Theology of Liberation*. Maryknoll, NY: Orbis, 1998.

Pope, Stephen J. "Proper and Improper Partiality and the Preferential Option for the Poor." *Theological Studies* 54 (1993) 242–71.

Premawardhana, Shantra D. "Christian Openness to Interreligious Dialogue." *Tikkun* 26 (2011) 1–2.

Rah, Soong C. *Many Colors: Cultural Intelligence for a Changing Church*. Chicago: Moody, 2010.

Bibliography

Rahner, Karl. "Experience of the Holy Spirit." In *Theological Investigations*. Vol. 18, *God and Revelation*, by Karl Rahner, 189–210. New York: Crossroad, 1983.

Root, Andrew. "Regulating the Empirical in Practical Theology: On Critical Realism, Divine Action, and the Place of the Ministerial." *Journal of Youth & Theology* 15 (2016) 44–64.

Root, Andrew, and Kendra Creasy Dean. *The Theological Turn in Youth Ministry*. Downers Grove, IL: IVP, 2011.

Santrock, John. *Adolescence*. 11th ed. New York: McGraw Hill, 2007.

Schneiders, Sandra M. *The Revelatory Text: Interpreting the New Testament as Sacred Scripture*. 2nd ed. Collegeville, MN: Liturgical, 1999.

Sedwick, Jay. "Teaching for Adoptive Ministry." In *Adoptive Youth Ministry: Integrating Emerging Generations into the Family of Faith*, edited by Chap Clark, 302–15. Grand Rapids, MI: Baker Academic, 2016.

Segovia, Fernando F., ed. *Discipleship in the New Testament*. Philadelphia: Fortress, 1985.

———. "Introduction: Call and Discipleship—Toward a Reexamination of the Shape and Character of Christian Existence in the New Testament." In *Discipleship in the New Testament*, edited by Fernando F. Segovia, 1–23. Philadelphia: Fortress, 1985.

Senge, Peter M. *The Fifth Discipline: The Art and Practice of the Learning Organization*. New York: Doubleday, 1990.

Sergiovanni, Thomas J. *Moral Leadership: Getting to the Heart of School Improvement*. San Francisco: Jossey-Bass, 1992.

Smith, Christian. *Soul Searching: The Religious and Spiritual Lives of American Teenagers*. New York: Oxford University Press, 2005.

———. *Souls in Transition: The Religious & Spiritual Lives of Emerging Adults*. New York: Oxford University Press, 2009.

Smolarski, Dennis C. *Sacred Mysteries: Sacramental Principles and Liturgical Practice*. New York: Paulist, 1995.

Sobrino, Jon. *Spirituality of Liberation: Toward Political Holiness*. Maryknoll, NY: Orbis, 1990.

Sofield, Loughlan, and Carroll Julian. *Collaboration: Uniting Our Gifts in Ministry*. Notre Dame, IN: Ave Maria 2000.

———. *Principled Ministry: A Guide to Catholic Leadership*. Notre Dame, IN: Ave Maria, 2011.

Spear, Karen. "Contemplating Integrity: Nurturing Franciscan Servant-Leadership through Contemplative Prayer." *The Journal of Association of Franciscan Colleges and Universities* 10 (2014) 8–19.

Spears, Larry C. "Tracing the Growing Impact of Servant-Leadership." In *Insights on Leadership: Service, Stewardship, Spirit, and Servant-Leadership*, edited by Larry C. Spears, 1–13. New York: John Wiley & Sons, 1998.

Stier, Greg. "The Gospel Advancing View of Youth Ministry." In *Youth Ministry in the 21st Century: Five Views*, edited by Chap Clark, 3–34. Grand Rapids, MI: Baker Academic, 2015.

Strommen, Merton, and Richard A. Hardel. *Passing on the Faith: A Radical New Model for Youth and Family Ministry*. Winona, MN: Saint Mary's, 2000.

Synod of Catholic Bishops. *Young People, the Faith, and Vocational Discernment*. Vatican City: Libreria Editrice Vaticana, 2017.

Tacey, David J. *The Spirituality Revolution: The Emergence of Contemporary Spirituality*. New York: Brunner-Routledge, 2004.

Bibliography

Thoreau, Henry David. "Walden." In *Walden and Civil Disobedience*, edited by Paul Lauter, 39–264. Boston: Houghton Mifflin, 2000.

Tickle, John. *Discovering the Bible: 8 Simple Keys for Learning and Praying, Book One*. Liguori, MO: Liguori Publications, 1977.

———. *Discovering the Bible: 8 Simple Keys for Learning and Praying, Book Two*. Liguori, MO: Liguori Publications, 1980.

Tillich, Paul. *Dynamics of Faith*. New York: Harper, 1957.

United States Conference of Catholic Bishops (USCCB). *Brothers and Sisters to Us*. Washington, DC: USCCB, 1979.

———. *Co-Workers in the Vineyard of the Lord: A Resource for Guiding the Development of Lay Ecclesial Ministry*. Washington, DC: USCCB, 2005.

———. *Renewing the Vision: A Framework for Catholic Youth Ministry*. Washington, DC: USCCB, 1997.

———. *Sons and Daughters of the Light: A Pastoral Plan for Ministry with Young Adults*. Washington, DC: USCCB, 2012.

United States Conference of Catholic Bishops, and the Committee on Evangelization. *Go and Make Disciples: A National Plan and Strategy for Catholic Evangelization in the United States*. Washington, DC: USCCB, 2002.

Webber, Ruth, Andrew Singleton, Marie R. Joyce, and Arrigo Dorissa. "Models of Youth Ministry in Action: The Dynamics of Christian Youth Ministry in an Australian City." *Religious Education* 105 (2010) 204–15.

White, David F. *Practicing Discernment with Youth: A Transformative Youth Ministry Approach*. Cleveland: Pilgrim, 2005.

Whitehead, Evelyn Eaton, and James D. Whitehead. *Christian Life Patterns: The Psychological Challenges and Religious Invitations of Adult Life*. New York: Crossroad, 2001.

Whitehead, James D., and Evelyn E. Whitehead. *Method in Ministry: Theological Reflection and Christian Ministry*. San Francisco: Harper Collins, 1990.

Zalot, Josef D., and Benedict Guevin. *Catholic Ethics in Today's Word*. Winona, MN: Anselm Academic, 2011.

Epilogue

> *Build your lives on one model that will not deceive you. . . . Open the Gospel and discover that Jesus Christ wants to be your "friend" (cf. John 15:14). [Jesus] wants to be your "companion" at every stage on the road of life (cf. Luke 24:13–35). [Jesus] wants to be the "way," your path through the anxieties, doubts, hopes, and dreams of happiness (cf. John 14:6). [Jesus] wants to be your God (cf. Matthew 16:13–17).*[1]
>
> Pope John Paul II
World Youth Day, 1995

As Pope John Paul II reminds us above, although there may be many models for the Christian community to use to help facilitate personal faith and communal spirituality, such as those discussed earlier in the book by various theologians' models of Jesus (John F. O'Grady), models of the church (Avery Dulles), models of Eucharist (Kevin W. Irwin), models of God (Sallie McFague), and now models for Christian youth and young adult ministry. Ultimately, there is truly only *one* paradigm for the Christian faith to follow—Jesus the Christ. Nevertheless, it would be unwise and shortsighted if there were no mention of other possible models of youth and young adult ministry for the future.

Possible Future Models

The future is ripe for Christian youth and young adult ministry and the four models presented in this book are certainly not exhaustive by any means.

---

1. *Sons and Daughters*, vi. The actual quote is from Pope John Paul II, *Message of the Holy Father*, at the World Youth Day Mass in Luenta Park on Sunday, January 15, 1995.

Epilogue

Again, the four models addressed in this survey are: (1) the biblical-hermeneutic, (2) the servant-leadership, (3) the liberation, and (4) the Christian discipleship. I would like to propose several more models, perhaps for a sequel to this book or maybe simply for other pastoral theologians to contemplate and refine.

There are a variety of models that would work well within Christian youth and young adult ministry, but would also be extremely suitable and ecumenical for other Christian denominations. Like all the models discussed in this book, there are strengths and limitations to the following models. However, the focus here is simply to introduce youth and young adult ministers and the readers to other possibilities, with the caveat being that each model must have its own theology, and the ability to be integrated into parish youth ministry, college campus ministry, and young adult ministry, and possess several pastoral implementation strategies.

There are a few additional models for consideration for youth and young adult ministers to study, integrate, and implement into their ministry with young people. Some possible other models are as follows: (1) the friendship model, (2) the liturgical-initiation model, (3) the Marian model, (4) the service and social justice model, (5) the pastoral care and counseling model, and (6) the Christian leadership model.

Each of these models could be integrated into youth and young adult ministries. All of these models are also highly ecumenical, except for the Marian model, which would unfortunately attract only Catholic, Orthodox, and Anglican Christians, and of course, that would be a real shame. At this time, I have only begun to work on a couple of these models, but most likely in the near future I will begin actively researching, writing, and presenting workshops on these models.

About the Author

Arthur David Canales, DMin, is a third generation Mexican-American. Art and his wife Tanya have three children: Alex, Anna, and Albert. They live in Indianapolis, Indiana, where Art is associate professor of pastoral theology and ministry at Marian University. He is considered one of the foremost Catholic adolescent ministry scholars and educators in the United States.

He began his education career at Ohio University (Athens), and transferred and earned a bachelor's degree from Florida International University (Miami), Master of Arts from University of Miami (Coral Gables), Master of Divinity from the Catholic University of America (Washington, DC), Master of Arts in Liturgical Studies from the University of Notre Dame (South Bend), and a Doctor of Ministry from the Catholic University of America (Washington, DC) with a major emphasis in pastoral theology and liturgical and sacramental theology, and a minor concentration in pastoral care and counseling. His doctoral dissertation is titled, *Toward a Theological, Liturgical, and Pastoral Understanding of Sunday Parish Worship with Deacon and/or Lay Presiders* (CUA Press).

Art has previously served as a parish youth minister (Miami, Florida; Washington, DC; and Beltsville, Maryland), a college campus minister (Coral Gables, Florida), diocesan director of youth and young adult ministry (Austin, Texas), and as an assistant/associate professor of theology and ministry at Silver Lake College of the Holy Family (Manitowoc, Wisconsin) and Saint Edward's University (Austin, Texas). Art is also the creator of and an instructor for the Diocese of Austin's Youth Ministry Certification Program.

Dr. Canales has written over forty pastoral/theological educational essays for the Manitowoc, Wisconsin, *Herald Times Reporter* (2000–2006). He has written over thirty scholarly articles for various publications. He has contributed a chapter titled "Early Adolescence: Venturing toward a

About the Author

Different World" in the book *Human Development and Faith: Life-Cycle Stages of Body, Mind, and Soul* (Chalice Press, 2015). He is coauthor of *Keeping the Cup Full: Financial Stewardship for Teens and Young Adults* (Cornerstone Financial Education, 2009) and author of *A Noble Quest: Cultivating Spirituality in Catholic Adolescents* (PCG Legacy, 2011).

Dr. Canales is a member of National Association of Catholic Youth Ministry Leaders (USA), the Association of Youth Ministry Educators (USA), and the International Association for the Study of Youth Ministry (UK). He is involved with the National Initiative on Adolescent Catechesis (USA) and is a consultant for *Fe y Vida* (USA). Dr. Canales is a contributing editor to a joint USCCB and NFCYM document titled *The Joy of Adolescent Catechesis: A Letter to Those Who Minister with Catholic Teenagers in the United States*. Moreover, Dr. Canales is a member of the editorial board of the *International Journal of Sports and Christianity*. Finally, he is an AAPC certified pastoral counselor and a member of the American Association of Pastoral Counselors (USA).

Dr. Canales has presented over twenty-five keynote speeches and over one hundred workshops, seminars, and academic papers in more than thirty-five dioceses around the country and abroad. He is a highly sought-after keynote speaker and a popular workshop presenter on areas of Christian discipleship, pastoral theology, stewardship, and youth ministry. Currently, Dr. Canales is working on issues that focus on ministering to, with, and for LGBTQ Christian youth. He also provides ministry mentoring and pastoral supervision with youth ministers and campus ministers throughout the Archdiocese of Indianapolis and around the country.

Index

absolute mystery (God),
    experiencing, 126
academic adolescent ministry
    scholars, 16
academic calendar, 141–42
acceptance, within servant-
    leadership, 64
"acculturation," compared to
    inculturation, 96n25
action, models as modes of, 31
action-reflection, 142n84
A.D. (2015) television mini-series, 51
adolescence
    defined, 6
    distinguishing emerging adults
        and young adults from, 7
    focusing liberation theology on,
        92–93
    representing a transition, 3
adolescent catechesis, 42
adolescent ministry scholar, author
    as, 2
adolescents
    as advocates of liberation
        theology, 91
    ages of, 4
    defined, 5
    developing into authentic
        Christian disciples, 149
    growing up in a culturally diverse
        society, 100
    lives in constant flux, 131
    from various racial and ethnic
        cultures, 101

adult catechists, becoming servant-
    leaders, 83
adult education principles
    (andragogy), 68
African-American young adult
    ministry, 59
agape, 75
ageism, 91
Agosto, Efrain, 66, 78, 81
Aguilera-Titus, Alejandro, 101, 102
Ahasuerus (Xerxes I), 50
alienation, leading to division, 160
all-of-us-together languages, 102
Almsgiving, 48
anawim (those overwhelmed by want
    and poverty), 47, 66
Anderson, Ray S., 21
andragogy, 68, 68n30
apartheid, 96n25
Arnett, Jeffrey J., 7
articulation, around servant-
    leadership principles, 67
artists, loving what they create, 135
Arzola, Fernando, Jr., 95
Asian minorities, teaching, 109
Association of Youth Ministry
    Educators, 16
authoritarian powers, keeping world
    religions from dialogue, 103
auto-theme biography, 108
awareness
    coming with young adulthood, 9
    as a servant-leadership
        characteristic, 69

Index

baptism, 124
Barabbas (1964), 50
Beatitude principle, faithfulness to, 48
Beatitudes, acting out, 46
believer, disciple synonymous with, 128
Ben Hur (1949), 50
Pope Benedict XVI, 32
Bergler, Thomas E., 7
Bevans, Stephen B.
   on models of contextual theology, 19, 20
   on participating in theology contextually, 106
   work on models, 16
Bible. *See also* Scripture
   authoritative to Catholics first and foremost, 17n2
   as the book itself, 33
   capitalized to demonstrate respect, 32
   daily reading and meditating of, 44
   indispensable for youth and young adult ministers, 34
   interpreting from the margins, 40
   knowledge areas supported by the RTV, 41–42
   as a living word, 36
   as necessary for a youth and young adult minister, 39–40
   as object of study, 35
   as a timeless book, 54, 55
   understanding and interpreting, 38
   uses of, 39
The Bible (2013) television mini-series, 51
Bible courses, coupling Scripture with discipleship, 143n85, 143–44
Bible pericope. *See* pericope
Bible studies, goals of, 37
Bible study theme, of Discipleship and the Scriptures, 143
Bible-centered, faith-sharing groups, leadership of, 38
"biblical," as a term, 33

biblical characters, exhibiting servant-leadership, 80
biblical cinema series, ten-week, 49–50
biblical criticisms, 56, 56n25–57n25
biblical curriculum, 42
"Biblical Heritage" course, 51n24
biblical images, of servant, 64
biblical interpretation
   as deductive, 39
   illustrated, 38
   individual and denominational, 56
   learning, 43
biblical message, helping young people absorb, 35
biblical narratives, 27, 35
biblical roots, of servant-leadership, 80
biblical spirituality, 43–44, 54
biblical text, exegeting, 43
biblical themes, four-week series on various, 45–46
biblical values and gospel principles (*koinonia*), creating a community on, 130
biblical-hermeneutic approach, steps of, 46
biblical-hermeneutic method, integration into ministry, 40–43
biblical-hermeneutic model, 32–59
   biblical themes mentioned in, 51n24
   characteristics of, 29
   described, 27
   essentials of, 36–37
   facilitating adolescents and young adults learning, 38
   facilitating young people's faith-life experience, 59
   strengths and limitations of, 53–57
biblical-hermeneutical circle, 37–40
Bonhoeffer, Dietrich, 120, 126
Borgman, Dean, 10, 43
Bosco, John, 141

Index

bounding circle, 128
"breaking new ground," theological task of, 18
builder of community, as a servant-leadership characteristic, 69

Cahalan, Kathleen A., 22
"cardinal," deriving from the Latin word *cardo*, 70n38
cardinal virtues, listed, 71n38
Carotta, Michael, 129
case studies
    based upon real scenarios, 31
    for the biblical-hermeneutic model, 57–59
    for Christian discipleship, 151–53
    for the liberation model, 116–17
    for the servant-leadership model, 85–86
catechetical series, welcoming an Asian population, 109–11
Catechism of the Catholic Church (CCC), 124, 124n13
The Catholic Bible: Personal Study Edition, 34n5
Catholic Bishops (US). *See* US Catholic Bishops
Catholic Church
    high regard for other world religions, 102–3
    Vatican II changed the face of, 17n2
Catholic faith community, drawing young people to participate in, 156
Catholic insights, on youth ministry and young adult ministry, 2
Catholic young people, exposed to discipleship in various ways, 122
CCC. *See Catechism of the Catholic Church* (CCC)
Cesar Chavez: Mexican-American Labor Leader (1995), 78
cessation, truth of, 110n74

The Challenge of Adolescent Catechesis: Maturing in Faith, 42
The Challenge of Discipleship (Kielbasa), 147
character and disposition, change in, 126
Chavez, Cesar E., 78
choices, for emerging adults, 7
Christ. *See* Jesus Christ
"Christian apologist," 159
Christian catechesis, as *sine qua non* (absolutely indispensable) for Christian discipleship, 124
Christian Church, mission of, 10
Christian disciples. *See also* disciple
    empowering young people to live as, 156
    as made, not born, 129
    task of raising-up, 153
Christian discipleship. *See also* Christian discipleship model; discipleship
    allowing young people to experience God, 123
    case study, 151–53
    components of, 130–39
    conversion process fostering, 132
    described, 122
    developing a theology of, 124–29
    elements of, 140
    as an expansive area of inquiry, 150–51
    as an experience in the risen Christ, 128
    fostering through leadership initiatives, 146
    as the foundation for all other models, 121
    at the heart of all ministries, 124
    implementing, 149
    integrating a two-year curriculum, 152
    methodologies for implementation of, 140–41
    only a few components of usually stressed, 151

Index

Christian discipleship (*continued*)
    as a paradigm and measuring-stick of Christian living, 149
    as a practical and lived theology, 129
    practical theology and model of praxis for, 130–39
    prayer essential in cultivating, 135
    as the primordial model, 120, 153
    as a "radical" call to follow Jesus Christ, 150
    situating in youth and young adult ministry, 121–24
    theological categories of, 139–40
"The Christian Discipleship and Leadership Challenge," sessions of, 147
Christian discipleship model, 120–53. *See also* Christian discipleship
    characteristics of, 29
    described, 28
    implementation strategies, 141–48
    implementing, 152–53
    making good theological and pastoral sense, 153
    as the primordial model, 121
    strengths and limitations of, 149–51
    teleological (end) goal of, 120–21
Christian faith. *See* faith
Christian identity, spirituality, and faith, increasing, 11
Christian leadership, learning about the major models of, 146
Christian leadership institute, 146–47
Christian leadership model, 172
Christian ministries, as the work of God, 21–22
Christian paradigms, 28
Christian precedents, for appropriating Scripture, 35
Christian service, levels of, 136
Christian stories, teaching with an Asian "twist," 110
Christian theological response, to a given lived reality, 90
Christian unity, call to, 159
Christian youth and young adult ministry. *See* youth and young adult ministry
Christianity, as exclusivist, 104
Christians, in dialogue with people from other religions, 103
Christology
    models for, 18
    types of, 109n72
Chupungco, Anscar, 98
Church
    connecting young adults with, 123
    mission of, 1, 156
    models of, 16–18
cinema, introducing servant-leadership themes, 76
cinema series, offering, 78–79
circle of servant-leadership, 83–84
circle of trust, creating, 69
Civil Rights Movement, foundation laid forth by, 115
classic Christology, difficulty with, 109n72
coercion approach, to leadership, 63
cognitive development, of middle adolescents, 93
collaborative facet, of ministry, 158–59
commitment, 70, 125
Committed Traditionalist type, of emerging adult, 8
community
    building at various levels, 69
    characterized by gospel values, 130
    defined, 5
    referring to youth and young adult ministry, 101
    role in discipleship, 131
community component, of Christian discipleship, 130–31
community of disciples model, of the church, 17
compassion, 71, 82
Compassion in Exile (1992), 78

Index

"comprehensive," describing the approach to ministry with Christian young people, 121
comprehensive youth and young adult ministry, 157
conceptualization, as a servant-leadership characteristic, 70
congregational ministers, knowing core young people, 159
congregational-life committees and councils, young people taking initiative in, 68
congregation/congregations, defined, 5
contextual theology, 20, 106
contextualization, as the *sine qua non* (absolutely necessary) process, 106–7
contextualization process, of Christianity, 97
conversion component, of Christian discipleship, 131–32
conversion process, steps in, 131
cost, of commitment for God, 125–26
The Cost of Discipleship (Bonhoeffer), 140
Cousins, Ewert H., 21
Covenant, summer weekly gathering focusing on, 52
Co-Workers in the Vineyard of the Lord (USCCB), 125n17
Creation, four-week series on, 45
Crosby, Michael, 46
cross-cultural experiences, 113
cultivation, of servant-leadership, 67
cultural diversity, 113, 160
cultural information and social sciences, importance of, 24
cultural minority, sociohistorical context of, 108
cultural or racial backgrounds, exchange among different, 99
culturally diverse facet, of ministry, 160–61
culture
   in Asian countries, 110n73

instilling the gospel into contemporary, 97
stages of, 99–100

Dalai Lama, 60, 78
Daloz-Parks, Sharon, 9
David, movie about, 50
Day, Dorothy, 78
day of reflection, focusing on prayer, 142–43
de Kock, Jos, 113
De La Torre, Miguel A., 39, 118
deanery, 157
Delilah, 50
denominational bigotry, leaving behind, 160
denominational contexts, for ministerial work, 23
desire, truth of, 110n74
destiny, as the ultimate goal for a servant-leader, 84
Deus impossibilia non iubet ("God does not command the impossible"), 135
development, of servant-leadership systems, 67
"developmental" learning, 113
developmental themes, for youth and young adult ministry, 104
diakonia (Greek), 11–12, 136
differences, perceiving as reasons for growth and complementarily, 99
dignity, connected to the reality of being human, 63
dimensions
   of Christian discipleship, 129
   of praxis-based education, 74n46
disciple. *See also* Christian disciples
   "following" Jesus, 122
   meaning of, 28
   as synonymous with the word believer, 128
discipleship. *See also* Christian discipleship
   categories of, 130n35
   discussing the themes of, 142

Index

discipleship (*continued*)
  echoing the Christian faith (catechesis), 124
  establishing, 39
  expanding and contracting, 127
  involving a cost, 126
  living a life of, 124
  predominant paradigm for Christians, 28, 122
Discipleship in the New Testament (Segovia), 144
Discovering the Bible: 8 Simple Keys for Learning and Praying, Book One (Tickle), 51n24
Discovering the Bible: 8 Simple Keys for Learning and Praying, Book Two (Tickle), 51n24
"Discovering the Bible through Film" cinema series, 49
disenfranchised, realism of, 118
diversity
  embracing unity in, 161
  inculturation affirming, 98
dogmas, attesting to Christ's divineness, 109n72
domus ecclesia ("domestic church"), community and, 131
Downie, Alison, 103–4
dreaming, by youth and young adult ministers, 81
dukha, truth of, 110n74
Dulles, Avery, 16–18, 22

early adolescence, defined, 6
early adolescents, defined, 5
ecclesial dogmas and doctrines, dissemination to cultures of other religious traditions, 97
ecclesial integration, Christian denominations embracing, 160
ecclesial ministry, models of, 30
ecclesiastical community, interpreting sacred texts, 33, 38
ecumenical facet, of ministry, 159
ecumenism, present impasses, 18

Eightfold Path of Enlightenment and Liberation, 110n74
Eleanor Roosevelt: A Restless Spirit (1994) documentary, 79
Election, focusing on, 52
emerging adult tribes, Bergler's, 8
emerging adult value shifting, markers for, 9
Emerging Adulthood (Arnett), 7
emerging adults
  ages of, 4
  defined, 6, 7–10
  lives in constant flux, 131
  US Catholic Bishops' documents for, 42
emerging adults and young adults, driving force of, 93–94
empathy, within servant-leadership, 64, 70
Empowered by the Spirit: Campus Ministry Faces the Future, 86
Empowered by the Spirit: Empowering Campus Ministry, 42
empowerment, of servant-leadership, 67
"enculturation," compared to inculturation, 96n25
Entertaining Angels: The Dorothy Day Story (1997) movie, 78
environment, respecting, 72
Esther (1999), 50
ethical and social justice standards, in the Scriptures, 37
ethnic diversity, as cultural gifts, 99
ethnicities, all benefiting from the Asian culture, 111
Eucharist, models of, 19
Evening of Reflection, planning an ecumenical, 75
exclusivism, 104
experience of God, 126, 127
experiential leadership development, 134
experiential living (*lex vivendi*), 124
experimental models, for youth and young adult ministers, 22

Index

faith
    coming from God's revealing word, 35
    emerging adults keeping their options open, 8
    fostering within the lives of young people, 132
    as a gift from God, 133
    growing and maturing, 59
    in Jesus, 128
    living a life of, 125
    one paradigm for, 171
    understanding in terms of a particular context, 106
faith component, of Christian discipleship, 132–33
faith-sharing groups, formed around various populations, 108–9
Faix, Tobias, 106–7
Fassati, Pier Giorgio, 141
female adolescents and young adults, engaging in self-reflection, 108
feminist Hispanics, 108
feminist models and interpretations of God, 19–20
Ferch, Shann, 63
field trip, to a mosque, 113
Fields, Doug, 12–13
film series, on biblically based themes or persons, 49
"first-person" thinking and awareness, moving to abstract abilities, 93
Five Pillars of Islam, 112
flower petal image, for servant-leadership, 84
foresight, as a servant-leadership characteristic, 70
form criticism, 56n25–57n25
Four Noble Truths, 110, 110n74
4 Little Girls (1998) documentary, 111
Francis of Assisi: Performing the Gospel Life (Cunningham), 140
Francis Zaire Washington case study, 57–59

friendship model, 172
friendship-maintaining community, enhancing, 130–31
fundamentalism, 56, 115

Gallio, Marcellus, 50
Gandhi (1982) movie, 78
Gandhi, Mohandas, 75, 78
global awareness, transforming people, 81
Gloria Catalina Sanchez case study, 116
goal setting or finding, as the prime requirement of leadership, 81
God
    addressing youth and young adults through the Scriptures, 54
    as the artist of everything, 135
    available to everyone, 126
    caring more about the person, 13
    Christian ministries as the work of, 21–22
    experiencing, 126–27
    having a deep abiding commitment for, 125–26
    revealing God's self to the people, 34
God's call, 124–25, 139
Golden Rule, encapsulating, 87
Gonzaga, Aloysius, 141
Goretti, Maria, 141
Gospel Advancing View of Youth Ministry (Stier), 39
Gospel message, sharing, 41
gospel priority, in youth gatherings, 39
Gospels
    depicting Jesus as a servant-leader, 64
    knowledge for adolescents suggested by the *RTV*, 42
Gotama the Buddha, similarities with Jesus Christ, 110
Great Servant-Leaders Series, 78, 79
The Greatest Story Ever Told (1965), 50

Index

Greenleaf, Robert K.
    encapsulating servant-leadership, 65
    as the "founder" of servant-leadership, 61
    on the inward journey of the servant-leader, 84
    on the leader seen as servant first, 61
    modeled servant-leadership after the ministry of Jesus of Nazareth, 64
    on servant-leaders, 81
Greenleaf Center for Servant-Leadership, 73
guerilla warfare, liberation theology and, 92
Gutiérrez, Gustavo, 28, 88, 90, 107

habits, conjuring negative images, 71n38
hajj (the once in a lifetime journey to Mecca), 112
healing, as a servant-leadership characteristic, 71
hermeneutic
    of a crucified people, 110
    as a term, 33
hermeneutical circle, 33, 38
hermeneutical process, of interpreting sacred Scripture, 34
Herrera, Marina, 99
high descending approach, to Christology in John, 109n72
high school years, defined, 6
historical criticism, 56n25
holiness, living the call of, 128–29
Holy Spirit, 131, 138
holy young people, lives of, 141
homosexual people, 111, 117
horizon, changing one's, 127–28
hospitality, facets of, 104
"hyper-connected generation," 7
Hypostatic Union, Dogma on, 109n72

I Ching (perfect realization of Change), recognizing Jesus the Christ as, 110
imago Dei (the image and likeness of God), 13
Imam (Muslim minister), 113
immersion trip, experiencing a third-world country, 145
inculturation, 96–99
    compared to acculturation and enculturation, 96n25
    cultivating open-minded evangelization and catechesis, 98
    dimensions of, 97
    as helpful to youth and young adult ministry, 98
    leading to the principle of independence, 99
    as necessary, 97, 99
    as significant to youth and young adult ministry, 98
    within a liberation framework, 95
independence, principle of, 99
indigenous communities, situating the message of Jesus to, 98
initial calling, to serve neighbor as a disciple, 125
Innocence of Muslims (2012), 112
instability, as a theme for emerging adults, 9
integration, liberation principles for, 105
intellectual conversion, 132
intercultural ministry, 160–61
International Association for the Study of Youth Ministry, 16
interreligious openness
    Downie's schemata for, 104
    importance of, 102–5
    within a liberation framework, 95
introspection and self-awareness, leading to self-discovery and transformation, 142n84
invitation, from God to serve God, 124
Irreligious type, of emerging adult, 8

Index

Irwin, Kevin W., 16, 19
Islam, month-long series on, 112–13
Islam, as a multifaceted Arabic word, 112n79
Islam: Empire of Faith (2000), 112

Jackson Johnson ministry vignette, 25
Jesus and Prayer, focusing on, 143
Jesus Christ
    attachment to, 126
    as an authentic servant-leader, 81
    biblical-hermeneutical model used by, 34
    calling Christians to the fullness of Christian life, 125
    as the centerpiece of the Christian religion, 54
    claimed his own authority, 34
    connecting young adults with, 123
    as the definitive servant-leader for Greenleaf, 65
    following, 129, 171
    as a human person first, 109n72
    issues of imitating, 122
    on the kingdom of God belonging to young people, 155
    leading by serving others, 27
    message as a servant-leader, 64–65
    models of, 18–19
    movie on, 50
    as the primordial sacrament of God, 121
    primus inter pares or first among equals, 65
    putting servant-leadership into fundamental practice, 81
    as the quintessential servant-leader, 77–78
    situating in an Asian context, 109
    as the ultimate servant-leader, 64
    as unifying center of Christian discipleship, 28
    wanting to be your "friend," 171
    washing the feet of the Twelve, 65
    young people becoming his disciples, 140
    young people developing personal faith in, 132
Jesus Christ Superstar (1973), 50
Jesus of Nazareth (1976) film, 49, 78
Jesus' Sermon on the Mount or Beatitudes, focusing on, 46–48
Jesus the Person Incarnate, 33
"Jesus the Ultimate Servant-Leader," example six-week series, 78
Jewish slaves, washing the feet of another person, 65
Jihad, 112
Joan of Arc, 141
Pope John Paul II, 128, 171
Joseph, biblical story of, 50
Joseph in Egypt (1995), 50
journey, conversion referred to as, 131
Judeo-Christian heritage, four-week series on, 46
justice, 47, 103

Kageler, Len, 104–5, 105n58
Kelly, Margaret, 62
Kielbasa, Marilyn, 147
King, Martin Luther, Jr., 75, 100
King David (1985), 50
Kowalska, Mary Faustina, 141

language of the heart, prayer as, 135
Las Hermanas (The Sisters), on the spirituality of liberation of women, 108
late adolescence, defined, 6
Latin America, majority both poor and Christian, 88
Law, summer weekly gathering focusing on, 52
lay ecclesial minister, 85
Layla Kim case study, 151–53
leader, relationship with followers, 82
leadership
    based on serving, 66

Index

leadership (*continued*)
    development, 67, 133
    meanings of, 133
    prototypes of within Christianity, 134
    skills, 66, 133
    training for youth and young adults, 68
"learner" and "teacher" model, Christian discipleship treated as, 122
lectio divina (divine reading), 48
Left Behind (2014), 50
Left Behind Trilogy (2004), 49
Letter from Birmingham Jail (King), 75
lex vivendi (law of Christian living), 123, 124, 156
LGBTQ high school students, life experiences of, 111
liberation
    born of shared vision to abolish unjust situations, 28
    components of, 90–91
    emphasizing human response to the invitation of salvation, 27–28
    as an excellent model, 91–92
    experienced as action, 40
    integrating and implementing, 115–16
    modeled on the ministry of Jesus of Nazareth, 114
    as a movement within Latin America and with minority groups, 114–15
    as a paradigm within the Christian experience, 116
    practical components of, 118
    reminding United States citizens of civic responsibility, 115
    as a spiritual journey, 95
    themes of, 89
    as theologically and pastorally relevant, 115
    truth of, 110n74
liberation ministry, with youth and young adults, 94–96
liberation model, 88–119
    characteristics of, 29
    described, 27–28
    engendering hope and justice to minorities, 117
    focus of, 106
    as an integrative approach, 118
    methodological strategies for implementation of, 107
    moving youth culture to a culture of grace and mercy, 93
    principles integrating into Christian youth ministry, 94
    strength and limitations of, 114–16
liberation motifs, 28
liberation principles, 96
liberation themes, integration of selective, 89
liberation theologian, catechizing, 107
liberation theology
    complementing and completing youth and young adult ministry, 89
    in the context of youth and young adult ministry, 90–92
    described, 28, 90
    dimensions of, 95
    dynamics of, 91
    emphasizing with emerging and young adults, 93–94
    first uttered by Gustavo Gutiérrez, 90
    focusing on adolescents, 92–93
    integrating into Christian youth and young adult ministry, 95
    not always seen in a positive light, 92
limitations
    of the biblical-hermeneutic model, 55–57
    of the Christian discipleship model, 150–51
    of the liberation model, 115–16

Index

of the servant-leadership model, 82–83
listening, 27, 71
literary criticism, 57n25
liturgical (public) prayer, 135
liturgical (worship) ministry, 159
liturgical-initiation model, 172
Live to Tell (1995) movie, 111
lived reality, discipleship as, 129
locations, for Bible studies, 37–38
Lonergan, Bernard J. F., 127–28, 132
Lorenzen, Thorwald, 16, 19, 20
Love, summer weekly gathering focusing on, 52
low ascending Christology, 109, 109n72

Malcom X (1990), 112
Mandela, Nelson, 79
Mandela the Man (1996) documentary, 79
Marian model, 172
marriage, adulthood beginning with, 8
Martin Luther King Jr.: A Historical Perspective (2002), 75
Marxism, liberation theology and, 92
mathetes, meaning "disciple" of "pupil," 122
Matthew, relevance of the Gospel of, 47
McFague, Sallie, 16, 19–20
meaning of one's life, 9
Medina, Lara, 108
meekness and violence, focus on, 47
mercy, focus on, 47
Mere Discipleship: Radical Christianity in a Rebellious World (Camp), 140
The Message (1977), 112
Messiah, summer weekly gathering focusing on, 52
metanoia and conversion, 36, 36n6
methodological strategies, using within a liberation model, 114
methodology, for youth and young adult ministry, 23–25

middle adolescence, defined, 5, 6
middle adolescents, 93
middle school years, defined, 6
minister, of youth and young adults, 11–13
ministering, to culturally and ethnically diverse young people, 101–2
ministry. *See also* youth and young adult ministry
facets of, 157–61
improving the quality of, 23
model for, 15
put forward by God's initiative and God's personal ministry of revelation, 21
situating an exact model within youth and young adult ministry, 25
understood as service or *diakonia* (Greek), 11–12
of youth and young adults, 10–11
minjung ("the popular mass"), Jesus as, 110
mission, within youth and young adult ministry, 101
mission of the church, connecting young adults with, 123
mission relief organization, trip in conjunction with, 145
mission trip, 98, 145
missional typology, describing "tribes" of emerging adults, 8
missionary activity, respecting indigenous culture, 97
models
benefits of, 156
for Christian youth and young adult ministry, 21–23, 25–30
of the Church, 16–18
creation of new, 30
of the Eucharist, 19
investigative use of, 18
of Jesus, 18–19
for ministry, 15
other theological, 19–21
possible future, 171–72

Index

models (*continued*)
   presented in this book, 156
   understanding and mastering, 16
   for youth and young adult ministry, 20–21, 30, 155
"Models for Adolescent Ministry: Exploring Eight Ecumenical Examples" (Canales), 120n2
"Models of Christian Leadership" course, 62n8–63n8
Models of Contextual Theology: Faith and Cultures (Bevans), 19
Models of God: Theology for an Ecological, Nuclear Age (McFague), 19
Models of Jesus (O'Grady), 18–19
Models of Revelation (Dulles), 17
Models of the Church (Dulles), 16–17
Models of the Eucharist (Irwin), 19
Mooz-lum (2010), 112
moral conversion, 132
moral instruction, 134
"moral" virtues, 71n38
morality component, of Christian discipleship, 134–35
Mordecai, 50
Mother Theresa, 78
Mother Theresa (1986) documentary, 78
mourning and comfort, focus on, 47
movies
   allowing empathy and compassion for minority groups, 111
   following-up with theological reflection and small group faith-sharing questions, 51
   highlighting servant-leadership themes, 76
Moyaert, Marianne, 104
multicultural and a multi-faith society, 105
multiculturalism, 99–102
   as a component of liberation theology, 100
   fostering a spirit of, 111
   within a liberation framework, 95

Muslim, 112n79
Muslim mosque, field trip to, 113
Muslims, introducing the worship life of, 113

National Catholic Young Adult Ministry Association, 158
National Federation for Catholic Youth Ministry, 158
"new period," emerging adulthood as, 9
non-Christians, spiritual and moral truths found among, 103
non-liturgical (personal) prayer, 135
Nostra Aetate, 102–3
nurturing, servant-leadership concepts, 67

Ocean of Wisdom (1991), 78
O'Grady, John F., 16, 18–19
Old Testament, knowledge for adolescents suggested by the RTV, 42
One-on-One Retreat, 147–48
oppressed peoples, emancipating, 28
oppressive governments, keeping world religions from dialogue, 103
oppressors, loving, 75
oral tradition, preserving the narrative, 33
organizational change, within Christian youth and young adult ministry, 105
outdoor wilderness course, 145–46
outreach activities, 136
outside stimuli, shaping teenage values, 6

paradigm shift, making, 127
parish priests, knowing core young people, 159
parish/parishes, defined, 5
Paschal Mystery, identification with, 122

Index

pastoral activities, on non-catechetical nights, 47
pastoral care and counseling model, 172
pastoral community, 30–31
pastoral outcomes, 29, 30
pastoral work, 21
Apostle Paul, 44, 80–81
Paul and his letters, knowledge suggested by the *RTV*, 42
peace, making, 47
pedagogical strategies, on Christian discipleship, 148
peer community, connecting young adults with, 123
peer ministry
    developing, 68
    discipleship likened to, 122
peers, forming faith communities of, 131
people of God
    interpreting sacred texts, 33–34
    practicing their faith, 38
pericope
    daily reading and meditation upon a particular, 43
    defined, 33n3
    interpretations of, 35
persecution, from the world, 47
personal experience, importance of, 24
personal narratives, sharing, 108, 109
persuasion, as a servant-leadership characteristic, 72
Peter & Paul (1981), 49
Petralla, Ivan, 118
Phan, Peter C., 108
"plan of action," for a college and campus ministry, 85
Pontius Pilate, 50
poor in spirit, focus on, 47
poor monk, identifying Jesus as, 110
"poor religiousness," 109n73
pop-culture, using the Scriptures to dissect, 43
possessions, gaining more, 40

practical ministry, models focusing on, 16
practical theological interpretation, task of, 22
"the practice of interpretation," 43
pragmatic suggestions, regarding the Bible, 44
praxis, wedded to a particular context, 106
praxis-based education, 74, 74n46, 137, 137n70, 146
prayer
    component of Christian discipleship, 135–36
    day of reflection focusing on, 142–43
    making into a big deal, 39
    services concluding weekly summer sessions, 52
Premawardhana, Shantra D., 103
prescriptive method, providing tangible examples, 105
present moment, living in, 110n74
primordial, defined, 121
private prayer, focusing on, 143
"program leaders," defined, 67n26
prophetic spirituality, described, 95
Proverbs, reading from daily, 44
prudence, 70
psalm, reading one daily, 44
public prayer, focusing on, 143
purity of heart, achieving, 47
purposing leadership style, 72

Qur'an, 112n79

racial differences, as cultural gifts, 99
Rahner, Karl, 127
reality, models of, 16
redaction criticism, 57n25
Redemption, summer weekly gathering focusing on, 52
regional events, "boycotting," 158
reign of God, 47, 97
relational evangelism, equipping teenagers for, 39

Index

relational servant-leadership behavior, 77
relationship-making, community enhancing, 130–31
religious and spiritual matters, categories for emerging and young adults, 94
religious conversion, 132
religious fundamentalism, 56, 115
religious language and symbols, as models, 21
religious mystery, accessibility of, 21
religious object, taken to mean God, 104
religious other, forcing reflection on personal faith, 105
religious people, all committed to the same religious object, 104
religious types, of emerging adults, 8
Renewing the Vision: A Framework for Catholic Youth Ministry (1997), 41–42, 66, 86
resignation, as confirmed desperation, 63
Resurrection and Discipleship: Interpretive Models, Biblical, and Theological Consequences (Lorenzen), 19
Resurrection of Jesus, models for, 20
retreats. *See* weekend retreats
revelation
    Dulles's models of, 17
    summer weekly gathering focusing on, 52
revolutionary movements, liberation often confused with, 115
Riebe, Francette, 51n24
Rita Rutledge case study, 85–86
The Robe (1953), 50
rock climbing services, 146n93
Romero (1989) movie, 78
Romero, Oscar, movie on, 78
Roosevelt, Eleanor, 79
Root, Andrew, 24, 105–6
ropes courses, 145n92
Rosary, praying, 48–49

RTV. *See Renewing the Vision: A Framework for Catholic Youth Ministry* (1997)

"Sacra Pagina" (sacred page) retreat, 48
sacred Scripture
    integrating into youth and young adult ministry, 41
    interpreting, 34
    as *norma normas non normata* (the norm-giving norm that is not under any other norm), 54
    word of God interpreted as, 32
sacred text, preserving stories, 33
saints, as positive role models for young people, 141
Samson and Delilah (1949), 50
Savio, Dominic, 141
scope, determining educational aims, goals, and outcomes, 42
scriptural foundation, for young people, 43
scriptural themes, for weekly summer sessions, 52–53
Scripture. *See also* Bible
    all inspired by God, 45
    capitalized to demonstrate respect, 32
    consisting of real stories about real people, 54
    coupling discipleship with, 143
    "digging" deeper into, 44
    flexible character of, 54–55
    interpretations of individual pericopes of, 35
    liberation motif rooted in, 114
    living life according to, 37
    from a non-dominant youth and young adult ministry perspective, 40
    reading for personal transformation, 36
    study of, 58–59
    weaving into the curriculum, 25

Index

Scripture and tradition, as integral components for Christianity, 24
Scripture scholars, hermeneutics and, 33
Second Vatican Council (1962-65) (Vatican II), 17, 17n2, 102–3
secularization, 94
seeing God, blessedness of, 47
Segovia, Fernando F., 126, 144
Selective Adherents type, of emerging adult, 8
self-absorbed and self-centered existence, moving beyond, 63
self-actualization, 24, 131
self-actualizers, 142n84
self-awareness
    as a gradual process in young people, 119
    importance of, 43
    journey of, 69
    leading toward self-discovery, 54, 142n84
self-discovery, 54, 131, 142n84
self-preservation, concern with, 40
self-reflection, giving purpose, 108
sensus fidelium (sense of the faithful), 23
sequence, determining educational aims, goals, and outcomes, 42
"The Servant as Leader" (1970) (Greenleaf), 61
servant dimension, fundamental for servant-leadership, 66
servant-leader(s)
    attributes of, 81
    exploring the life of a heroic, 75
    famous, 76
    goals and, 81
    inward journey of, 84
    Jesus as, 77
    rising above and beyond personal weaknesses, 80–81
    traits characterizing, 62
    youth and young adult ministers viewing themselves as, 83
servant-leadership
    attributes of, 80
    backbones of, 27
    background on, 61–62
    biblical foundations and theology of, 64–66
    crucial characteristics, 81
    curriculum, 86
    definition of, 62–63
    difficult to put into practice, 83
    empowering integrity and dignity, 63
    experts, inviting to speak, 79
    familiarity with the philosophy and principles of, 82
    foci in the Franciscan tradition, 63–64
    goal of integrating, 67
    helping young people become empowered, 82
    ideals, 63
    implementing pedagogical and pastoral methodologies for, 73
    integrating into a campus ministry, 86
    as a model for youth and young adult ministry, 73
    as part of global awareness, 81
    pedagogy, 75
    as a philosophical concept or a leadership construct, 83
    putting the subordinate first, 64
    situating in youth and young adult ministry, 66–72
    studying, 73
    themes, previewing in movies, 77
    theological characteristics of, 68–73
    as a theory, 63
    traced back to Jesus of Nazareth's public ministry, 134
    traits offering a framework, 62
    types of behavior, 77
    young people highlighting small acts of, 76
Servant-Leadership (Greenleaf), 73

Index

Servant-Leadership: A Journey into the Nature of Legitimate Power and Greatness (Greenleaf), 61, 82
Servant-Leadership: Jesus & Paul (Agosto), 78
servant-leadership model, 60–87
    characteristics of, 29
    as a community of equals, 83
    described, 27
    strengths and limitations of, 80–83
servant-leadership project, organizing and implementing, 74–75
servant-leadership theory, premise of, 63
servants, youth and young adult ministers as, 11
service, benefits for young people, 137
service and social justice model, 172
service component, of Christian discipleship, 136–37
service learning, social justice learning not tantamount to, 137n68
service projects, empowering others to transform their lives, 136
service-learning experiences, young people leading, 74
service-type ministry, 159
sin, summer weekly gathering focusing on, 52
small acts of servant-leadership, examples of, 76n51
Smith, Christian, 8, 94
Smolarski, Dennis C., 66
social justice learning, 137, 137n68
social level, liberation theology impacting adolescents on, 91
social service projects, involvement in, 136–37
Sola Scriptura, as rallying cry of Protestants, 53–54
solution-finding, adopting attitude of, 62

Sons and Daughters of the Light: A Pastoral Plan for Ministry with Young Adults, 42, 86
Sons and Daughters (US Conference of Catholic Bishops), 10n22, 123–24
South American liberation theology, of Gustavo Gutiérrez, 28
Sower and the Seed, Jesus' parable about, 59
Spear, Karen, 63
Spears, Larry C., 68
spiritual awakening, coming to, 69
spiritual communal meditation, 48
spiritual leadership, traced back to Jesus of Nazareth's public ministry, 134
spiritual maturity, helping emerging adults reach, 7–8
spirituality
    of discipleship, 102
    of openness, 103
    path to, 138–39
Spirituality of the Beatitudes: Matthew's Challenge for First World Christians (Crosby), 46
Spiritually Open type, of emerging adult, 8
status quo, maintaining, 40
stewardship, 64, 72
Stier, Greg, 39
stories
    helping youth share, 39
    telling of tragic, 108
strangers, welcoming, 161
The Strangest Way: Walking the Christian Path (Barron), 140
strategies
    for Christian discipleship, 141–48
    facilitating a quality servant-leadership curriculum, 74–80
    for implementation of the biblical hermeneutic method, 45–53
    for implementing the liberation model, 108–13
strengths

Index

of the biblical-hermeneutic
model, 53–55
of the Christian discipleship
model, 149
of the liberation model, 114–15
of the servant-leadership model,
80–82
subordinate, putting first, 27
suburban youth, entering into a
liberation motif, 96
suffering, putting an end to, 110n74
Suffering Servant motif, 110
summer months, service and
leadership during, 144
summer weekly youth and young
adult gatherings, focusing
on various biblical themes,
51–53
Sunday Eucharist, focusing on, 143
Sunday worship, constituting several
areas of prayer, 136
Synoptic Gospels, as distinct from the
Gospel of John, 109n72

task servant-leadership behavior, 77
teacher(s), in young adult ministry,
122
teenage values, outside influences
shaping, 6
"teenage years." *See* adolescence
teenagers, 5, 91
The Ten Commandments (1956), 49
10 percent rule, adhering to, 39
terms, defining, 4–13
textual criticism, 56n25
theologians, 16, 171
theological categories
of Christian discipleship, 150
integration of, 129–39
theological framework, for youth and
young adult ministers, 88
theological models
helping situate and better
understand the practice of
ministry, 22
used by Dulles, 17

theological models and methods,
15–31
theological objectives, 29, 30
theological organizing frameworks,
models as, 31
theological reflection
assisting youth pastors and young
adult ministers, 23
described, 137n69
encouraging, 111
framing movies theologically and
socially, 76–77
on ministry experiences, 137
model of, 15
theology
designating, 39
importance of models, 21
new way to do, 90
for youth and young adult
ministry, 124–29
A Theology of Liberation (Gutiérrez),
88, 88n1, 107
theoretical models, for youth and
young adult ministers, 22
"third-person" abilities and thinking,
developing, 93
Thomas Aquinas, 135
Thoreau, Henry David, 63
thorn in the flesh, given to Paul, 80
Tickle, John, 51n24
Tillich, Paul, 133
tolerance, fostering a spirit of, 111
traditional criticism, 57n25
Transcendent, experiencing, 104
transformational leadership, 134
trends, shaping teenage values, 6
tribes, of emerging adults, 8

"Uncovering Your Bible Heritage"
summer, 51–52
"undesirables," interacting with,
47–48
unitive facet, of ministry, 157–58
universal events, participating in, 158

Index

US Catholic Bishops
   on Christian discipleship is a major goal of youth ministry, 123
   documents for emerging and young adults, 42
   guidelines for ministering to Christian youth, 121n3
   guidelines for youth and young adult ministry, 86
   helping shape young adults, 9–10
   on multiculturalism, 100
   on nurturing service in young people, 137
   Sons and Daughters, 10n22, 123–24
utopianism, 118

value shifts, as a theme for emerging adults, 9
values of a culture, compatible with the values of the Bible, 97
Vashti, 50
violence, liberation theology and, 92, 115
"virtue," deriving from the Latin word *habitus* meaning "habit," 70n38
virtues
   hinging on lesser virtues, 71n38
   of youth and young adult ministers, 12
A Vision of Youth Ministry (1976), 40–41
vocation (life's calling), of youth and young adult ministers, 12

washing the feet, of the Twelve, 65
weekend retreats
   boosting a young person's interior life, 77
   centering on the Scriptures, 48
   developed around servant-leadership ideas and principles, 76
   offering Christian discipleship, 147
   suggested, 26n20
we-they language, leaving behind, 102
Whitehead, Evelyn E., 15
Whitehead, James D., 15
wilderness trips, taking a variety of groups on, 145n91
word of God
   described, 32–33
   fundamentalist interpretation and literalistic comprehension of, 56
   interpreting, 39
   as a major component for Catholic youth ministry, 41
   manifesting the divine, 53
   as a powerful representation of God's love and compassion, 53
Word of God, denoting the Second Person of the Holy Trinity, 33
"Word of God" retreat, 48
work-camp organizations, for Protestant and Catholic youth and young adults, 144
work-camp trip, providing a great service opportunity, 144
work-camps, success with, 144n86
workshop, on liberation theology, 107
worship, as an important element of prayer, 136

yin/yang philosophy, Taoist concept of, 110
young adult ministry, of the author, 1–2
young adulthood, 9, 10
young adults
   ages of, 4
   defined, 7–10
   distinguished from emerging adults, 9
   as the object of liberation theology, 91

Index

US Catholic Bishops' documents for, 42
young people
  becoming involved in two ministries, 159
  becoming servant-leaders, 67, 83
  committing themselves to God, 125
  contributing to the community, 130
  defined, 4
  describing today's, 6–13
  developing interpersonal skills, 102
  emphasizing the needs of others, 87
  empowering people of different lifestyles and color of skin, 111
  empowering to live as disciples of Jesus Christ, 123, 140
  encouraging to pray, 135
  experiencing the larger Christian community or diocese, 158
  exposing to Christian discipleship, 123
  fostering Christian discipleship in, 153
  fostering the growth of, 156
  helping become authentic Christian disciples, 150
  integrating into the larger life of the community, 159
  journaling about perceptions of servant-leadership, 77
  learning experiential ways to become advocates of change, 142
  mutual awareness of unity among all, 160
  needing to experience the larger life of the parish, 159
  One-on-One Retreat encouraging, 148
  rekindling the spirit of, 3
  significance of spirituality for, 138
  training to become Christian leaders, 133
Young People, the Faith, and Vocational Discernment, 7
younger teenagers, defined, 5
youth, defined, 5
youth and young adult minister(s), 4–5
  adapting a strong prayer regiment within their ministries, 135
  allied to other youth and young adult ministers in their region or deanery, 157
  becoming familiar with the lives of extraordinary holy people or saints, 141
  called to serve, guide, and lead young people, 12
  commitments list, 12–13
  conceptualizing, 70
  conducting Bible studies, 37–38
  continuing their own study of Scripture, 56
  counteracting prejudice, racism, and discrimination by example, 102
  defined, 5
  distinguished from youth and young adult ministry, 10
  empowering young people to identify with the conversion process, 131
  facilitation sessions by, 146
  fostering the personal and spiritual growth of young persons, 132
  having a good comprehension of the Scriptures, 44
  having a mid-week Bible study, 143
  having theologically educated and pastorally trained, 151
  helping young people discern God's call upon their lives, 125

Index

youth and young adult minister(s) (*continued*)
- helping young people galvanize and gravitate toward liberation theology, 96
- helping young people see the cost of following God, 126
- hosting catechetical workshops, 142
- implementing the Bible into ministries, 35
- infusing the word of God into activities and programs, 37
- initiating various contemporary topics and themes from the Scriptures, 55
- intentional virtues of, 12
- inviting local theologians to come and speak, 45
- involving in a peer Bible study with other ministers, 45
- linking ministry efforts with other efforts, 158
- as a minister of the Christian church, 11
- most too busy to entertain other world religious traditions, 102n48
- needing adequate training in Scripture studies, 56
- needing encouragement to begin to think about liberation, 105
- not making a mission trip into an adventure in tourism, 145
- practicing empathy, 70
- preliminary reading and studying on Christian discipleship, 140
- primary functions of, 12
- promoting servant-leadership, 67
- providing strategies for integrating sacred Scripture into the lives of young people, 35
- purchasing a Christian high school curriculum on the Bible, 42
- reenvisioning Christian discipleship, 149
- shaping experiences of God for young people, 127
- supporting commitment to God, 125
- taking a class on Christology or Soteriology, 141
- taking care of themselves before giving to others, 13
- thinking and doing ministry "outside the box," 161
- training teenagers and young adults in leadership, 134
- as undereducated in theology and biblical studies, 57
- using the Bible with young people, 43

youth and young adult ministry
- benefiting from various models and methods of theology, 15
- "big picture" of, 4
- challenging the *status quo* within, 3
- Circle of Servant-Leadership for, 83–84
- components for doing, 40–41
- components of, 157
- described, 10–11
- dynamics of servant-leadership for, 60
- education illuminating the discipline of, 23
- enhancing spirituality, 138
- evening/gathering described, 25n20–26n20
- facets of, 157
- falling under Christian ministry, 5
- implementation strategies for, 45–53
- integrating the word of God within as essential, 41
- intersecting dimensions or themes, 11
- journey of, 155–61
- keeping at the forefront, 156

Index

liberation theology in the context of, 90–92
methodology for, 23–25
models for, 21–23, 25–30
models within, 155
primarily concerned with Christian discipleship, 141
purpose of, 161
purpose of models, 21
rarely homogeneous in North America, 100
as remedial functions of the Christian Church, 10
role and purpose of, 10–13
Scripture woven through, 44
shifting into becoming a community driven by servant-leadership, 87
started from "scratch," 2
students hesitant to conduct Bible studies with youth, 39
studies enriching, 20
themes worthy of discussion for, 100
those interested in, 23
typical methodology, 40
uniting to the larger church, 158
weekend retreats and days of reflection, 26n20
as the work of the Holy Spirit, 156
youth and young adults
empowering to change theological horizons, 128
as the present and future of each community, 130
youth culture
free of biblical and Christian underpinnings, 6, 92
moving to a culture of grace and mercy, 7, 93
youth pastor, 4–5. *See also* youth and young adult minister(s)
youth pastors and young adult ministers, models assisting, 26

Zakat (almsgiving or tithing), 112
Zeffirelli, Franco, 78

www.ingramcontent.com/pod-product-compliance
Lightning Source LLC
Chambersburg PA
CBHW021731220426
43662CB00008B/800